8-24-1998

Friends are my Health

A H Brooks

Family are my Treasure

For: Charleston University
From: a 1937 graduate of Morris Harvey College
Best Wishes
Arthelia H. Brooks

The Backside of Yesterday

THE BACKSIDE OF YESTERDAY:
My Life and Work

by

Arthelia Hilleary Brooks
"Tillie"

Celo Valley Books
Burnsville, North Carolina

Cover illustration by Ann Swift.

The photos in this book were partially funded by donations from: Willis Hertig, Noriko and Minoru Yamada, and Tommy Tyson.

Copies of this book may be obtained by sending $25.00 + $4.00 postage/handling for each copy to: Ms. Arthelia Brooks, 529 Green Mountain Drive, Burnsville NC 28714. If you live in North Carolina, please include an additional $1.50 for sales tax.

Library of Congress Catalog Card Number 94-71713
ISBN 0-923687-32-7

Copyright © 1994 by Arthelia H. Brooks.
All rights reserved.
Printed in the U.S.A.

No part of this book may be reproduced, in any form or by any means, without permission in writing from the publisher.

To Arle Brooks, my husband of fewer than nine years, and to his family, whose devotion to me and to my girls has never changed.

To my own Hilleary family, where I grew up loved and happy.

To my three daughters, my three grandsons, and my two great-grandsons.

and,

If you are a Methodist woman, this book is also gratefully dedicated to you, and to all the Methodist women who have gone before you.

TABLE OF CONTENTS

List of Illustrations ix
Foreword xi
Acknowledgments xv
Introduction xvii
My Mentors xix
List of Abbreviations xxv
Chronology xxvii

Section I: Family Stories
    My Mini-Autobiography 9
    The Colonel McDowell Place 25
        Pre-Celo Community, Inc. 25
        Laurel Cove — CCI, Inc.-Era Residents 27
    Children 67
        Births 67
            Paula — 1945 67
            Maryla / Marla — 1947 68
            Dena — 1949 70
            Kittens of Mitzi, the Cat 71
            Robbie and Jeremy 72
        Child Rearing 73
        The Sayings of My Small Children 77
    The *Toe Valley View* Newspaper and WTOE Radio 89

Section II: People
    Lydia Holman 101
        Introduction 101
        Early Years 103
        Serving as a Nurse in Mitchell County 106
        Personal Interviews with Miss Lydia Holman 113
        Finis 116
    David Salstrom 121
    Francis Ballew 127
    Juanita Presnell / Mitzi Presnell Shook 129

/ vii

viii / CONTENTS

    Bea Thomas 131
    Alvin G. Jones 133
    Estelle White 135
    Laughruns / Rays 143
    Memories from Jack's Creek 153
    Tragedies 161
        Judy Shuford 162
        Darrell Gibbs 163
        Unnamed girls 164
    Someone Had Listened 167
    Younger Friends 171
    The West Kentucky Years 183

Section III: Arle Brooks
    Biography of Ernest Arle Brooks 201

Section IV: Trips
    Texas in August 235
    Points West and the Unexpected 239
    The Far East — 1966 245
    My Japanese Families 255
    New England 265
    A Bus Trip Home 269

Section V: Special Occasion Writings
    Healing Service 283
    My Tribute to the Women of the Methodist Church 297
    Scarritt College and Scarritt-Bennett Center 301
        My Personal Involvement in Scarritt's History 302
        Memorable Scarritt Classmates 304
    Favorite Sermons 309
        Just One Chapter 309
        Womankind's Special Debt to Jesus 311
        The Importance of a Name 315
    A Eulogy for the Dear Departed 321
    A Good Friday Prayer 325

Section VI: Today
    Weathering the "Storm of the Century" on Styles' Hill .. 331
    The Unsolved Stones Mystery 337

Afterword 341

LIST OF ILLUSTRATIONS

Photos for Chronology/Autobiography (Arthelia/Tillie) 3–8
Map 18
Col. McDowell's Grave 19
Log House 20–22
Celo Community, Inc. 23
Hertig Family 57–58
Hilleary Family 59–64
Births / Rearing Children 65
Yancey County Friends 87
Toe Valley View 88
People
    Lydia Holman, David Salstrom, Alvin Jones, Estelle White 96
Friends Near and Far
    Carolyn Scott, Ian and Katelin Kennedy, Joe and Helen Donahue, Jude and Rachel Craddock, Liz Evans, Marshall and Mary Buckalew, Arthur and Esther Russell, Catherine Ezell and Martha Almon 97
    Kay and Chuck Sittig, Muriel Clark, Jean Quinn, Dorothy Robinson, Katie McDaniel 98
Laughruns/Rays and Jack's Creek 140
Jack's Creek 141
Younger Friends 169-170
West Kentucky Years
    Louisville Conference 176
    Disaster Team Training, Texas, Myrta Davis 177
    UMRF, General Conference, Memphis Conference 177
    Church and Community 178
    Lakeland Parish 179–180
    Lakeland Wesley Village 181–182
The Ernest and Mary Brooks Family 191–192
Arle Brooks 193
Arle and Tillie Brooks and Children 194

/ ix

Tillie and Older Girls
    Paula 195
    Marla 196
    Dena 197
Brooks Reunions 198
Favorite Scenes 232–233
Far East Trip 243
Japanese Families 253-254
Marla Brooks Lang 275–276
Marla Brooks Hoover 277–279
Methodist Women 292–293
Higgins Memorial UMC 294-295
"Methodist Woman" Cover 308
Eulogies
    Troy Howell, Juanita Brandon, Greta Maddox 324
On Styles Hill 328–329
Stones 336

FOREWORD

When I retired in 1985, I returned to Burnsville, North Carolina. There, in many settings — both in groups and with individuals — I shared some of my life experiences, as older people are wont to do. My friends often reacted to my stories by saying something like, "Tillie, you should write these stories down."

I had not done any writing (except talks or sermons) since 1956, when I wrote the "People I Meet" column for the *Toe Valley View*, a now defunct local newspaper. From that year of writing, though, I had one leftover assignment hanging over my head: the one about Lydia Holman, a nurse who had served the people of Mitchell County for over fifty years. She had refused to allow me to write her story then because of adverse publicity in her early years, but she did give me material to use for an article, and asked that it not be published until after her death. The materials she gave me were annual reports published by the committee that funded her work, reports circulated to contributors with the goal of getting more contributions. In anticipation of the article being written, I interviewed both Lydia and people who knew her. The interviews were enlightening, as some of those I talked to loved Lydia, and others were highly critical of her methods. Lydia died in 1960.

I carried the annual reports and interview records with me through many moves, for thirty-two years, always meaning to write the article. So when I started writing this book in 1992, I started with that article, thinking that the book was going to be mainly about Lydia Holman and people like her.

But the book has turned out to be about my total life experience, of which Lydia's story is only a minute part. As I wrote, I began to recall many significant persons, places and events I had been involved with personally, and I became aware that it might not be such a simple task to decide which ones should go into the book, and which ones shouldn't. I asked Lloyd Bailey (a friend reared on Jack's Creek who is now a professor at Duke University) if anything definitive had yet been written about Lydia Holman, and I also expressed my dilemma about what to leave out of my own life story. Lloyd has published several local histories, and I honor his advice. He said he didn't think there was yet anything substantial on Miss Holman, and that he'd like to use some of my material for his own forthcoming book, *The Heritage of the Toe River Valley*, which is coming out in the fall of 1994. (I gave him permission.) In answer to my question about my own experiences, he said, "Don't leave anything out!"

Looking at the length of the present book, I'm inclined to think I didn't.

In the early days of writing this narrative, I was telling my daughter Marla and her son, Jamie, some of my experiences. "How can you remember all that stuff, Grandma?" Jamie wanted to know. The answer to that question is my sources: I have a collection of letters from Arle, which he wrote to me before we were married, and I also have a collection of letters I wrote to his family during the years of 1941 through 1965, which Arle's sister Elva sent back to me in 1987. I have used them in this book, designating the former as LA, and the latter as LF. In addition to these sets of letters, I have many friends who have helped me get names and facts as correct as possible. In particular, Mildred Ray and Betty Motsinger of Burnsville, North Carolina, were called on more than once.

Some of the other remembering came harder, after searching for days and even weeks, in my "mind's computer" for a name. I was often amazed that the answer came in the waking hours of the night, when I would write it down immediately, lest it leave me before morning. In fact, this book was first written in my mind, before it ever got onto paper, mostly during the night when I thought I should be sleeping. Many times I said to myself, sometimes even aloud, "This book will be the death of you yet!" But dire results have been avoided because I've had the freedom to take a nap in the day if I felt the need.

This book has been two years in the writing — all handwritten. I know it is long, and I am under no illusion that everyone will find all of it of interest to them. (If there *is* even one person who does, please let me know!) I have tried to include the most interesting aspects of my experiences. There may be a place or two that seems comparable to the "begats" in the Old Testament. I know there is a roll call of the people written about in my column, "People I Meet" and also a list of names of all those who spent some time with Arle and me at the Celo log house we called Laurel Cove.

I will tell you one reason this book is long. In her letter of summation and instructions when the writing was considered done, my editor, Diana, said, "In general I think the book now says pretty clearly what (I think) you're trying to say. As I mentioned, I'm still not clear on the driving force that's gotten you through, though I assume from knowing you it's your relationship with God. I feel a little sad to hear what a good teacher you are, and not see that in this book. But perhaps that's another book." To which I reply, "No way, José!"

I did make quite a few additions to answer Diana's concern about me, the author: the chronology of my life; the list of people I consider my mentors, the list of books of enduring significance in my life. The article on child rearing was added to answer her plea, "Can't you share some of your experiences that would help mothers of young children?" And parts of many articles were expanded to give more details that Diana requested.

But I also want to explain that part of Diana's problem is simply one of trying to understand a personality such as mine. Tom Lea once told me, "Tillie, you are the least complicated person I have ever met." And Sandy Stubbs put it, "Tillie, you are so *boring!*" Having had a loving family, what I considered a happy childhood, and loving friends all my life, I have been secure about who I am, and about God's love for me. I adjust rather easily to whatever the existing circumstances demand, and have gotten along with people without undue controversy or severed relationships. If there was a misunderstanding, I took the first opportunity to clear it up, and I feel I failed in this in only two instances of my life. When a problem comes along — a trauma with my children, or anything else — I worry only one day about it, lose sleep over it for only one night, and then I say, "Lord, if there's anything I can do to help in this situation, tell me. Otherwise, I just trust you to meet the need."

I am basically a happy and optimistic person who has found my faith in the goodness of those I've met to be justified. I've lived my life relatively free from fear, and I am not aware of anyone who has ever tried to harm me, so there is no call for me to forgive. I feel I have lived under the special protection and blessing of God. How else can I explain such a wonderful life?

I have, however, had some concern about one of Jesus' woes: "Woe to you, when all men speak well of you, for so their fathers did to the false prophets." (Luke 6:26) I have never been hated, excluded or reviled for righteousness' sake, nor have I suffered. So perhaps I have not been bold enough for Christ to engender enmity. It is something I do not understand. I only know I have tried to serve

Him. I cannot think of any person I have ever hated in my whole life, and anger is not a disturbing part of my nature (except when people mistreat other people or animals or the good earth by throwing trash out of their cars).

I did not intend this book to be about me, but mostly about those who have been a part of my life. It has blessed me again to think about what they have meant to me. I hope the many pictures which I have selected from my twenty-two albums will help make the book more meaningful for you.

I will quote from Edith Deen's preface to her book, *The Bible's Legacy for Womanhood*, "As I now conclude my task, I rejoice that I shall no longer have to discipline myself to . . . research and writing [and wakeful nights]. And yet in a little while I know I shall feel as lost as a mother who has seen her child marry and leave home for good. [My detached nature *may spare me*. . .] I hope that readers will feel as I did as I wrote that God, the supreme power of the universe, is very much alive in our world, just as he was in the time of creation and through the New Testament church."[1]

— Arthelia "Tillie" Brooks
June 6, 1994
"B-Day"

NOTE

1. Edith Deen, *The Bible's Legacy for Womanhood* (New York: Doubleday, 1969).
2. Ibid.

ACKNOWLEDGMENTS

Without the help of friends this book could not have gotten to first base. Jenifer Morgan offered to make the facilities at Rural Southern Voice for Peace available and David Salstrom did all the first draft on the computer and Jenifer did some additional typing — all free. The Celo map is the contribution of Robert (Gred) Gross. I'm indebted to these friends and to Joel Robertson at Yancey Graphics, who has done the pictures with care and personal interest in the final outcome of the book. It would be awesome to contemplate what the actual cost would have been.

I'm appreciative of the encouragement Lloyd Bailey gave me at the start of this undertaking. The pictures are a real labor of love. From my twenty-three albums (after many yes or no decisions) I have selected these pictures so that years later my great-grandson, Jeremy Hoover, will have a pictorial history of his ancestors and of the life and work of his "Grandma B."

I am doing the pictures album style so I can do the page layouts myself, and thus save hundreds of dollars. If persons appear in the text the page number is noted beside the photo.

The generosity of four persons has paid for the pictures — my only living uncle, Willis Hertig, my Japanese "daughter - son," Noriko and Minoru Yamada, and my friend of more than forty years, Tommy Tyson. Marla has done the printing for picture identification for me. Additions and most imperfections are mine.

I want to express my gratitude for 129 persons who had enough faith in the end product to place prepublication orders (Robert Lenski ordered twelve copies and Betty Ann Banks Young ordered five); and on the Hilleary side of my family, a very heartfelt thank-you to my niece, Rebecca Jackson Long for her vote of confidence.

I am indebted to county libraries, Holcombe Brothers Funeral Home and many friends who made special efforts to secure facts for me, to Frances Higgins for the introduction to this book, and to Ann Swift (who shares the same birthday I have) for the cover art.

To Diana, my editor, who helped me make necessary changes

and encouraged me to "tell more," I am grateful. Because of her expertise I offer this book to you with confidence and pride.

Arthelia / Tillie Brooks
June, 1994
Burnsville NC 28714

INTRODUCTION

When I first met Tillie Brooks, she had already been living in Yancey County for about six years. She was working as a deaconess with the United Methodist Women of the Western North Carolina Conference in the Methodist Churches of Yancey County.

During this period of time she had added another daughter to the two she already had, and had lost her husband of nine years. Arle Brooks died of a brain tumor on July 6, 1953.

What particularly intrigued me about Tillie was her undaunted determination to carry on and make a life for herself and her little family, while at the same time giving so much of herself to those around her. One wonders what sparks the determination and creative flame in someone like Tillie, whose life work touched so many people.

She has seen the best of times, as well as the worst, and somehow developed the unusual ability to readily adjust to whatever the situation demanded emotionally or physically. The situations have been varied and many but she has always managed to make the most of what came along — for herself and for others.

The *Backside of Yesterday* is far more than the recalling of times and places and deeds done, it is the summary of a remarkable life that has been well-lived in every sense of the word.

When this wonderful and inspiring woman informed me that she was writing a book about her experiences after she made her home in this area, I was flattered and extremely pleased to be asked to write the introduction. The stories that follow are a tribute to Tillie Brooks and how one woman's life came to shine so bright in this little part of the world.

— Frances Higgins

MY MENTORS

These are some of the persons whose deep faith and commitment to Christ and His church have influenced my life at many important points of decision. They've brought me satisfaction and joy as fellow sojourners and co-workers during my years of service.

A.J. (Jack) Walton	Dr. Walton was my World History teacher at Morris Harvey College in Barboursville, West Virginia in 1933, and through the years I saw him as he served in different capacities. A fellow West Virginian, he left Morris Harvey to serve on the M.E. Church, South, board in Nashville; he later became executive of the Duke Endowment Fund, and finally he served as visiting pastor for West End Methodist church in Nashville. It has just been the *essence* of Jack Walton that has sustained my regard for him through the years.
John Hollister	John was the minister of the Methodist church in Barboursville when I made my commitment to Christ in 1934. He was the first to *lift up* Christ and say to me, "Look at Him. He is worthy! Dedicate your life to His service," instead of trying to *scare* me into the Kingdom.
Verna Fannin	Verna helped me to understand that a St. Paul type of conversion was not appropriate for me.

Toyohiko Kagawa	In 1935 I represented Morris Harvey at a 5,000 member youth conference in Memphis, Tennessee. Toyohiko Kagawa was the speaker. To us, he was *the* outstanding Christian in the world. He was late coming to the platform that day. We later found out he had been tidying the restroom the boys had trashed in their hurry to hear this great man. Since then, I have always left a public restroom as neat or neater than I found it.
Emily Olmstead	Emily was my sociology teacher at Morris Harvey College in Barboursville, West Virginia (before the college moved to Charleston). Emily led me, in 1937, to consider training at Scarritt College in Nashville for full-time Christian service.
Albert Barnett	My New Testament teacher at Scarritt, Albert Barnett was accused of destroying his students' faith. He challenged me to *think*, to put my faith on a firm foundation.
Harry Denman	A layman, head of the Department of Evangelism of the M.E. Church, South. Harry was a good organizer and speaker, but he is best remembered as a person-to-person evangelist. He autographed a devotional book for me.
Bro. Quessenberry	On my first appointment, Bro. Quessenberry was our pastor at the Methodist church in Marytown, West Virginia, between 1940–43. Bro. Quessenberry would say to the congregation of nine or ten, "Well, I had prepared (such-and-such) a sermon, but since there are so few here, I will just . . ." One day I said, "Brother Quessenberry, do you ever expect more than ten or twelve of us at Marytown on Sunday morning?" "No, I guess I don't," he replied. "Well, please do us a favor and don't tell us if you are not giving us your best." And he never

	did again. I learned *not* to let numbers be so important.
Fanny B. Crowell	Mrs. Crowell was the WSCS "Conference Mama" when I worked as a Rural Worker in the WNC conference, 1953–55. She had to comfort *me* when I visited her in the hospital in Asheville in 1961. I could not understand why one so caring was dying of cancer! I'm glad a portrait of her will still comfort me at the Brooks-Howell Home when I go there to live.
Joe Petree (and Ginny)	Joe was pastor of the Newdale charge (1953–55) in North Carolina. (The Newdale charge consisted of Martin's Chapel at Newdale, and smaller churches at Windom and Celo, North Carolina.) One of the several experiences we shared was the retreat he organized to go to South America in 1971, after I had moved to Kentucky. On the way to South America, due to a snowstorm in Greensboro, our plane was late in arriving at Miami. We decided to get on the plane to Ecuador without our luggage — I learned to do with "less" for five days.
Lucy Norton	I became acquainted with Lucy (and her saintly mother) when I was on the Asheville district WSCS executive committee in the mid-sixties. Lucy was our Spiritual Life leader. From there she was called into the ordained ministry. She was a pioneer in getting women accepted by the churches, she served on the High Pastures retreat center board here in Burnsville, North Carolina, and she also led retreats in this conference and elsewhere. We were able to spend an evening together at a retreat in the Memphis conference. Every thought of Lucy blesses me.
Louise Wright	Louise was a member of the Asheville district WSCS executive committee, and twenty-five

xxii / MY MENTORS

	years later she is still giving of herself as freely as ever. She's on the Brooks-Howell board as chairperson of its auxiliary committee. She has celebrated her ninetieth birthday, and is writing a review of this book for the *North Carolina Christian Advocate*.
Tommy Tyson	A WNC conference evangelist in the early fifties, Tommy introduced me to the real ministry and to the power of the Holy Spirit (see the Tragedies section of this book).
J.R. Dawkins	J.R. was pastor of the Newdale charge when Marla and her age group were baptized in the South Toe River and joined the Church.
Thomas E. Rutledge (and Mary) Philip Nordstrom (and Lola)	Thomas was the Celo pastor when Dena was sprinkled and joined the Church. Tom shared with Philip Nordstrom in performing Marla and Jerry Hoover's wedding. The Nordstroms were CCI members and are still valued friends who now live in New York, near their daughters.
Don Noblitt (and Joretta)	Don was the minister of the Bald Creek charge (1961–63). The insight that came from the eventual separation of this couple was: Joretta had married a factory worker, and she did not share his call to the ministry. The adjustment was too great! I later met Don's new wife, who had always worked in the Church.
Thomas W. Weeks (and Carol)	Tommy followed Don as minister of the Bald Creek charge, and these two demonstrated to me what *real* commitment sometimes demands. Tommy was almost blind. (see Jack's Creek stories, later in this book.)
WNC Conference Leaders: John Christy	As a Church and Community worker, and as treasurer of the UM Rural Fellowship for eight years, I held many of our church leaders

Ben Steele
Garland Young
H. Claude Young, Jr.
Garland Stafford
Hubert C. Clinard
Wilson Nesbitt

in high esteem because of their dedication to the small membership church, and enjoyed working with them to strengthen this largest segment of the UM church.

Other SE Jurisdiction Leaders:
Carl Judy
William Appleby
James Sells
Earl Brewer
Harold McSwain
Gladys Campbell
  (CCW)
Ralph Nichols
  (CCW executive)
Gene Holdridge
Walter German
William Morris

Charles Rogers
  (and Nancy)

Charles was the pastor of the Grand Rivers Methodist church when I went to Kentucky in 1968. He was very successful in enabling the lay people of his church to be in the ministry. I helped him "walk the floor" at the hospital, waiting for his wife Nancy to deliver Carla, the first girl in the Rogers family in eighty years. I also shared the joy with the proud Rogers grandparents.

Joe Piercey
  (and Mary Ann)

Wright Pillow (and Jo)

Fred French
  (and Margie)

Jimmy Stubbs
  (and Sandy)

I worked in the development of the Lakeland Parish in western Kentucky with these wonderful people. [See the West Kentucky Years section, later in this book.]

Joe Geary (and Karen)	Joe was my minister at Union Ridge UMC, and the second person around whom I saw an aura of light when he told about his spiritual debt to a gift of the Bible. He and Karen gave me a book with blank pages that I call my Serendipity Book. I have written my most momentous happenings since 1979 in it.
Geraldine (Jerry) Hylemon	Jerry was the National Division of UMBGM representative to our CORE leadership team (the executive committee of CC Workers) while I was on it. I have never ceased to marvel at the devoted service of Methodist women! Jerry had us to her home in Williamsport, Pennsylvania. We saw the stadium where the Little League Baseball World Series is played, and every Christmas I hang the colored bells she knit for me.
Ralph Jacks (and Miriam)	Ralph was at Higgins Memorial UM church in Burnsville, North Carolina, while I was in Kentucky, but I was sent the newsletter. Ralph wrote lovely eulogies for some of my dearest friends, and I wish he would get them put together for me and others who would cherish them.
Don Shuman (and Margie)	Don was the minister at Higgins when I returned to Burnsville in 1985. He edited *A History of the Methodist Church in the Toe River Valley*, and I count the whole family as my friends.
Billy Hunter (and June)	Billy served Higgins after Don left. I've told him, "After having listened to sermons all my working life, I liked yours best." Some of us attended his retirement party, Sunday, May 23, 1993.
Robert (Buzz) Scott (and Jamie)	Buzz is my present pastor at Higgins. Maybe it is my age, but I feel closer to Buzz than to any pastor in the past.

ABBREVIATIONS USED IN THIS BOOK

AFSC	American Friends Service Committee (a Quaker social action group)
A.M.E.	African Methodist Episcopal
AMS	Arthur Morgan School, in Celo, North Carolina
CC	Church and Community (Worker)
CCI	Celo Community, Inc. (an intentional community in Celo, North Carolina)
CCW	Church and Community Workers (United Methodist)
CO	conscientious objector
CLT	Core Leadership Team (CCW)
CPS	Civilian Public Service
EUB	Evangelical United Brethren Church. (In 1968 this church joined with the Methodist Church to form the United Methodist Church.)
FDR	President Franklin Delano Roosevelt
HUD	U.S. Department of Housing and Urban Development
ICU	Intensive Care Unit
LBL	Land Between the Lakes, Kentucky
LBLAM	Land Between the Lakes Area Ministry

LWV	Lakeland Wesley Village (a UM retirement facility in western Kentucky)
M.E.	Methodist Episcopal Church, North
MECS	Methodist Episcopal Church, South
MP	Methodist Protestant Church

The above three bodies joined to form the Methodist Church in 1939.

PMR	polymyalgia rheumatica
T.C.U.	Texas Christian University
TVA	Tennessee Valley Authority (electrification)
UM	United Methodist
UMBGM	United Methodist Board of Global Ministries (also known as the General Board of Global Ministries)
UMC	United Methodist Church (formed in 1968 in union with EUB)
UMRF	United Methodist Rural Fellowship
UMW	United Methodist Women
UNC	University of North Carolina
UNCA	University of North Carolina-Asheville
WNC	Western North Carolina
WPA	Work Projects Administration
WSG	Wesleyan Service Guild
WSCS	Women's Society of Christian Service
WS	Women's Society
WSG	Wesleyan Service Guild (for working women of the Methodist church; this group ended when UMW began.)

CHRONOLOGY

February 11, 1915 Randolph County, Alpena, West Virginia	Born the eldest of seven to John Edward Hilleary and Gertrude Hertig Hilleary. Paternal grandparents: John Augusta and Arthelia Smith Hilleary. Maternal grandparents: Christian Hertig and Susan Von Allman Hertig. Siblings: Lucille, Fred, Oma, Ruth, Olive and Edward.
1915–1920	Family lived at Weese Crossing, West Virginia, on location of Father's logging job. Mother cooked for men who worked for him.
1920–1921	Family lived at Kingsville, West Virginia. I started first grade there. My teacher was my Mother's brother, Bill.
1922	Family moved back to Weese Crossing, then to Maryland. I finished first grade at my grandmother's, at Alpena, West Virginia.
1922–1925	Family lived at least two places in western Maryland, one being Vindex. I went to school there for the third, fourth and fifth grades.
1925–1926	Family returned to West Virginia, I think to Red Creek, West Virginia. I attended sixth grade at Alpena, while living with my grandparents. Lucille stayed with Uncle Herbert in Elkins, West Virginia.
Fall 1926–1927	Had typhoid fever while at Red Creek, West Virginia.
1927	Family lived temporarily at Holly Meadows, near Parsons, West Virginia.
1927–1928	Family moved to Pheasant Run, Tucker County, West Virginia. I finished the eighth grade there, and started high school at Parsons, West Virginia.

1928	Family moved across the mountain to Cheat River, R.F.D. Kerens, West Virginia.
1928–1929	Stayed about two months with Aunt Jennie in Holly Meadows, then went to Parsons with Aunt Annie for the first year of high school.
1929–1930	Stayed with Aunt Annie in Parsons for my second year of high school.
1930–1931	During my third year of high school, our daily trip to school (and back) was quite involved. To go to school, Lucille, Pearl Wingfield and I would walk, then ride with a teacher, then take the train for a total of 9 miles. On the way home, the process was reversed, except it was a bus we took, instead of a train.
1931–1932	I drove the three of us to school in the family's four-door Chevrolet for my senior year in high school. Had a car wreck.
1932–1933	Stayed with Uncle Willis and attended Morris Harvey College in Barboursville, West Virginia.
1933–1934	(Depression years) Lucille and I stayed home and took care of our younger siblings, and the school teacher who boarded with us, while our parents were away on a logging job. The house burned March 17, 1934. (How the family fared after the fire is a blank.)
1934–1935	Went to stay with the Fannins *very* soon after the fire. I helped during the summer with Mrs. Fannin's difficult pregnancy. In return, they paid for my sophomore year expenses at Morris Harvey College.
1935–1936	Helped the Rigglemans during the summer of 1935. The college moved to Charleston, West Virginia that summer, and that fall I worked for room and board with two families to attend my junior year at Morris Harvey College.
1936–1937	Worked part-time at West Virginia Agricultural Laboratory, rented a room across from the state Capitol. Finished my senior year and graduated from Morris Harvey College *magna cum laude*.

1937–1938	Worked full-time at the laboratory, where Fisher Key was one of my co-workers, and paid for my room and board with Tom and Mary Stout. My sister Oma was then in school at Morris Harvey College.
1938–1939	On scholarship from the W.V. Methodist women at Scarritt College in Nashville, Tennessee, working toward my master's degree. I worked during the summer at Vashti School near Thomasville, Georgia.
1939–1940	Finished work on my master's degree, including my thesis. Was consecrated a Methodist deaconess in New Orleans in March 1940. Soon thereafter, I met Arle Brooks when he visited Scarritt and proposed marriage. I refused because of my commitment to work for the Methodist women for four years in return for my scholarship to Scarritt. In July, 1940, in Chicago, I attended the United Methodist commissioning of missionaries and deaconesses. Arle went to trial in Philadelphia for refusing to register for the draft. Walter Longstreth was his lawyer. In July, 1940, I was appointed to work in West Virginia coal mining areas in the Bluefield district. I lived with my co-worker, Myrta Davis in Roderfield, West Virginia.
1941	I continued to work in Roderfield, West Virginia. On January 10, 1941, Arle was sent to Danbury (Connecticut) Prison. In July, Arle was sent to a CPS work camp in Patapsco, Maryland.
1942	Still in Roderfield, West Virginia, I requested a new appointment because of sinus problems from the coal dust and anemia. On January 20, 1942, Arle, having finished his sentence at the Patapsco, Maryland, work camp, arrived at the cooperative farm in Wesson, Mississippi. In December, 1942, Arle was arrested for not carrying his draft card, and was put in the county jail in Jackson, Mississippi.

1943	In January, 1943, Arle is sent to the federal prison in Texarkana, which is on the Texas-Arkansas border. In August, 1943, between appointments with the Methodist women, I made a trip to Texas and got an acute case of food poisoning. Visited Myrta Davis and her sister, Mary Frances, in Tyler, Texas; Arle's folks in San Marcos, Texas; and Arle in prison in Texarkana. In September, 1943, I was appointed to Scarritt Rural Training Center at Crossville, Tennessee, at the request of Mabel K. Howell, who was its director. My sinuses improved, but the anemia persisted.
1944	Arle was paroled from prison in July, 1944. I visited Arle and his folks in San Marcos, Texas, to get to know him in person (rather than by mail). We decided to marry. In September, in Crossville, I went for my Wasserman test. The doctor who administered the test had been a missionary in India. I asked her about my anemia. She tested for amoebic dysentery, a common cause of anemia in the East, found +2 amoebic dysentery, and cured it with six hydrochloric acid shots. Arle and I were married in Arle's family home, October 22, 1944.
1945	I lived with Arle's parents while Arle worked in Philadelphia for American Friends Service Committee (AFSC), who had helped him through his draft-resistance problems. *Our daughter, Paula, was born August 28, 1945* on Arle's thirty-sixth birthday. I was thirty. Arle and his dad planted a huge fall garden. Dad Brooks and I harvested the garden after Arle returned to work for American Friends Service Committee in Philadelphia.
1946	Paula and I joined Arle in Philadelphia in May, where we all stayed at the Brudercoop.
1947	We visited my family for Christmas, since Arle was still with AFSC. I stayed with Paula at a house owned by Harry and Gene Wolf that was meant to be a fledgling intentional com-

munity. Met Dave Salstrom there, and Arle came there, too, after finishing his contract with AFSC in late February. *Our daughter, Marla, was born March 17, 1947* in the hospital at Elkins, West Virginia.

The Brooks family of four arrived in Celo, North Carolina, on May 4, 1947, to become part of the intentional community there, Celo Community, Inc. We stayed in the McDowell cabin, and Dave Salstrom joined us there that fall.

At CCI, Dave Salstrom knit and I embroidered argyle socks as a cottage industry.

Arle and I made preparations to receive guests at what we called the Laurel Cove Retreat Center, which consisted of our own cabin, the barn, and the (corn) crib cabin, which we moved a little way from the house.

1948

Dave Salstrom moved to the Foor cabin in the fall of 1948, and Peg Calbeck moved into our front room. The CCI block-making cottage industry began in 1948. Ruby and Doug Moody lost their baby.

1949–1950

Our daughter, Dena, was born on August 21, 1949 in the front room. I delivered her myself, and Dr. Elpenor Ohle cut the cord. We got electricity to the log house.

Symptoms of Arle's illness were becoming more apparent, but in the summer of 1950 he came nearest to realizing his dream for Laurel Cove. Many young people stayed with us, one of whom, in the fall of 1949, was Peace Pilgrim.

1951

I call 1951 the worst year of my life. Arle became seriously ill while in Texas visiting his family. I went to him, leaving my three young children with CCI families, and was able to bring him home on the bus. A month later, Wen Hinkey and I drove him to Philadelphia where he was operated on for a brain tumor, December 6, 1951. Emily Longstreth, Walter

Longstreth's wife, made my stay in Philadelphia as easy as was possible, considering the circumstances. After Arle was able to travel, we stayed, with the children, at my parents' home for Christmas.

1952　Returned to Celo the end of February. Arle was handicapped now, unable to do so many of his favorite things — reading, writing, speaking — but he enjoyed gardening.

1953　I returned to work with the Methodist women of the WNC conference on June 1, 1953, working with the Methodist churches in Yancey County. Arle's tumor showed signs of returning as Arle spent more time in bed, with more frequent headaches. He died July 6, 1953. I had my job with the church to support the girls, taking over Peg Calbeck's position when she retired to marry Phil Neal in October, 1953.

1955　I quit my job with the Methodist women, and worked with *Toe Valley View* newspaper and WTOE radio.

1957–1960　Upon the demise of the *Toe Valley View*, I taught fifth grade at a Spruce Pine elementary school for three years. I worked at the desk of the Nu-Wray Inn during the summer of 1958.

1960　I went back to work for the Methodist women in Yancey County.

1962　Michiko Tonegawa from Hokkaido, Japan, visited me for ten days to gain experience in rural work. She was sent by the Methodist Women's Division.

1965　My brother, Fred Hilleary, and Emily Longstreth died in March.

1966　From March through May, Betty Motsinger and I made the trip to the Far East. I financed my trip with a bequest from Emily Longstreth. We visited Michiko and met Noriko (Nora) Satsuma and Minoru Yamada, who had just become engaged.

	In the first week of August, Nora arrived for a visit.
	In September, Marla married Charles Lang.
1967	Nora returned to Japan in the last week of July.
1968	Charles Lang went to Vietnam in April. His son, Robert (Robbie) Lang was born to Marla on July 5, 1968 at the Burnsville hospital.
	At the end of August, I left for Kentucky to work in the Louisville conference, and took up residence in Grand Rivers, Kentucky.
1969	My second grandson, Derek Lang, was born to Marla at Spruce Pine Hospital, November 24, 1969.
1970–1971	Left for South America on December 31, 1970 on a month-long retreat with my former minister from Celo UM church, Joe Petree, and his group. While there, I visited Machu Picchu in Peru.
	Began serving as executive secretary to LBLAM, which I continued doing until 1980.
1972	I moved across Kentucky Lake from Grand Rivers, Kentucky, to live in Aurora, Kentucky, and work in the Memphis conference with the Lakeland Parish, mostly working with elderly people.
1973–1980	My third grandson, James Arle Hoover, was born October 2, 1973. Also worked with Kentucky's Conference council, youth camps, mentally retarded children and adult camps and served on the executive committee of the Kentucky UMW Conference. Also served as secretary to the Marshall County Advisory Committee on Aging (1973–1985), and as treasurer of the UM Rural Fellowship (1972–1980). Received citation at 1980 Memphis Annual Conference.
1980	Retired from the National Division, UMBGM. Helped recruit residents for the Lakeland Wesley Village near Benton, Kentucky, which

	was in the process of being built. Wrote a history of the LBLAM, and helped the new executive secretary get oriented.
1981	In July, moved from Aurora, Kentucky to the Lakeland Wesley Village and served as resident manager until 1985.
1985	In May, I retired *again* and returned to Burnsville, North Carolina. I took up residence in Keith Styles' ground floor apartment. Also took hospice training in the fall of 1985, and served as a Mountain Friend for a year for Carolyn Scott.
1987	Made a trip back to Japan to visit Yamadas and Michiko Tonegawa.
1988	Helped arrange for Emi Yamada to study at Brevard College in Brevard, North Carolina, for two years.
1990	Emi's mother, father, and sister Nozomi came for Emi's graduation in May of 1990.
1991	My great-grandson, Jeremy Hoover, was born in Norfolk, Virginia, on January 13, 1991.
1992	Nozomi Yamada spent a lot of the summer with me before entering Brevard that fall. Late summer, 1992, I made a trip to Oregon, Alaska, and California; also to New York City.
1992–1994	Worked on this book!!!

Section I
FAMILY STORIES

Chron./Auto Bio. I

Gertrude, Lucille and Arthelia Hilleary P. 9 about 1917

Walter Wingfield and Arthelia P. 12 1931

Aunt "Jennie" Long P. 11 about 1929

(M. Ward banquet dress) Arthelia and Mom 1932

Uncle Plummer Phillips 1968

Aunt Annie Phillips with Marla and Paula P. 11 about 1950

Cousin Fred Long 1968

Chron. / Auto Bio II

Arthelia And Esther Burns in Cheat River P. 11

Parsons W. Va. High School - graduated 1932 Pic 1968
P. 11

Barboursville Meth. Ch.
Pic 9-76   P. 13

Verna and Chester Fannin with Arthelia
Pic 10-67 P. 13

Scarritt College Nashville, Tn.
L to R → Ester Banks, Arthelia, Mattie Lula Cooper
P. 303
Pic. 1939

Vashti School Thomasville, Ga.
P. XXIX

Chron/Auto Bio IV

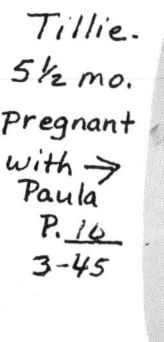

Loghouse Celo, NC 5-4-47
P. 2?

Tillie.
5½ mo.
Pregnant
with →
Paula
P. 16
3-45

Tillie -
← Work
Photo
2-64

Tillie - Lydia Holman's
← Altapass, N.C.
P. 116

Tillie - Celo UMC - Celo, N.C.
↓ Photo by Toge Fujihira

Chron / Auto Bio V

Tillie - Dag Hammarskjöld Lounge church Center for U.N., N.Y.
6-65

Tillie - Aurora, Ky. (mother - daughter blouse material from → Noriko
3-17-74

Celo ↑ log home
3-68

fenton Deaconess Home P. iZ →
Chautauqua, N.Y.

Exec. Comm. Marshall Co. Adv. Comm. on Aging
- L to R - ↓
J. Workman,
S. Reynolds,
T. Brooks,

P-187

C. Laechett,
M.J. Mitchell
(Dir)
4-9-80

Chron. / Auto Bio VI

Tillie - Styles apt. Burnsville, N.C. (first permanent and P. m. R) 10-91

Tillie - at Jean Quinns "shirt painting session"

Robbie, Jeremy and "Grandma B"

Tillie - "Senior Prom" with Jesse Rabek 5-7-94

Tillie - Sermon Higgins Mem. UMC. 4-10-94

MY MINI-AUTOBIOGRAPHY

I am a second generation American, at least on my mother's side of the family. My maternal grandparents, Christian Hertig and Susan von Allman Hertig were born in Switzerland and came to this country when they were eleven and nine respectively. They settled in the most mountainous part of West Virginia, in Randolph County. The community was called Alpena (Little Alps) and included other Swiss families — Ratzer, Knutte and Schmidlen. They spoke a dialect of German. I was born about seven miles from the Alpena post office/grocery, two-room school and Presbyterian church.

My mother, Gertrude Elizabeth, was the third child in the family of four boys and four girls. The children were: Herbert, John, Gertrude, Marie, Carl Christian, Mamie, Lula and Willis. The youngest, Willis, was only seven years older than I. He came to see me when I was born, and made this prophetic statement: "Well! I don't think she'll ever amount to much." He is the only one of the eight still living. At our Hilleary reunion, June 29 – July 5, 1992, we celebrated the July birthdays in the family. Willis was eighty-four on the twelfth. Mother's youngest sister, Biddy (Lula Hertig Burns), helped care for me as a newborn baby and thus formed a special bond that lasted until her death on October 12, 1977.

My paternal ancestors were Irish and English. Grandfather John Augustus Hilleary was probably an O'Hilleary, according to my speech teacher at Scarritt, and the O would have been dropped when the family came to America. Grandmother Arthelia Smith was English, and I was named for her. As far as I am aware, she died several years before I was born. Grandfather died when we lived at Weese Crossing, West Virginia, when I was about five. My father, John Edward Hilleary, was the youngest of three children — two girls and one boy, as far as I know. He was a logging contractor. Not the kind who worked from an office, but one who worked with the men in the woods, usually in some remote place.

I am the eldest of seven — Lucille, Fred, Oma, Ruth, Olive, and Edward. (Fred died in March, 1965.) When I was six and needed to go to school, Pop decided he would try farming, so we moved to

Kingsville, West Virginia. The school was near our home and both Lucille and I went, with Mom's brother Bill (formally named Carl Christian) as our teacher. He asked us not to call him "Uncle Bill" but of course we did, and so did the rest of the pupils. I remember him doing the Russian Bear Dance around the school room.

However, we did not go to that school very long. It was copperhead country; and when Mom saw my sister Oma holding onto the tail of a snake trying to keep it from going under the house, she refused to live there any longer. The family went back to Weese Crossing and I went to my grandmother's to finish my first year of school with my Uncle Willis, who was finishing eighth grade at the Alpena school. (I later went there for the sixth grade and had as my teacher George Cunningham, who had also taught my grandmother.)

The next segment of my life is dim in my memory. We lived several different places in Maryland where Pop had logging jobs. One distinct memory was a terrible case of poison ivy — especially on my knees and face. I couldn't walk, see or eat properly. My face was at the scab stage when someone came by selling Cloverine and Rosebud salves. Mom bought a box of each. That night she soaked the scabs with the whole box of Rosebud salve, and made a mask with a piece of sheet. The next morning my "scab face" was in the mask and I had new pink skin.

I do remember Vindex, Maryland, a mining town that was pretty rough. It was there that Mom decided she'd better tell me a few things about sex when she overheard us ten-year-olds talking about our planned chestnut hunt as a time to get together sexually. She was horrified when I had to go to court because I, a girlfriend, and two boys had looked through the keyhole of a church before meeting and we had seen the preacher with his hand up a classmate's dress. Of course we talked.

We moved back to West Virginia when I was eleven, and soon after the move I came down with typhoid fever. Dr. Wyatt, who really believed in "feed a cold / starve a fever," was my doctor. All I was given to eat was buttermilk. My sister Lucille, who later became a nurse, was sure I would have starved if the kids had not slipped me food from the table. In addition to no food, Dr. Wyatt's healing remedy was repeated doses of castor oil. After weeks of illness, I had to learn to walk again, my hair came out and came in curly. The curls didn't last, though. I remember Mom cutting off the last curl after we moved to Pleasant Run in Tucker County, West Virginia, where I finished the eighth grade.

The summer before my freshman year in high school we moved to an old log house on Cheat River. Pop had built on a new two-story section. Dark clouds and ominous wind still bring back memories of the late Sunday evening hailstorm that left us with a damaged roof and only one dry bed.

We all learned to swim in the Cheat River. I bless my mother, who was afraid of the water, for allowing us to enjoy it. She took us to the swimming hole and instructed us, "Wade out until the water is up to your chest and then swim back." It worked. She never knew that we often rode our inner tubes when the river "came down." Perhaps the Indians named the river "cheat" because of it had cheated many of them out of their lives when it "came down" so unexpectedly. With heavy rains above us, we would hear this great roar and then a huge *wall* of water would come down. After it levelled out we rode the inner tubes. I don't know how we found out that if we got in on our side of the river it would take us to the other side by the swinging bridge just around the bend — so we could walk back and do it again. (The Cheat is not a big river, so I was surprised to learn that in November 1985 it demolished downtown Parsons, and flooded all other areas along its northward course through West Virginia. In the mountain valleys the water had nowhere to go.)

I attended high school in Parsons, West Virginia. During the first two years I stayed with my father's two sisters; the first few months of my freshman year I was just outside Parsons with Aunt Jennie Long, then I moved into Parsons with Aunt Annie and Uncle Plummer Phillips until the end of my sophomore year. Aunt Annie baked huge loaves of bread, took me to all the Western movies of the early thirties, and made sure that I was given the information that I was an "eighth month baby."

For my junior year in high school I moved back home. My sister Lucille and our neighbor, Pearl Wingfield, and I made the daily nine-mile trip in three stages. We walked the first three miles up and down low-gear roads, rode four more miles with Marjorie Irons, who taught elementary school at Porterwood, and then a train took us the last two miles for a dime. On the way home, the school bus brought us back the two miles to Porterwood, and then the trip was reversed. In winter, we left and returned in the dark. This schedule took us through the eight months that Marjorie taught, but high school went for nine; so in the ninth month we walked the seven miles, and a few times skipped the train ride to save the dime.

One thing we both hated was carrying the lunchbox we shared.

Why couldn't we just eat enough in the morning to last all day? It was also the source of my last physical fight with Lucille. As children, we fought so often that Aunt Annie, who lived with Mom when we were very young, later told me that whenever they heard Lucille go "yi, yi, yi," Mom would say, without needing to look at us first, "Run, Annie, stop them before they hurt each other." From the time Lucille was old enough to sit up until this day walking home on the country road we fought. That day the argument was over who had had the bigger piece of a cinnamon roll and a piece of mince pie at noon. For the first time, I realized how silly we must look, and I vowed never to let it happen again. It didn't.

My senior year in high school I drove a Chevrolet over the roads we three had walked the year before. One morning I got too close to the edge of the dirt road and the dirt gave way. The car turned over once and lodged against a tree. We all crawled up the bank and since we were not far from home, we walked back there. I was the only one who had a scratch, so Mom pulled the cut on my knee together with tape before we were taken on to school. I don't know how a doctor in town heard about it, but he called me into his office off the street and stitched it together. I still have the scar — now 1½ inches above my knee.

I was accused of driving off the road because I was looking across the river for a glimpse of Walter Wingfield, my first serious boyfriend, Pearl's brother. I never told anyone that I *had* had a momentary mental lapse, but not due to Walter. I remember there were two more incidents when I became aware that the moment before had been a void. It got to a point where I wondered if I should continue driving a car; but then it didn't happen any more.

I graduated from high school in 1932 during the Depression. We didn't have many special events — no yearbook or a senior banquet. I did have a class ring. (If we had had a yearbook, it might have agreed with the comment my Uncle Willis made about me when he was seven. I was not part of the in-crowd in high school. It was a bit of an ego trip when I went back for my thirty-fifth reunion to find I was the only girl who had a master's degree — and that only one boy had gone on to college.)

Now I was ready for college — but *where, how*? Willis came to the rescue. He was teaching in Barboursville High School, the town where the Methodist-affiliated Morris Harvey College was located. I could stay with him and Marie, and help care for their baby. I also did babysitting for the principal of the high school — Chester Fannin and his wife, Verna.

What would have been my next year in school, 1933–34, was still in the Depression. Pop had a logging job away from home and Mom went to cook for his workmen. I no longer remember where the job was exactly, but it was probably between thirty and fifty miles away from home. Lucille, who had finished high school, and I stayed at home to help out. Not only did we have responsibility for ourselves, the home, two sisters and two brothers (Oma was with Aunt Annie going to high school), we also boarded the young man who taught our local one-room school. The arrangement ended when we burned the house down on March 17, 1934. A piece of paper blew onto the pan of coals that was smoking our thousand pounds of pork in the old kitchen. The fire destroyed the house, our dried beans and canned food. Practically nothing was saved. I clearly remember my little brother Edward, then five years old, hanging onto my skirt and crying, "Where will we live now?" I know I never lived at home after the fire, but don't clearly remember where the family lived immediately after the fire.

The Fannins, whom I had babysat for during my stay in Barboursville, heard that our home had burned. They wrote to say, if I would come immediately and help Verna during her difficult pregnancy throughout the summer, they would pay my school expenses in the fall. I went at once because I loved this couple and felt it was an answer to my need. It was a mutually helpful arrangement.

The big event of my sophomore year was the commitment I made to Christ during the ministry of John Hollister. Afterward, I was concerned, though, that there was so little feeling of great *change* in my life or awareness of Jesus' presence with me. Verna said, "You don't have to make any dramatic turnaround, but through the years when you are at the point of meeting someone's need, you will be aware of God's presence with you." That proved to be true. In a personal, unpublished book where I've recorded "My Faith Journey," I've written of these special times.

During the summer after my sophomore year, I also met Donald Dillon. It was a very brief friendship, but it is memorable because after he went to New York City he wrote very beautiful letters. I kept one that included such a lovely poem. He did not say who the author was — himself or some unknown writer — but I think it is worthy to be remembered.

> If I should feel that when I go away
> The miles between our hearts were any more;
> If when I spoke your name or knelt to pray

A fear crept into my heart not there before;
How could I go, or face tomorrow's dawn
Unless I knew, that parting brings me closer, dear, to you?

I miss you, dear. The crowding hills rear their
strange heads between your heart and mine.
And yet at night o'er God's blue window sill
The same soft star-lamps shine.

So lift up your hands, far off, lift up your hands
Toward that blue distance I am lifting mine.
For I have climbed the tallest peak that stands,
Unto the utmost pine and snow-capped peak,
That I may be nearer the Heaven that shelters you and me.

Between my sophomore and junior years of college, Morris Harvey College was in the process of moving from Barboursville to Charleston, the capital of West Virginia. During that summer I stayed with the president's parents and sister, the Rigglemans. I felt as if I was caught in the middle of a controversy. Since the college was related to the Methodist Church, and two dormitories had been built rather recently, the church people were very upset at the separation — including Chester Fannin, whose father was a Methodist minister. They thought that Dr. Riggleman and the faculty, who fully supported the move, had delusions of grandeur.

They contended that this was a small school — four or five hundred students — and it was only twelve miles from Huntington, West Virginia, and the state-supported Marshall University. They could not compete. The faculty was devoted and loyal, but had been paid very little for years. The businessmen in Charleston were certain the opportunity for service and success were greater there. The transition was difficult! Faculty offices, and some of the classes, were held in the old library building and other buildings in the inner city. But the move proved to be a success. Today the college is called Charleston University. Thousands of students attend the beautiful campus across the Kanawha River from the state Capitol. On April 9, 1992, I had dinner with Marshall Buckalew and his wife, Mary. He was my classmate in the 1937 graduating class and I had not seen him since, though he served as president of the college after Dr. Riggleman.

During my junior year, in Charleston, I stayed in private homes and worked for my room and board. The last year I worked part-time in the State Agricultural Laboratory and rented a room across the street from the Capitol building.

The year after graduation I worked full-time at the lab and had a room with Tom and Mary Stout. I wanted to help my sister Oma a little (three of my four sisters graduated from Morris Harvey) and save money to go on to graduate school — Scarritt College in Nashville, Tennessee.

My sociology teacher, Emily Olmstead, who had been the personal secretary to the founder of Scarritt [see the article on Scarritt College later in this book], had encouraged me to go to Scarritt and prepare for home mission work. The women of the West Virginia Methodist Conference gave me a full scholarship for two years with the understanding that I would then work at least four years. I later refused Arle Brook's marriage proposal in order to honor that commitment. [See the story of Arle, later in this book.]

After graduating from Scarritt in 1940, my first appointment was to the coal mining area of southern West Virginia. I lived and worked three years with Myrta Davis at Roderfield, where we served four churches, and lived in the mining camp there. Myrta was forty that year and had been working with the church for seventeen years (she was ninety-one in 1991). I was only twenty-five, so she was the one with experience. However, when she came to see me in Kentucky forty years later, our mutual friend, Greta Maddox, asked Myrta, "How well did you two get along living together for three years?" Myrta said, "Oh, we had no trouble. Tillie just went her way, and I went *hers!*" I suppose it may have been a little that way, because I *was* a more practical person. But she mustn't have minded, because we certainly enjoyed those years together and felt very close to each other until she died on September 17, 1991.

After three years, though, I requested a move because the coal dust was severely affecting my sinuses. I was also having a problem keeping my red blood count up, and spending almost all I made ($75 monthly) on iron tonics and shots. At the request of Mabel K. Howell, who had been my missions teacher at Scarritt and was a native of Asheville, North Carolina, I was sent to the Scarritt Rural Training Center at Crossville, Tennessee, which Miss Howell then directed. I worked there with Martha Almon and Dick and Juliet Milk. The change helped my sinuses, but not my anemia. Four doctors gave up on finding a cause.

At the end of that fourth year I decided to marry Arle. When I went to the Presbyterian clinic at Pleasant Hill for my Wasserman test, I was treated by a woman doctor who had served in India. I asked her if *she* could find the cause of my anemia and she said, "In the East, the first thing we look for is amoebic dysentery. If you can give me a stool sample, I'll test for it." It tested as plus two amoebic dysentery; six hydrochloric acid shots eradicated it. We assumed that the amoeba had been a "gift" from some Scarritt student from the East.

I married Arle at his home in San Marcos, Texas, October 22, 1944. We lived at his home for a year and a half, where Paula was born August 28, 1945. Marla was born March 17, 1947, in Elkins, West Virginia, before we moved to Celo Community in North Carolina on May 4, 1947. Dena was born in Celo on August 21, 1949. [Detailed stories are told in the Births chapter, later in this book.] Arle died July 6, 1953, one month after I had returned to work for the Methodist Women's Division in Yancey County, North Carolina.

I worked altogether eleven years in Yancey County. Between 1955 and 1960 I worked with a weekly newspaper, the *Toe Valley View*, and with WTOE radio. When these no longer seemed viable, I taught fifth grade for three years at a Spruce Pine school in nearby Mitchell County. One summer, I also worked at the desk of the Nu-Wray Inn, which is in Burnsville, North Carolina.

A couple in Philadelphia, Walter and Emily Longstreth, had befriended Arle and me in many ways. In March 1965 Emily died and remembered me in her will. It was put to many uses — one being a two-month trip to the Orient (March–May 1966) with Betty Motsinger. We went on our own, but while there, I visited several of our mission workers. Our itinerary included Texas, California, Hawaii, Tokyo and three other cities, Hokkaido Island, Okinawa, Taiwan, Philippines, Hong Kong, Singapore, Kuala Lumpur, Malaysia, Bangkok, Thailand, and home by Alaska and Seattle. [Details are in the Trips section, later in this book.]

In 1968, with all daughters gone, I was sent to Western Kentucky. I worked three years in the Louisville conference. In 1971 with additional money from Emily's estate, I went to South America with a retreat group of twelve to try to encourage English-speaking missionaries in Ecuador, Peru and Bolivia. I took a side trip to see Machu Picchu — an abandoned Inca stronghold, and my lifetime favorite tourist attraction, alongside Mt. Fujiyama in Japan.

In 1972 I was transferred to the Memphis conference. As part of my "ministry to tourists" I served ten years (1970–1980) as executive secretary of the Land-Between-the-Lakes Area Ministry Council, composed of nine interdenominational ministers (men). It provided worship leaders and chaplains for the TVA and the many state campgrounds in that recreational area. Before l left I wrote a history of the organization.

I formally retired from the National Division in 1980, but with my Social Security income, I could afford to stay on to help recruit residents for the Lakeland Wesley Village that opened in July, 1981. I served as resident manager of the 96-apartment complex until May of 1985, and wrote a history of its beginnings for the Conference archives.

I returned to North Carolina, where I've lived in Keith Styles's apartment, been near Marla and my grandsons, enjoyed old friends, and found some new ways to be involved in church and community.

In 1987 I revisited Japan at the invitation of Noriko Yamada, whom I had met at Michiko Tonegawa's on Hokkaido in May of 1966. Michiko was one of our mission workers. Nora had came and lived with me at Celo from August 1966 to July 1967 and now, twenty years later, she was married, had grown daughters, and she wanted me to come see them. She and her husband offered to help pay expenses.

I served at Fenton Deaconess Home at Chautauqua, New York, as co-hostess with Lois Marquart, the summers of 1988, '89 and '90.

Possibly the great trip of my later years just happened — August 18–September 9, 1993. I flew to Portland and Paula and I took the ferry *Columbia* up Alaska's inland waterway to visit my sister Olive's family. We flew back and I took AMTRAK to Los Angeles to visit with Dena, with a one-day stop-over in Klamath Falls, Oregon, to be with my "bus friend," Muriel Clark, and a return visit to Crater Lake. I worshipped on Sunday morning at the Crystal Cathedral while in Los Angeles. I flew home; and to use my last two Delta coupons, went to New York City September 27–October 2 to visit my sister Lucille and see a Broadway play.

The Woman's Division has approved my application to live in Brooks-Howell Home in Asheville, where I expect to spend my last days. As long as I can drive I am in no hurry to leave this pleasant place and my family and friends here.

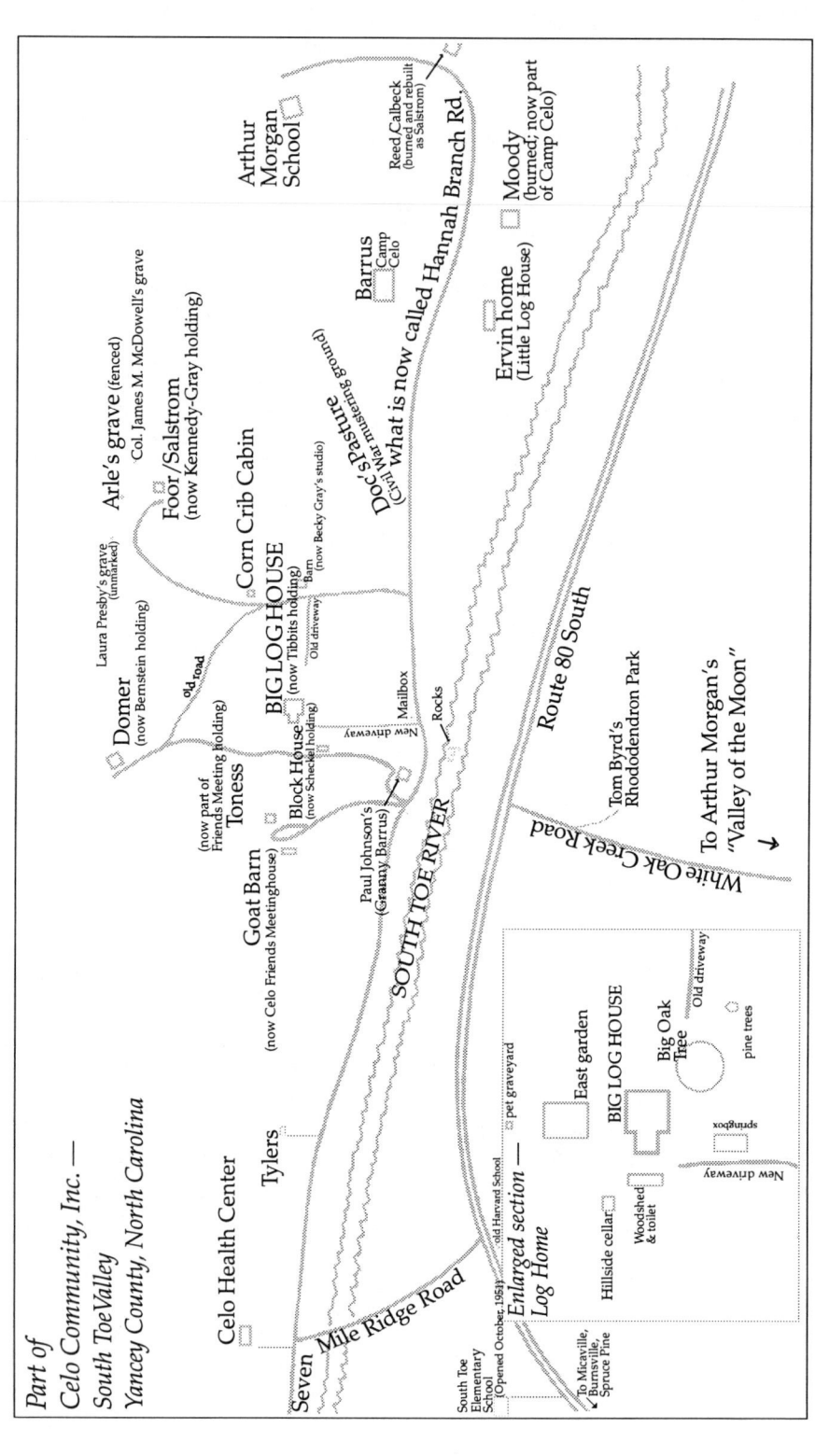

Col. J. M. McDowell's grave at Celo, N.C.
Marla and Paula Brooks
Born - June 22, 1794
Died - May 29, 1854

Log House / Laurel Cove I

David Moody, Paula, Myrtle and Joyce Foor

Peg and Paula home from nursery school P 34

Peace Pilgrim P. 39

Marla - ready for the Journey

Charles Teems and family P. 47

Log House II

Log house from back

Tillie, with Father, Christine Mother and Isobel Smucker P.59

Jim, Midge, Dave and Teresa Wyman 1967 P. 36

Christeen Steen → P. 41

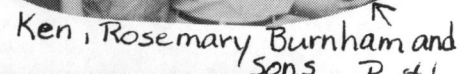

Ken, Rosemary Burnham and Sons P. 41

At Nordstroms
Top G. Graham,
F. Smucker,
L. Nordstrom, I. Smucker,
C. Steen, F. Tyson,
M. Smucker,
B. Motsinger,
C. Smucker, T. Tyson
O. Graham,
Bottom
K. Tyson,
P., M., and A.
Nordstrom P.51

Log House III

Maxine Grindstaff, Paula and Marla Brooks
Betty Jean Grindstaff, and Dena Brooks
P 50

Gladys Young P.53

Remodeled Log house

Arthur Morgan P.53   8-67

A.M.S. Girls - Debbie Denenfeld, Margie Pierce, Becki McLay, Carol Brooks and Carol Ann Swann
P. 52

Tillie with Reva and John Griffith P.37

C.C.I.

Barbara, Paul and Pearl Geouge, Lola, Marilyn Nordstrom, Bob Barrus, Harold, Elva stringer, Roy Rose, Arle, Tillie, Marla Brooks, Mary Jane, Horace Reed, Ernest, Mary Brooks, "Grandma" Erickson 6-49
Geouge, Nordstrom, Reed Children   Paula Brooks and Hazel Rose

Wendal Bull and Lola Nordstrom 12-75

Phil Nordstrom and Margit Hirschenhauser   P. 31, 4b

Paul, Susan and Mary Ohle

Ed and Nancy Whetstine with Mother and Father Smucker

Root Critters →

THE COLONEL McDOWELL PLACE

PRE-CELO COMMUNITY, INC.

Sandra Jean Higgins, of Burnsville, North Carolina, is a woman of the eighth generation from the original McDowell settler in North Carolina — "Hunting" John McDowell. She has shared with me information about this illustrious family. McDowell County was named for Joseph McDowell, a son of "Hunting" John, and in Asheville the McDowell family once owned all the property where the two hospitals, Memorial Mission and St. Joseph, now stand. William Wallace McDowell's home in Asheville is on the National Register of Historic Places. It was restored in 1980 and is open to the public. McDowell Street bears the family's name.

My chief interest in this family stems from the fact that they once owned the land where I lived in a log house in Yancey County's South Toe Valley for twenty-one years. Mary Ohle, my friend and neighbor there, traced the deeds of ownership at the courthouse for me. She thought the original owner may have been a Lattimore family from Pennsylvania who sold it to a George Rowan, but, to be sure, one would need to check at the Burke County courthouse before 1833 when Yancey became a county. We didn't do that.

In the Yancey County records the first owner of this South Toe property was Isaac T. Avery, who sold it to James M. McDowell in 1839. James was the son of Joseph, and the grandson of "Hunting" John. It stayed in the McDowell family until Sarah McDowell Silver (Sandra Higgins's grandmother) sold it to H.W. Davis in 1908. Davis sold it to Claudia Ervin Powell, and the American Friends Service Committee bought it to establish Celo Community, Inc. (CCI), in 1937. Within Celo Community the "owners" do not actually own property, but use "holdings" instead. The Ervins retained legal ownership of one small plot with what I'll call the little log house on it, next to the Moody/Barrus holding. Sitting squarely within the land otherwise held by CCI, this piece of land is still privately owned, and is now in the care of Clark, Joe, and Holt Ervin.

The first McDowell to occupy the farm, which at the time included the holding I was to occupy as well as the land the Ervins came to own, was Colonel James Moffitt McDowell. He lived in a frame house on the bank above the spot where what I'll call the big log house now stands. Sandra's information says he lived there from 1831–1854. (Yancey County records say he bought it in 1839. Perhaps he lived there while Avery still owned it.) He died May 29, 1854, and was buried on the hill nearby. His grave is near CCI's Foor/Salstrom/Kennedy holding, and slaves are said to have been buried at the foot of that hill. The McDowells were known to have owned a hundred slaves before the Civil War.

After Colonel McDowell's death the family apparently rented the farm to local people. Hattie Silver told me that her grandfather, John Autrey (a Baptist minister and the first person buried in the cemetery at the South Estatoe Baptist Church), lived on the place and trained soldiers for the South during the Civil War. The mustering ground was about where Doc's Pasture is now.

In 1894 James Alburto McDowell chose a mate, Delilah Ann Holcombe, who was displeasing to his aristocratic family in Asheville. The couple decided they would feel more comfortable on the South Toe farm. So they came with their three children and during the thirteen years they lived there, three more were born. James' brothers did come to see about the family and brought provisions regularly. They would camp under the big tree [see photo] and hunt during these visits. James farmed and ran a grist mill, and Delilah was known as a granny woman who delivered babies and cared for the sick. One of the six children of James and Delilah was Bessie, who married a Ballew and visited me in the summer of 1947. She told me that my log house, the big log house referred to earlier, was about thirty-five years old and that it must have been built after the McDowells sold the land. Her family had lived in a frame house just above it (that was no longer there), and she was a descendent of Colonel McDowell whose grave was nearby.

After H.W. Davis bought the property in 1908, his wife's sister, Annie Stowe, her brother Boyce and her sister, Beulah (Mrs. Sam) Thompson, lived on the property. Probably Boyce and Sam got Whit Ballew, of Seven Mile Ridge, to help build the big log house about 1912, and they were the first to live in it. At any rate, when they left, the property was purchased by the Ervin family, but I'm not certain the Ervins ever lived there year-round. Some who did live in the little log house (next to the Barrus holding) were Bascom Gibbs and the Ericksons (Ruby Moody's parents). In the big log house Arthur Patton possibly moved there somewhere between 1915 and 1924. Hattie Silver felt sure he was there in the year 1924; then preacher Plyler McMahan moved in. Henry and Hattie Silver moved there in 1929 and lived there until the property was sold for Celo Community in 1937. The eldest of Hattie's children, Dale, was born in the middle room of the big log house. Her daughter, Marjorie (now Gibbs) told me in 1991 what happy memories she had of the years they lived in that house, of their playing in the hay in the barn and helping to make molasses each year. Marjorie recognized the log house in the painting hanging in my living room. I gave her the snapshot that my friend, Estelle White, had used as a guide to paint the picture. The other children were Velma (Shuford), Gilberta (Stepp) and Marshall.

A couple of families lived in the big log house after Hattie left. She thought Lee Whetstine was one, perhaps Nola Westall was another, and I think Robert (Bessie's son) Ballew and his wife Florence were the ones who had just moved in December 1946 when Arle visited the Moodys in March and was told the house had just been vacated. So, Robert Ballew was the only McDowell descendent who actually lived in the big log house.

LAUREL COVE — CCI, INC.-ERA RESIDENTS

1947

The first part of this story ended with Celo Community having purchased the McDowell property as part of the 1250-acre tract comprising Celo Community, Inc. The founders of CCI were William H. Regnery, president of Joanna Western Mills Co., Chicago; Arthur E. Morgan, president of Community Services, Inc., Yellow Springs, Ohio; and Clarence E. Pickett, executive secretary of American Friends Service Committee, Philadelphia, Pennsylvania. The land was purchased in 1937.

In an article, "About Celo Community," by Ruby Moody and Louise Toness, they said that the vision for the community in "broad outlines might be expressed like this: to live among like-minded people, striving for honesty in all human relations . . . to pay allegiance to our common humanity overshadowing religious, racial, economic, or political differences; to rear children in a wholesome environment where they can become acquainted with nature and be stimulated by intellectual freedom . . . to grow from these roots a life that is full and integrated rather than shallow and fragmented."[1]

By the time Arle and I arrived at Celo Community, a two-story plus basement health center had been built on the community's property.

Arthur Morgan, who was the "brains" of the Celo Community venture, first conceived it as a kind of agricultural cooperative with a manager. He thought the manager might perhaps be my husband, Arle Brooks, who visited the community in 1940, but Arle was not at all interested in that format. For a time in the early years of the community, Ben Brost was the manager, but apparently Brost's managership did not suit the Celo Community, Inc. residents whom Morgan recruited in the early forties, many of whom were conscientious objectors to war, because the manager idea was soon given up.

In March, 1947, Arle, on his way back from a speaking engagement at a Friends college in Greensboro, decided to stop by Celo Community to see his friends, Douglas and Ruby Moody. Doug told him about the log house in the community that had just been vacated. Arle liked what he saw and learned about Celo Community. He brought back an application form for Celo Community membership for us to fill out. We were accepted for membership, and my brother Fred took us in my sister Ruth's new car to Celo.

We arrived in Celo in May with our baby girls — Paula, twenty-one months old, and Marla, less than two months. Our home was by the South Toe River. I walked through the dark rooms with few furnishings and decided I would just get in the car and go back to my brother's home. But then I went out the front door and saw the majestic Black Mountains before me and the huge, welcoming oak tree in the front yard. I decided that a house could be changed. The mountains and the oak tree would be there to encourage and inspire me.

Before I came to Celo, I knew nothing about the area, but through the years I have come to realize that the Toe River Valley is a very unique section of the diverse state of North Carolina. Bill Sharp, writing in *State* magazine once called it "the valley on the roof of North Carolina"[2] Hugh Sidey, the author of the *Life* article, "A Time of Trouble in the Toe Valley," described our part of the world in this way: "The valley is a softly beautiful dip in the Blue

Ridge Mountains along the Tennessee border. Through it the Toe River and its two branches run toward the Mississippi. . . . Few travelers enjoy [its] lovely vistas and pure, cool air, for the valley is off the beaten path. This isolation suited the early English settlers fine. They laid a neat patchwork of small farms along the hillsides. The old families married among themselves, preserving to this day one of the purest Anglo-Saxon strains to be found in this country."[3] [The story of Hugh Sidey's almost-visit to Laurel Cove is included later in this chapter.]

In western North Carolina, the two counties of Mitchell and Yancey, and part of Avery county, are included in the Toe River Valley today. But it fits no description that lowlanders or dictionaries have for valleys. This one has an average elevation of nearly 2,500 feet and is a valley only by virtue of its drainage system and the higher ridges that hem it in. These ridges are part of the Appalachian Chain — the oldest in the United States — which has more than two hundred peaks over 5,000 feet. Two of its highest peaks (Mount Mitchell at 6,684 feet and Roan Mountain at 6,286 feet) are claimed by the Toe Valley area. A section of the 469-mile Blue Ridge Parkway, which follows the crest of the Blue Ridge Mountains from Shenandoah National Park in Virginia to Great Smoky National Park in North Carolina and Tennessee, forms the valley's eastern boundary. The Black Mountains, a spur off the Blue Ridge, define the southern border, and they are the ones to claim the highest peak east of the Mississippi River, Mount Mitchell. The Bald Mountains, the Unakas, and Roan Mountain fill out the northern and western confines of the valley.

The North and South Toe rivers converge near Micaville to form the Toe River. After being joined by many small creeks as well as the Cane River and Big Rock Creek, the Toe River escapes into Tennessee as the Nolichucky River by way of a 1,750-foot gorge hewn through the Unakas. It is the only water exit the Toe Valley has. This narrow channel, and a similar one in the adjacent Avery County valley that allows the Linville River passage through the Blue Ridge, have led some to think this valley may have once been a huge inland lake.

John Griffith, son of a Methodist minister in South Carolina, and David Jensen from Iowa had arrived in Celo Community before us. We had sent money to buy some necessary household items, but my May 17 letter to my family tells what we found, "1st room —

mattress with two sleeping bags, suitcase, cardboard box, orange crate, and a lantern; 2nd room — mattress and springs with two sleeping bags; kitchen- long table, three burner oil stove, stovetop oven, two oil lamps, pan, old coffee pot, two water buckets, one dipper, broom, two scrub brushes, soap, two plastic-handled forks, knives and spoons, and a clock. The food supply consisted of a box of breakfast oats, two cans of soya beans, one of turnip greens, one of condensed milk. There were a few potatoes, a jar of molasses, and twenty-five pounds of whole wheat flour. And I mean *period*." Before I finished this letter the French Broad Electric Membership Company had put up a pole in our yard.

John had figured out that *all* one's nutritional needs were met by eating oatmeal twice a day with blackstrap molasses and then turnip greens, soya beans, and whole wheat bread for the third meal. I think that David was quite relieved when I arrived and varied the menu. He soon left to go to California. John soon left, hitch-hiked to Iowa and married Reva on May 24th. They returned to live in the front room until they left in November.

During the summer of 1947 a large garden was planted, and Arle experimented with novel building materials. He had a formula from Jack Bays for making "RBR slate" from newspapers run through a hammer mill and mixed with melted asphalt, which could then be troweled onto wood or concrete floors. The finished surface was linoleum-like. It was put on our front room floor and also used in some new buildings in the community. Jack Bays had also recommended using sawdust with cement to make building blocks, so a block making form was purchased. These blocks had some real advantages: (1) they were light in weight, easily handled; (2) they did not conduct heat and cold as readily as blocks made with sand; (3) nails could be driven into them with relative ease. They were used in our guest-cabin on the hill near our house and in the Celo Community house built for the Schwintzer family. The blockmaking was done in our barn.

In September the community members were invited to a picnic with Arthur and Lucy Morgan at their cabin in the "valley of the moon" — a cove at the top of what is now White Oak Creek Road. I was interested to see the large photo of President Franklin Delano Roosevelt on the wall with the inscription, "For Arthur Morgan from his old friend, FDR." I knew that Arthur Morgan had been Roosevelt's first chairman of the TVA. Through the years I often wondered if the French Broad Electric Membership Corp. was connected with the TVA, but I never asked, not even when David Salstrom and

I went to Marshall, North Carolina, to help them observe their fiftieth anniversary in 1990. When I began to write the story of my years in North Carolina in the spring of 1992, I called the Burnsville office of the French Broad Electric Membership Corporation to ask her. The lady who took my call referred me to Florence Ramsey in Marshall, who gave me this information: "There is no connection with the TVA. We once tried to buy power from them, but the distance was too great. The first provider of power to this valley was the Northwest Carolina Utilities, a private company with headquarters in Virginia. They served only the larger towns of Burnsville, Spruce Pine, and Bakersville — straight lines, no service to rural areas. French Broad bought that company in 1940. Mark Bennett had been with Northwest, and when ownership changed, he came to the Burnsville office with French Broad. Because of World War II, it was hard to get materials to extend lines to the outlying areas." The foregoing explains why electric power did not come to our place in Celo Community until 1948.

The girls and I spent most of the month of October at my home in West Virginia to be with my father who had fallen from a horse and fractured his hip. Reva was able to keep things going at Celo. We visited in Charleston and Barboursville, West Virginia before returning. John and Reva decided to leave in November to get work, which left the way open for David Salstrom to come from Sky Valley, North Carolina. He slept upstairs over the kitchen and knit argyle socks on a machine in the front room. I embroidered them during the winter months. It was so mild I was able to do much of it while sitting on the front porch in the good light of the sun. That was the first time I became fully aware of the low arch and setting time of the winter sun and measured its going down by the peaks of the Black Mountains.

1948

Phil Nordstrom wired our house according to a letter to family dated January 26, 1948, so I presume we got electricity about that time. I noted that I started going to the local Home Demonstration Club to get to know the valley people.

Arle named our place Laurel Cove. The six acres of bottom land was ringed by a hill covered with trees, laurel and rhododendron. He set forth his purpose and dream for the place in a brochure: "Laurel Cove is a place where people may give time for prayer, study, and work that may assist them to find greater meaning in life, and a deeper spiritual awareness. . . . There are three periods of corporate prayer, 6–7 A.M., 11–12 noon, and 6–7 P.M. Many persons may not be ready for three hours a day for prayer . . . each must begin at his own level and use the time and method that will be of greatest help to him. . . . It seems that to learn to enjoy physical labor is one of the early requirements for the life of the spirit, else a person may be tempted to spend time in prayer because he dislikes hard work. Work at Laurel Cove is for spiritual exercise, a relaxation for the body and mind from hours of prayer and study. The three hours of work are for gardening and for improving the physical facilities of the place."

In order to prepare for persons to participate in this retreat program we fixed the shed side of the barn as a guest room. Probably we also moved the corn crib to the edge of the woods and made it into the "crib cabin" with cooking facilities and a sleeping loft. The barn loft was also used for sleeping.

In April of 1948 Harry and Julia Abrahamson moved their vitamin business from Chicago to the basement of the Health Center. Harry's partner was Lloyd Tyler. He and Phyllis moved next door to us with their children Ann, 7, and Ty, 5 years old. This family has figured importantly in my life as unfolding events will show; so they are introduced even though they were not residents of Laurel Cove.

A sad event of the summer was the death of Ruby Moody's baby due to the RH negative blood factor. I wrote: "Arle and I and two neighbors went to see Doug and Ruby for just a few minutes, and Ruby wanted me to stay with her the next day while Doug went to [the hospital] for the baby [girl]. I went about 8:30 and stayed until after 4:00. He brought the baby about 1:30 and we buried her right away. Phil Nordstrom had made a nice little box and her granddad [Erickson] dug the grave a little way from the house. If anyone ever says to me 'The picture of grief,' I think I shall always see that graveside scene with just Ruby, Doug, her parents, and me present. Just before Doug nailed the box shut, Ruby asked to hold the baby. She was wrapped in a blanket so Ruby could not see her. Since she was not embalmed, she felt almost alive. Gee, at that moment I thought I would surely burst with grief. It wasn't just that *this* baby was dead, but the chances of having any more were about hopeless. To me this disease was something I *read* about, not something that happened to my friends. Phyllis Tyler has lost two or three from the same RH negative factor. She is pregnant now but hasn't too much hope that she'll be able to carry it. It is due in Feb."[4] (Several years later I found I was also RH negative.)

In July, Thelma Stoner arrived for a visit and slept at the barn. David's sister, Jessie, visited with him for a week. She slept and had her breakfast at the Tylers. Florence ("Sunny") Hickman from a mainline Philadelphia Quaker family spent a week with us and slept in the crib cabin.

David moved with his knitting business to the Foor cabin in September, and Margaret (Peg) Calbeck came to live in the front room in October. She worked some with Dave in the sock business, and met Philip Neal, the "boss" of the enterprise, when he came for a supervisory visit.

In early December (1948) I left Marla with Arle, and Paula and I visited friends in Crossville, Tennessee — the last place I worked before we married — and Scarritt College in Nashville, my alma mater, where I had lunch with President Cuninggim. I also found out on this trip that I was pregnant again.

1949

"Thelma [Stoner] plans to return in May (to attend Penland School of Handicrafts) . . . and Cora Belle Hunter, who visited Peg this Christmas, hopes to spend half of her summer here and would like for us to furnish lodging and some of her meals. Edward [Mickle] says he would like to spend some time the latter part of the summer."[5] "Arle is making blocks for the cabin we plan to build this spring."[6] "Phyllis [Tyler] left last Tuesday by plane for Chicago. She is to have her baby there under the care of two doctors who have specialized in RH negative cases. I practically outfitted her, she said. She took the bed jackets that Lucille and Edith gave me, three of my gowns, a good slip, and the black maternity dress. I spent Monday finishing a skirt that she took, and put a bodice on an aqua wool skirt that Mom sent before Christmas. . . . We have had her family for two meals and will probably have them more."[7] Baby Seth was successfully delivered on February 28, 1949.

Peg probably vacated our front room about the last of June, when she moved to the house the Reeds had exchanged for a larger one across the river. Our block cabin on the hill *was* built and the blockmaking ceased. There are records that the Celo Friends Meeting was held in the barn in June, 1949. With young children I never did attend, so I missed the black snakes mating under the eaves during Meeting.

The Celo Friends Meeting was held in the barn in summer and the meeting room at the Health Center in winter until the goat shed on the Toness holding was remodeled in 1956, where the meeting has been held from then until now.

It was raining hard the night of August 20. I felt I had prepared well for the birth of my third child. I had read *Childbirth Without Fear*[8] and had followed the diet and special exercises. Now everything was in readiness in the front room. Because of the rain I delayed calling Arle as long as possible because I knew he had to walk to get to the doctor. Finally about one in the morning. I called, and he got Cora Belle (from the cement block cabin on the hill) to come stay with me while he went for Dr. Ohle. Arle got back before the baby was born, but the doctor had not arrived. I received her, announced that it was a girl, and wrapped her in a blanket before the doctor came to cut the cord, etc. Dena was born at 2:00 A.M., August 21, 1949. Later Cora Belle said, "You were *beatified* when you announced her birth." Ignoring the middle-of-the-night house call, Dr. Elpenor Ohle said the bill was *one dollar*. When I protested, he said, "You had done all the hard work before I got there. The dollar is for the length of hose used for the enema bottle."

In Arle's letter telling his parents about Dena's birth, his mother detected that he was not well. Before sending it to his sister Elva she wrote on the top, "Bet Arle was not feeling well when he wrote this." As early as April I had noted that his headaches had returned. He had been working hard making the blocks and continuing construction of the buildings and certainly was not following the contemplative life he had envisioned for Laurel Cove. [See the separate story on Arle, later in this book.]

1950

This year came the nearest to fulfilling Arle's dreams for Laurel Cove being a retreat for young people. Many came. I have definite records of who stayed there with us, but have given up figuring out where everyone slept. Some were with us for only a meal or a brief visit, others came for months or even a few years. I want to include every name here, for the record. Those who had a bearing on my life beyond that brief summer, I will follow to the conclusion of our relationship.

Sunny, who had visited a week two summers before, had married a fellow Duke student, Bill Davidson, on August 30, 1949. She says they spent three months at Celo the summer of 1950. They were true spiritual seekers. In a 1981 letter she says, "I remember Arle saying he wished a *guru* would come over the mountain. I thought he was a fine guru, and no one finer could come."[9]

"Bill said, 'Tillie is even more impressive.' That winter we became Catholic and entered a different world. But I am still a Quaker, as well. I remember arguing with Dave Salstrom about whether cutting off squash blossoms [to fry] would cut down on the number of squashes and whether texture in food is as important as taste. . . . I loved it, and you."[10] The Davidsons now live in Maine, and with the Catholic influence, have *many* children.

Remembering my great regard for Mahatma Gandhi that summer, the Davidsons brought me a sketch their English friend, Clair Leighton, had done of Gandhi as he napped on the couch of her parents' living room in London, shortly before he was assassinated in 1948. Dena has asked for that picture. Sunny came to be with me when Arle was operated on in Philadelphia in December, 1951. We are no longer in touch at this time.

After I retired from the National Division (UMBGM) in September, 1980, I wrote to several people who had spent time with us at Celo. I was thinking I would write the account of Laurel Cove in my retirement; but my so-called retirement ended up being a five-year stint of working with Lakeland Wesley Village, and then the writing was been put off again until 1992. The above quotation from the Davidsons was one answer I received. The second important one was from Midge Smith, who had been engaged to a conscientious objector, David Wyman. He had been with David Jensen at Interns in Industry in Philadelphia. He heard about our place from Jensen.

The letter from Midge gives real insight into the 1950 summer at Laurel Cove. Excerpts from her letter follow: "I arrived during the first few days of June, 1950. . . . You gave me a room upstairs, over the kitchen in the log house. It was partially unfinished when I arrived, but we made walls from big sheets of cardboard nailed to the studs and then papered it with heavy, insulating craft paper — so it was real nice.

"Our day began with meditation in the chapel, then breakfast and work, lunch and work, supper, and another time of meditation in the evening. Maybe evening meditation was before supper.

"My work consisted of fixing up my own room, painting the outside of the cabin (the logs) with a mixture of old motor oil and red oxide pigment. (I always did think I got too much red pigment in one batch. I hope time mellowed it down.) I also helped in the garden and occasionally took care of Paula and Marla for an afternoon. I also went up to Dave Salstrom's cabin some mornings and knit argyle socks on his machine, for pay, I think.

"In mid-July, Dave [Wyman] arrived. . . . The guys lived in the loft above the chapel (in the barn) and did various maintenance and gardening jobs. I remember once you sent Dave and me up on Seven Mile Ridge to pick blackberries. *That* was a very nice day.

"At the time we felt we were being very useful, but in retrospect we realize that it was at considerable sacrifice, both economic and in terms of your own, private family life that you took us all in that summer. I don't think we have lived up to yours and Arle's hopes for us in living God-centered lives. But the input of your influence that summer was not wasted and has been reflected, at least to some degree, in our lives since then, both in that it opened new ideas and thoughts to us and made it possible for us to be together at that uncertain stage of our lives."[11]

Dave and Midge married soon after, and in July, 1967, they visited Dena and me "for a few hours with son Jim, not quite 16, and Teresa, just past 13. They [Jim and Teresa] enjoyed meeting you and seeing the beautiful log cabin they had heard about."[12]

We have stayed in touch, at least periodically, through the years. David served as Professor of History at the University of Massachusetts at Amherst until his retirement in 1991.

During the mid-1980s, I saw on TV references to lectures that David S. Wyman had given about his book, *The Abandonment of the Jews*. I kept promising myself I would borrow the book and read it. In February of 1989 an autographed copy arrived in my mail. The note on the title sheet said, "To Tillie Brooks — with admiration for your life and your example, with wonderful memories of times at Celo, with much love, and with gratitude for your patience with the very young, who thought themselves so very wise and mature. —David S. Wyman" (Dave . . . and Midge, too)

In his preface to the book, David said, "This book has been difficult to write. One does not wish to believe the facts revealed by the documents on which it is based. America, the land of refuge, offered little succor. American Christians forgot about the Good Samaritan. Even American Jews lacked the unquenchable sense of urgency the crisis demanded. The Nazis were the murderers, but we were the all too passive accomplices."[13] Prof. Randolph L. Braham, Director, Institute for Holocaust Studies, said, "*The Abandonment of the Jews* — it will certainly emerge as one, if not the only, definitive work of this highly controversial chapter of the Holocaust."[14] David served as a resource person for the filming of "America and the Holocaust: Deceit and Indifference," an episode of *The American Experience* series produced by the Public Broadcasting System (PBS) on April 6, 1994. It was good to see him in the film.

In a more recent letter, Midge wrote, "David retired from teaching, but not from lecturing, writing, and editing. He enjoys being under less pressure and having more time for his first love — baseball.

"In the fall of 1991 we spent our wedding anniversary with John and Reva at their home in Kansas City. That was a wonderful visit, with deep sharing as well as the joy of being together. . . . Our children and grandchildren are all well."[15]

Since Midge mentioned in one of her letters that John Griffith paid an overnight visit during the summer of 1950, and in another that she and David visited them, I will tell here of my relationship with John and Reva Griffith up to the present writing.

Sometime during the summer of 1947, John's parents and dog visited John and Reva. In 1963 [as told in the Trips section of this book], the girls and I visited them in Iowa on our trip to Minneapolis, Oklahoma, Texas, and Mexico. I think it was soon after that visit that they moved to Kansas City. We have at least exchanged Christmas letters through the years. In 1986 their oldest son, Chris, was murdered at a shooting range near his home (along with three other men) for no reason other than the bad luck of inadvertently witnessing a robbery. It made no sense to his sorrowing family. This devastated the whole Griffith family. I was able to express my sorrow with a hug when they happened to return to visit their "honeymoon house" on the 4th of May, 1990, while my Japanese family, Marla, and I were having a picnic at the log house.

John and Reva were on their way home from visiting his family in South Carolina and had planned to call and come by to see me, but they would have missed me. For all of us to have arrived there at the *same time* was a real serendipity!

To try to deal with the grief of Chris' death, Reva wrote a book about him. It was published by Celo Valley Books in 1992 and is called *This Song's for You*- a line from a poem written by his brother Ben. I bought a copy and let my friend, Dorothy Robinson, who had lost a daughter tragically, read it, too. She was so comforted by it that she bought her own copy. I hope the Griffiths will visit both Dorothy and me some day soon.

From my 1950 diary and letters to family there is a record of visits to Laurel Cove from the following:

7-15: Reba Hooks from South Carolina — referred to us by John Griffith's minister father. Dena and I spent a week in November with Reba's family in Bennettsville and attended her prayer group and returned to Burnsville with one of the members, Lem Crosland, now Mrs. Jim Anglin, living in Burnsville. [A story about Reba is told in the Healing Service story, later in this book.]

7-23: Raymond and Helen Binford — Quakers and parents of Naomi, Arle's former girlfriend, visited. Leland Standing and Russell Henderson, cousins of Reva Griffith, spent the summer months, also Burt Howard came in the fall.

Edward Mickle — lived in the crib cabin for about two years. He ate with us but fixed his own breakfast (late), cold cereal with "peanut butter milk" on it. He left in 1953 to serve as a clerk in the Mayflower Hotel in Washington, D.C.

Dick and Lois Ann Domer came in 1950. Their firstborn arrived in the same corner of the front room of the log house as Dena, my third. They lived in the crib cabin, then built a log cabin on the ridge above. Lois Ann had a beautiful voice and sang solo parts in the community production of the *Messiah* given in Burnsville, North Carolina. The Domers went to and joined the Brüderhof in 1954.

9-26: A 54-cubic-foot home-built freezer was constructed in the shed by Wendell Hinkey and John Robinson. John and his wife ate supper with us that night. John was an easy-going kind of mechanical genius. He could repair almost anything, but he was also a procrastinator — or else he promised more than he could get done. To finally get my radio fixed, I went into the shop and said, "I am going to stay here while you repair my radio." I had to do the same thing to get him to say what the bill was. His shop was in the old building on the east side of the square in Burnsville, later used by Troy McCurry and then torn down to build the main branch of First Union Bank.

10-8: Charles and Wanda Jackson visit, then spend the night in the log house. Some years later when Wanda was Wanda Lea, and then Wanda Austin, she made pottery and then worked for Social Services Department of Yancey County, from which position she is now retired.

10-12: Arthur Morgan ate lunch with us.

Thelma Stoner, whom we had known in Philadelphia first visited in 1948 but came to stay in 1950. She attended Penland School of Handicrafts to learn to weave. Most of the time she lived in the block cabin, did her weaving, and taught kindergarten to Paula and other community children at Grandma Erickson's house. She married Ralph Becherer, and they moved to New England in 1952.

Christine Steen spent some time in late summer of 1950, but a longer time the next summer when I really needed some help and moral support. Arle's illness had progressed, and Dena, not quite two, was so upset that even though she *had* walked and talked, she was not doing either now, and the only thing she would eat was a mixture of raw oats and apples with peanut butter and soya milk. While I helped cook at the Moody camp, Christine took complete charge of Dena. They formed a bond that lasted through Christine's years in a retirement home in Michigan.

When Julius Patton came to my home, taking the 1950 census, he said, "You know, this is the third census I've done here in the South Toe Valley, and I just ran across something I never heard tell of before. The Tylers down the road have three children, and everyone of them was born in a different state!" I said, "How would you feel if you met two in a row? Mine were born in Texas, West Virginia, and North Carolina." Julius just shook his head.

After the leaves had fallen in the fall of 1950, Mildred Ryder came and spent a week with us. She slept and ate with us in the log house. She was on a spiritual quest that culminated in her changing her name to "Peace Pilgrim" and starting on her life mission in January, 1953. I have pictures of her taken in our east garden when she visited again after her pilgrimage started. She wore tennis shoes, pants, a long-sleeved T-shirt, and over the shirt a kind of cobbler's apron. In the all-around pockets, she carried her simple possessions such as a comb, toothbrush, address book, and unanswered letters. The front of her tunic carried the words, Peace Pilgrim, and on the back, "Walking 25,000 miles for World Peace." On this visit I felt she was a little self-righteous, and it made me defensive.

"If everyone did what *you* are doing, who would provide a place for them to stop over?" I said to myself. Before her next visit, November 6, 1956, she had gone on a 45-day fast — nothing but distilled water. She came through as a truly enlightened, love-filled person, expressing no condemnation, but gladly accepting the God-given role others were playing. I felt the difference!

She really did walk 25,000 miles. (She counted the miles and would not accept rides while counting.) She walked in the North in summer and in the South in winter. She visited again when I lived at Grand Rivers, Kentucky (January 23, 1972). She came walking in, swinging her arms freely, while I was in the process of *sitting* on Dena's packed bag trying to get it closed for Dena's trip to Hawaii. Oh, the freedom of no excess baggage!

Peace visited me while I lived at Aurora, on the west side of Kentucky Lake, probably in the late seventies. She met with people who attended activities at the Lakeland Parish Center. They had been fascinated with the stories she told about her pilgrimage and were greatly anticipating her next visit.

In 1981, from Fort Worth, Texas, she wrote, "I'll be visiting you — which I guess will be in October. . . . I'll try to write you in a couple of months about an exact time for my visit to you in Kentucky. Lovingly and Peacefully, Peace."[16]

I had later word that she would arrive the last of September; but she was killed in a head-on collision on the way to a meeting with a Methodist minister in Illinois in July. So she was unable to keep that last appointment with me and our people. After all the dangers she had faced during those thirty eight years of her pilgrimage, as Dena said, "It is kind of ironic that she be killed in a stupid car wreck." But her influence continues in the things she has written and the thousands of lives she touched in person (as she did mine) and through TV, radio, and the posthumous publication of her writings in book form.

1951

If I were to choose the worst year of my life, it would undoubtedly be 1951. In a diary entry dated July 11, 1951, I said, "Arle's sick. Marla is not sleeping well. This is the lowest day of my earthly existence."

After the summer of 1950, when some aspects of Arle's dream for Laurel Cove had been realized, I wrote in *A Diary of Arle's Illness*, "He said he thought in the middle of the night, 'Why didn't we get rid of all our holding except our house and enough for a garden and not try to have a Retreat program?' because he felt he had nothing to give."[17]

The diary is a record of his struggle to earn a living at a job at which the diary says, "He is not skilled and feels inadequate and yet hasn't enough interest in or love for the work to become skilled. He dislikes the idle chatter and even worse the kidding that doesn't really seem like kidding." He was working with Celo Mountain Products, a cooperative work group, and helped to build the Schwintzer, Johnson, and Thomas houses. All the while his illness was increasing in frequency and intensity.

In the midst of all this, there were other happenings as my diary reports:

May 24: The Paul Johnsons arrived as next door neighbors.

May 26: I spent the morning with and had lunch in Asheville with Mabel K. Howell and met her brother and wife. (The Brooks-Howell Retirement Home is named for them.)

June 24: I started to work at Moody's summer camp.

July 4: David and Beverly White spent the evening.

July 22: My mother, my sisters Olive and Lucille, and my niece, Morna Lee, arrived and stayed until the 26th.

July 25: Arle went to Asheville for eye exam.

August 17: Margaret Taylor spent the evening.

August 19: Camp ended. Christine Steen had cared for Dena while I worked there.

August 25: Phil and Grace Neal to dinner, and Herbert Douglas arrived.

August 28: After almost a month of freedom from headaches, Arle left for Texas with Herbert Douglas to see his folks. Paula started first grade at the old Harvard School. Luna Ray was her teacher. (The new South Toe Elementary School opened on October 19, 1951, and Mae Chrisawn was Paula's teacher.)

Late in the afternoon Glenn, Anna Mae, and Glenda Miller arrived unexpectedly and found me in a "canning mess." They spent the night. Glenn was concerned because Anna Mae seemed to be having an emotional/mental breakdown. These folks were special friends from one of my churches at Crossville, Tennessee.

September 7 to 15: Russell Henderson (Reva Griffith's cousin) and Ann Yarrow spent a week.

September 12: Arle was ill when he arrived at his home in Texas. Finally Arle's sister Hazel wired me on September 21, 1951 that I would have to come to decide what to do about Arle.

September 25: I was elected chairperson of CCI.

September 27: With money from the CCI Emergency Fund, I went to Texas and brought Arle back on the bus with a two-night stop-over with the Millers in Crossville, Tennessee. We arrived home on the sixteenth of October. Community members had kept the girls during my absence. I *know* the Tylers kept Marla. *Probably* the Reeds kept Paula, and Ruby Moody kept Dena.

November 13: With the girls again with friends, Wen Hinkey and I took Arle to Friends Hospital in Philadelphia and returned on the seventeenth. The next day Ruby brought the phone message that Arle had been moved to Philadelphia General Hospital. I took Dena and went by train back to Philadelphia on the twenty-first; I stayed with the Ken Burnhams over Thanksgiving. We moved to a third floor apartment that Emily Longstreth rented for us ten blocks from the hospital on the twenty-seventh. She and other friends stayed with Dena while I visited Arle in the hospital. He was operated on for tumor of the brain on December 6; he walked to the apartment on the nineteenth, and my brother Edward came for us on the twenty-second and took us to my family's home in West Virginia. My brother Fred had brought the other two girls from North Carolina. We all enjoyed the holidays together and stayed on.

1952

In late February I wrote to Arle's sister Elva and her husband Harold, "We're back home and glad to be here. . . . We found plenty of wood and many other signs of neighborly love. [Mary Ohle had planted crocus by the spring.] . . . Arle is feeling fine and is enthusiastic about his gardening."[18]

One of my first thoughts when I was ready to write about the year 1952 was, "How did we subsist with neither of us working?" Again my habit of keeping records and writing letters came to my rescue. In March I wrote, "You know already both Arle and I worked for subsistence wages before we were married . . . believing that we should give all we could and take only what was needed for ourselves. . . . Part of our philosophy had been that when you *give all* you have to give, then your *real needs* will be cared for."[19] To be really honest, this was more Arle's idea than mine — although I gladly went along with him even to the extent of giving up any insurance I had carried. I felt that Arle's belief in this was justified because his real needs were met to the end, and to an unbelievable extent, the same principle has continued to hold true in my life.

I had kept a record of *every* gift from family and friends — from the $1000 from Mr. Regnery (one of the friends of CCI) to $25 from my Home Demonstration Club to two dollars from Francis Ballew. The record shows that the total of gifts received from September 28, 1951, to November 20, 1952, was $2,565.52.

We decided a good use for some of the money would be to put a pump in the spring, pipe water and put a bath in the cabin on the hill, making the cabin a possible source of rental income. Water was also piped to the outside of our own log house, and the barn was stuccoed and improved inside for sleeping space.

Arle was greatly frustrated because the part of his brain that controlled his speech and writing had apparently been removed, and he could no longer do the work that had been an important part of his life. But he did enjoy the gardening!

We had bought a rototiller, but he and mechanical things never did get along, so I did some tilling. I felt that nature pulled a cruel trick on him. He had planted a row of sweet potatoes down by the barn. When he dug the first hill, he came running to the house with a thirteen-by-eleven-inch sweet potato! It was the *only one!* All the rest were the size of a finger. It was *so* discouraging!

Both Thelma Stoner and Edward Mickle had left in the spring of 1952.

When the summer camp at the Moody place was over in August, Margaret Taylor and her two sons, Robert and John Paul, moved into the remodeled cabin, and Margaret taught music at the South Toe School. The cabin provided some income for us, with the Taylors staying until September, 1953.

In September, Arle and I were given a scholarship to attend a Camp Farthest Out near Hendersonville. The people there were a loving group, and many prayers were offered for Arle's recovery.

1953

January 24: "We (Home Demonstration Agent and I) drove all the way from Asheville in the snow . . . I was glad the snow wasn't so bad here. Arle worries enough even when conditions are the best when I am away. . . . Arle enjoyed working with his saw last week — even earned five or ten dollars. He's now sitting beside me sharpening the bow saw."[20]

April 1: "We had a letter yesterday telling us that our way was paid for Camp Farthest Out again this September." . . . I had a letter yesterday saying that I could with all safety feel that I would be the Rural Worker for Yancey County when Peg retires this fall to marry Phil Neal. I will also work half-time this summer. I will begin in June. . . . I will be furnished a car with $40 for car expense and $150 per month salary with two days a week off and one month vacation with pay."[21]

May 28: "I know you always want to know how Arle is . . . I hated to write when I was feeling discouraged about him. A couple of weeks ago . . . in the middle of one night I decided that I'd resign the job before they went to the expense of getting me a car; but when morning came, things looked a little brighter . . . He was dragging his right foot, and his articulation was very poor . . . If I find that my working affects him adversely, I will quit and trust that there will be some other way."[22]

June 26: "I just love my work. If Arle can just be well, there is much he can do to help in it. . . . Arle is pretty sick again . . . yet he looks so well, weighing more than at any time since we were married. . . . I sent him to be checked, and everything except *that head* was in perfect order."[23]

July 1: "Emma Robinson (age 12) helps me with the children.

... Arle is still in bed most of the time ... he is a little weak, but pressure in his head has lessened considerably."[24]

July 5: "So sorry to say that Arle is not better. ... He tries *so* hard to do little things to help me. ... He went with the kids to the river for half an hour this afternoon."[25]

Arle became ill that night, and I gave him a shot at 3:30 A.M., and he slept. I was due to start Bible school at Celo that morning so I asked Paul Johnson to come and sit with Arle. When Bill Ebeling came by to the freezer about 11:30, Paul asked him to go for Dr. Ohle. Elpenor (Dr. O.) arrived before Arle died at 11:50, a few minutes before I got home at 12:10. Having been warned at the Health Center that Dr. Ohle had been called because they thought Arle was dying, I had left the children with a neighbor. The cause of death was hemorrhage of the brain.

The funeral service was after the manner of Friends, held from the front porch of the log home, and Arle's body was buried on the hill above Colonel McDowell's grave. In August I prepared a special letter:

To those who have loved and befriended Arle and 'Tillie' Brooks.

> Tillie plans to remain in Celo Community with the three girls. She is most thankful for her job working with the Methodist churches of Yancey County under the Women's Society of Christian Service. She desires to express her thanks to God for your many evidences of love, especially during the last three years. Since Arle's death your words of sympathy and testimonies of gratitude for what he meant in your lives, have been indeed "the oil of gladness." God is indeed most merciful. May we all be blessed because a man named Arle Brooks was loaned to us for a time.

The notice in the *Yancey Record* said, "Funeral services for Arle Brooks, who passed away at his home at Celo, July 6, were held at the home on July 7 at 5:00 P.M., but those who knew him realize it was only his body that 'passed away.'" The real Arle lives on in his fuller, freer, eternal abode and in the hundreds of lives he touched in this and other countries in his short forty-four years.
As requested by Arle, he was buried very simply in a beautiful pine casket made by Wen Hinkey and Phil Nordstrom; the bed for his

worn-out body was made of fragrant pine boughs and a quilt sown by his mother. The service was partly after the manner of Friends, and Arle's body rests in a dogwood and rhododendron bower in Celo Community.

The return of the cancer (after more than a full year of freedom to do hard physical work) was gradually causing paralysis of all his faculties, yet only three times, and those in the last month before his death, did he have to endure great pain; one time being from midnight to 5:00 A.M. of the day he died. He did not move or regain consciousness from five o'clock until he was gone at 11:50 A.M. "Hemorrhage of the brain, a great blessing," the doctor said, sparing him and all those close to him the agony of suffering that might otherwise have been his lot. And so in death as in life, gentleness, peace and quiet unobtrusiveness found sanctuary in him.

We seem to give him back to Thee, dear Lord, Who gavest him to us. Yes, as Thou didst not lose him in Thy giving, so we have not lost him by his return. Not as the world givest, givest Thou, O Lover of Souls! What Thou givest Thou takest not away. For what is thine is ours always if we are Thine. And life is eternal; and love is immortal; and death is only a horizon; and horizon is nothing save the limit of our sight. Lift us up, strong Son of God, that we may see further; cleanse our eyes that we may see more clearly; draw us closer to Thyself that we may know ourselves nearer to our beloved who art with Thee. And while thou dost prepare a place for us, prepare us for that happy place, that where they are, and Thou art, we too may be, through Jesus Christ our Lord.
Amen.

— Archdeacon Wilberforce

With the three children and my work, I really did not have time to grieve, but I *did* go back to Camp Furthest Out in September and cried the whole week. Every time someone would ask about Arle I would start all over again. It was good to be among such loving people.

Peg and Phil Neal did marry at Higgins Memorial Methodist Church in Burnsville on October 4, 1953. Paula was the flower girl and got locked in the bathroom at the Nu-Wray Inn, and they had to go in from the roof to get her out. I doubt if Paula has ever locked a bathroom door since.

I rented the cabin for two weeks to the Andersons and for one week to Louise Toness's mother after the Taylors moved out in August.

I bought an electric stove for cooking and a small laundry stove for heating the kitchen of the cabin. Fannie Crowell, my "Conference Mama" persuaded me to let the Wesleyan Service Guild finance getting running water into the house with sink, hot water heater, and washing machine. That also involved putting in a septic tank. A group of Arle's friends from Mississippi providentially provided the amount of money Phil Nordstrom had estimated the job would require. This financial help came in October but the new facilities were not installed until early 1954.

1954

March 21: "Next Monday I am going to make a circuit in the middle of the state. I will speak to a women's group Monday, Tuesday afternoon, and evening. I will be back home Wednesday. Bertha and Paul Ballew will stay with the girls . . . and Paul will get my garden ready to plant."[26] I visited Bertha in the rest home in August of 1993. Paul is dead. Bertha was eighty-five years old and almost blind. She reminded me that she and Paul had stayed with the girls while I was away — and she made me fix Paul a bed downstairs because she was afraid in a strange house by herself. [Bertha died on December 10, 1993.]

Sometime during the summer — bean stringing time — Lura McMahan and I kept a pair of physically handicapped twins at my home for a few days while their parents took a trip. Also, Juanita Presnell spent a weekend with me after their home burned. [Both of these stories are told in the "People" section, later in this book.]

It was probably after Camp Celo closed in late August, 1954, that the great exodus from CCI to the Brüderhof took place. The Brüderhof is a Christian commune in South America, and it has an affiliated community, New Meadow Run, in Farmington, Pennsylvania. The Moodys persuaded the Barruses to take over the running of Camp Celo, so the Moodys could leave. Dave Salstrom and Margaret Taylor were married in my living room on August 28, and then they also left the community for the Brüderhof. They stayed for several months before returning to their former holding in Celo. "Pep" Hinkey, the Moodys and the Domers still live at the Brüderhof.

I recall that Dave and Margaret Salstrom were back in the community by the next spring because Dave helped Phil Nordstrom enclose one end of my back porch to install a bathroom there. They also worked together finishing the building of the Celo Methodist Church.

1955–1957

In the summer of 1955, John McConnell and his children, Cary and Connie, arrived in the community. As far as I know, no one in the community had heard of them before they arrived. John lived part of the time in crib cabin, and then in the block house on the hill above us. Some of the time Connie stayed with the Tom Leas, but a lot of the time with us. Cary stayed with us most of the time. I remember that I had stood up at PTA for five children in five different grades that year: Dena in first, Cary McConnell in second, Marla in third, Connie McConnell in fourth, and Paula in fifth.

John was enough of a "con man" to persuade Erling and Louise Toness that the Toe Valley could support another newspaper, and since I knew quite a few people through my church work, they convinced me that I would be a "big asset," so I quit my job with the Methodist Conference women. [This story is told in the account of the *Toe Valley View* and WTOE Radio, at the end of this section of this book.]

Wendal Bull moved to the community in October, 1956. He was a long-time friend of Arle's and had visited us with his wife, Ada, before Arle died. Wendal and Ada slept in the barn.

The entry in my journal dated November 10, 1956 tells of Paula's ten-day trip to New York City with Dorothy Barrus, and also notes that I went to the Yancey County prison camp twice monthly. I did this for eleven years. One of my favorite prisoners was Charles Teems. He was released in May, 1959, and that year we invited him to visit us at Christmas, but he was unable to come. He trained for the Baptist ministry at Fruitland and began serving churches. He visited us with his wife and one daughter in 1965. In the summer of 1967 he visited us again with his wife and two little girls. After a lapse of twenty-six years, I got a phone call from this "long-lost friend." I invited him to lunch on my birthday, February 11, 1993. After our three-hour visit, I found that he had served his congregation faithfully and creatively — now at a church near Newport, Tennessee. I told him *again* that it was worth every hour I spent at the prison camp if I had had any influence for good on his life. He said he had gotten my phone number in Kentucky from Phil Nordstrom, but I wasn't home when he first called. So now he had tried again.

Also in the November tenth entry, I said, "I have a special assignment to do for the community . . . one that I do not fancy — chair of a committee to try to work out something with the Tylers." They had moved from the community, and since property is held under a Holding Agreement instead of a deed, it sometimes takes some negotiating to get a matter settled to everyone's satisfaction. I may have been asked to do this because I had felt very close to the Tylers. I've already mentioned the birth of their son, Seth, and Marla's staying with them during Arle's illness, but we did not stay in touch after they left.

However, after I returned to Burnsville in 1985, I began to read stories and see notices of novels by Anne Tyler. Finally I asked Dave Salstrom "Is she *our* Anne Tyler?" and he said it was. In early December, 1990, I had a call from Elisabeth Evans. She was writing a biography of Anne Tyler and heard that I had been a neighbor of the Tylers — could she come and interview me. I told her that I remembered very little about Anne, but on the sixteenth she came anyway, and brought me a copy of Anne's novel, *The Accidental Tourist*. I rented the movie later after reading the book. Liz promised a copy of the biography, but I have not seen it.

April, 1957: "I had invited Hugh [Hugh Sidey, the author of the article on the Toe Valley cited later in this book, in the section on the *Toe Valley View* newspaper] and Paul, [his] photographer, to have supper with me on Friday of the night they were here . . . Mollie [Robinson], Emma's mother, came after she was through at the lunchroom and we worked like fighting fire. I was getting a lot of things done that should have been done a long time before. At five o'clock Dottie [Barrus] sent the phone message that they had been called back to Washington and regretted that they could not come. . . . We all just sighed, relaxed and enjoyed our nice clean house. Hugh says he's going to bring his wife down here for his vacation and is taking a rain check on the invitation. I was really going to give them quite an experience. I was including on the menu some of the things that grow *wild* around here." I had prepared Laetiporus sulphureus (also called chicken-of-the-woods mushrooms), lamb's-quarters (greens), and wild blackberry cobbler! (Hugh Sidey is still reporting, I saw on TV that he was on the plane with President and Mrs. Bush when they went home to Texas after leaving office; and later, as a panelist on the "Washington Week" in Review on April 29, 1994, I saw him representing *Time* magazine.)

In late summer of 1957, Robert Early, minister of the Spruce Pine Methodist Church, came to see me at the *Toe Valley View* office in Spruce Pine to say that they were short a fifth grade teacher at the Harris Elementary School, and they wanted me to consider the job. I think he knew that the newspaper wasn't paying me, and he was concerned. So even though I had no teacher training, I undertook the challenge. It was a help to me and my little family that, at the same time, my first co-worker (from Roderfield, West Virginia in 1940–43), Myrta Davis, wanted to study a year at Penland School of Handicrafts. She rented my block cabin and cooked the evening meal for the girls and me in exchange for her meal at our house from September, 1957 until September, 1958.

I signed the contract to teach the next year, and during the summer of 1958, I worked at the desk at the Nu-Wray Inn and sold World Book Encyclopedias. After Myrta left, Bill Ebeling's ex-daughter-in-law and three children lived in the cabin for about three months.

Early in 1959 Wendal Bull moved to the cabin on the hill. On June 16 he brought a thimbleful of frost from the top of my car for me to see — the latest frost we ever experienced at Celo. Some time during that year Don Fortenberry helped Wendal set out the pine trees on the bank above the house. Don and Ann lived in the crib cabin.

Toward the end of my first year of teaching I told my family, "One of the boys in my [class]room and the daughter of the man who runs our school store saved notebook paper wrappers (and had others saved by other people.)"[27] Together they collected 4,991 in the contest. Rebecca won first prize — a TV set, and Johnny won a bicycle. They also sent in their teacher's name. The thirteen highest in the United States won an expense-paid trip to New York City at the end of June for their teacher. I was one of the lucky thirteen. I was glad I had a sister in New York!

On the morning I was to leave, I was in my garden fixing a fence to keep the rabbits out, and I thought, "What a day of marvels I live in! Tonight I will be eating dinner in New York with sister Lucille and Bill." I flew from Charlotte, and it happened as I had thought. Today the marvels are even greater.

The Brooks clan visited in July. Granddad Brooks had died February 18, 1957; Mary had survived a broken hip, and Roy was using a new "voice box." During a family croquet game, Roy came in laughing and slapping his leg to tell me that Mary had done the impossible! She knocked her ball through the two starting wickets, and it went through the one on the right, too, without stopping!

From November 1 to December 1, Wendal took the wood

shakes from the roof of the log house and put on regular roofing shingles — my Christmas gift, he said. Emily Longstreth had sent the money for new shingles.

I decided I would teach at Spruce Pine one more year. Now there was an added difficulty. They were upgrading highway 19E across Chalk Mountain so we had to detour by Penland. Flora Belle Roberson who taught at Harris High and I took turns driving. We also took Mary Bennett who taught at Penland.

The school year ended with snow that lasted into April and May. I think we lacked only one day for being out a *straight month*, and when we did have school, only the pupils from town could get there. My class made a calendar of those months, using weather symbols, drawings, clippings, and dates. The calendar display included a picture of the class and teacher. It has been laminated and is in the Spruce Pine Public Library.

When Marla started to South Toe in 1953, two of her classmates were the Grindstaff twins, Maxine and Betty Jean, and during the late 1950s and early 1960s they were pretty much a part of the "Log House Family." They helped Marla celebrate her sixteenth birthday with a slumber party. (Betty Jean came to my seventy-fifth birthday luncheon in 1990 — "to honor my second mama," she said.) In the fall of 1960, I went back to work with the churches. It must have been very routine or else I was awfully busy because I didn't write that I had attended a short course at Scarritt in Nashville in January, 1962. I arranged to leave the girls with Mildred Ray's sister, Evelyn. But she turned out to be so afraid to stay alone in our home while the girls were at school that they told her she did not need to stay, so she left. Since Paula was a junior in high school, they managed without her.

We never had a TV while we lived at Celo. Sometimes my next door neighbor, Gertrude Barrus, would invite me for something special on NBC News with Huntley and Brinkley. During the *Bonanza* heyday, we would go on Sunday nights to watch TV with Willard and Mary Lee Hill who served as second parents to the girls. They feel the same way about them to this day. (Willard died October 2, 1993.)

Some time during the summer of 1961 I went to a three-day retreat at Brevard College. On Wednesday afternoon I was in the reception area when four rather strangely dressed people came in. Of course I wanted to be especially gracious to strangers in our midst. I found they were Mennonites from Ohio — father, mother, and daughters, Christine and Isabel. They told me they had driven down the Blue Ridge Parkway and just *wished* they could meet some of the "mountain people" who surely lived off the parkway. I said, "I am a mountain gal who lives about eight miles (as the crow flies) off the parkway. I guess you should go home with me."

I found that these people were the Smuckers (of "With a name like Smuckers it has to be good" fame.) Even though the strictest Mennonites did not traditionally drive cars, they justified driving their Buick by the fact that they were going to retreats where they sang the scriptures — especially the Psalms. We enjoyed their contribution to our retreat program. When we were ready to leave Friday, they said to me, "We appreciate your invitation. We will follow you home when you are ready to go."

I suppose I *meant* it, but I didn't *really* expect them to accept the invitation to go home with me. But home we went.

I gave the parents my downstairs bedroom. I think the girls slept in the barn. Isabel did some oil painting of the mountains and a picture of Marla from a snapshot I had taken. They stayed until Tuesday morning. I had taken them to see Ed and Nancy Whetstine (really *authentic* mountain people) and probably to Church on Sunday. One day we had a potluck dinner at the Nordstroms with the Grahams, Tysons, and Betty Motsinger.

Through the years when I've eaten Smucker's jam with someone, I've told this story and added the admonition "Don't ever issue an invitation unless you are prepared to follow through."

In the summer of 1962 the Woman's Division sent a Japanese woman, Michiko Tonegawa, who had been teaching in an agricultural college in Sapporo, to spend ten days with me to get some idea how we did rural work in the United States. That was the beginning of the saga of my Japanese Families [told in the Japanese Families section, later in this book]. Noriko Satsuma lived with me in the log house from August, 1966, until July, 1967. She married, and then after twenty-three years, came for her eldest daughter, Emi's graduation from Brevard College. The one place she *really* wanted her family to see was the log house, so on May 4, 1990 we went to the log house for a picnic with her family — her husband, Minoru Yamada, and daughters, Emi and Nozomi.

Elizabeth Morgan did a lot of the preliminary work in preparation for the opening of Arthur Morgan School (AMS) in the fall of 1962 — 7th, 8th, and 9th grades were included. Since it was predominantly a boarding school, and dormitories had not been built, the students were housed with community families. Dena went for her eighth grade that first year of the little, private school.

As nearly as I, Dena, and Bob Barrus can remember the following girls stayed with us sometime between the opening of AMS and my exodus to Kentucky. in September, 1968: Susan Campbell, Faith Morgan, Lisa Jasnowski, Margie Pierce, Becki McLay, Carol Anne Swann, Anne Beadenkopf, Riva Kieklighter and Debbie McPhee from Vancouver, Canada who had to be sent home early. Her last chance before being sent home was experienced with me. She burned my table putting hot candle wax in a milk carton. When the carton started to break, she poured the hot wax in the sink and then flooded the kitchen running hot water to try to wash the wax down the drain. Ernest Morgan came the next morning and got her "candle" out of my drain pipe. She peed on the rug by her bed. I could burn the rug, but getting the odor out of the wood floor was not easy. She sat in the bathtub and ate Fruit Loops by the hour. I've never liked the *sound* of them since.

She had been a similar *trial* to her family. She was not a mean child — just didn't seem to have common sense. Her mother did write to thank me for my patience — saying that Debbie had enjoyed living with me.

Paula graduated from high school in 1963, and I took the girls with me to Minnesota for a rural church meeting. [That story is told in the Trips section, later in this book.] We went on to visit Arle's folks in Texas. It was the first time I had been back since I went for Arle in October, 1951. The girls had been there to visit several times.

In March of 1965 my brother Fred died, and I went to West Virginia for the funeral. Our longtime friend in Philadelphia, Emily Longstreth, also died the same month. She remembered me in her will, as mentioned earlier, and also in the trips section, later in this book.

I had celebrated my "Golden Birthday" on February 11, 1965, and experienced a "reverse domino effect." The women of the Boring's Chapel WSCS gave me a four-place setting of china. This is what started me off on a course of giving attention to things around the house. Since there were already four of us in the family, I decided that, in order to have company, we needed an eight-place setting. So with the help of some women's groups, I got eight place settings and some extra pieces. Then I needed a place to put the china, so I got the china cabinet from the cabin on the hill and refinished it and the buffet to match. It became apparent that it would be nice to distinguish the dining room from kitchen; so I had Cartha Duncan crochet a twelve-by-eight-foot rug from nylon hose (she did a spectacular job of blending shades.) Then, it seemed, I needed a table and chairs. I went to Woodys, out of Spruce Pine, got eight chairs, and he sent down-state for a table to match. He let me pay by the month. I *did* have company, of course — in style! Marla now has the table, china cabinet, buffet, and chairs, and we still use them for family get-togethers. I still use the dishes, and the rug was sold at Lakeland Wesley Village.

In the fall of 1965, I got Marla off to Brevard College and Paula to Alaska. From March to May, 1966, Betty Motsinger and I went to the Orient. Dena stayed with Lois Doan, who had previously spent many nights with Dena.

It was probably during the spring of 1966 that Gladys Young spent a number of days at the log house recuperating from a rather lengthy burn-out/emotional breakdown. Not long afterward she returned to her former position as a court reporter.

On November 3, 1966, Marla married Charles Lang in Alabama.

In February, 1967, Connie McConnell returned and stayed in the crib cabin for a few weeks. I still hear from her about once a year. She has changed her name to Coronella Keiper and is an *avid* disciple of Christ (she never did *anything* in moderation.)

In the summer of 1967, Arthur Morgan spent the night in the log house. He had possibly come for the annual meeting of CCI. He was busy writing the book, *Dams and Other Disasters*, about the Corps of Army Engineers, published later in 1971. Earlier he had tried unsuccessfully, through litigation, to prevent the Corps from flooding the Seneca Indians out of the Allegheny River Valley in upstate New York.

I took his picture with my table, chairs and buffet. I think he had specified what he wanted for breakfast. I believe the menu included prunes. It was an honor for me to have this illustrious man as my guest. Arthur Morgan died in 1975 at age ninety-seven.

In the spring of 1968 Marla's husband, Charles, was sent to Vietnam; so she came home, and their first son, Robert, was born July 5 in the Burnsville hospital and came to the log house as home.

I took a leave of absence from Celo Community and went to serve the Methodist churches in western Kentucky as a Church and Community Worker. Charles came from Vietnam about Christmas. He lived in Celo Community and went to Mars Hill College until he and Marla separated in the spring. Marla was pregnant, and I came back to Celo Community when Derek was born.

Marla lived there with her boys, and some of the time Dena was there with her. By Christmas, 1970, John Thomas had built the sun room on the east end of the front porch.

Louise Cullison and I drove from Kentucky to help Marla prepare for her wedding. She and Jerry Hoover were married May 9, 1971, on the front lawn by Thomas Rutledge and Philip Nordstrom. Mary Rutledge supervised the breakfast served to twenty-six people after the ceremony.

But there was also a sad side to the festivities. "On the Thursday night before the Saturday wedding there was a dessert held at the Abrahamsons' in honor of Wanda Lea and Harvey Austin who had recently married. It was at this dessert that Gertrude Barrus told me that Elizabeth Morgan certainly needed my prayers. The cancer had returned, and she could not have any more operations. Elizabeth and Ernest came to the wedding. I was shocked at Elizabeth's appearance and could not keep back the tears when I embraced her. She asked me to come to see her if I possibly had time. I went the following Monday night, May eleventh. I sat with her while she soaked in the bathtub, and we had a good talk with no one else in the house. She has faced the reality of death very squarely. She was to leave Wednesday for examinations in Cleveland but feared that there were not too many options open to her. If she had to choose between prolonged, expensive treatments that will probably do no good, and death, she would choose death. They have just built a lovely home — the nicest she has ever had — and she has so much to contribute in the way of music to the lives of the children who come to the school!! I could certainly put my heart into a prayer for divine intervention in her behalf. Both she and I thought it was probably her only real hope."[28] Elizabeth died September 26, 1971.

I came back planning to be present when James Arle came into the world; but he did not cooperate. He waited too long, so I had to return to Kentucky before he was born. Of course he joined his brothers in the log house.

Some time around the mid-seventies Jerry planted the bottom fields in pine trees. To make the house warmer, he paneled the walls of the two front rooms and built a rock fireplace and mantle in the front room.

During most of the time that Marla lived there (in the log house) John Morgan lived in the crib cabin nearby. He was an expert nature photographer. When the new Terrace Hotel was built at Lake Junaluska, they used his pictures in the lobby and halls. An enlarged one of our red-roofed barn with a storm over the Blacks is predominant in the lobby.

Marla and Jerry separated in June, 1979, and she moved away. Becky Gray, who had her pottery shop in the barn, moved into the house. She let Paula and me stay there for our vacation in 1980 while she was away.

In 1980 Clark and Peggy Tibbits agreed to take the part of our holding that included the log house, the cabin on the hill, and the bottom land to the road. Becky Gray would take the part on the other side of the road that included the barn (now pottery studio) and crib cabin. Becky moved from the log house in early January of 1981, and the Tibbitses began the renovation of both buildings. They spent fifteen thousand dollars on the log house. They removed *everything* but the log walls! They even removed the front part of the roof, used all new materials, and put dormer windows upstairs.

They spent seven thousand dollars renovating the block cabin up on the hill — put a second story on it, and Judith Scheckel has improved the place more since she took it as a holding in January, 1991. Those who lived there after Wendal Bull left in 1981 until Judith moved there were: Phil Cope; Gred and Diana Gross with Brian, Micah and Meggie; Rio Alden; Miika Rolett and John Pertee with Isak and Aija; and Ruth Ostrenga.

On April 27, 1983, Dave Salstrom, as treasurer of Celo Community, wrote me a check in final settlement of my former holding, so my official relationship with CCI and the log house was ended.

It seems that Peggy Tibbits will be the resident owner and Celo Community member. Clark, Nathan, and Matthew Tibbits will be pursuing other interests.

On the morning of May 16, 1992, the house had a close call. The ashes that Clark put in a plastic bucket and took to the shed the night before were *not* dead as he had thought. They caught the shed on fire and the danger to the house was real, but it was spared.

Besides the Tibbits family, those who have spent brief and longer periods of time in the house were: Chris Franklin, Jason Yeager, Sylvain Lapostolle (a French student), Chris Kromardi, Josh Peterson, Randall Rountree, and Pace Phillips.

An even greater number have lived in the crib cabin besides John Morgan, who has been mentioned: Phil Cope, Randy Raskin, Jodie Pred, Linda Henry, Loy McWhirter with John Blood, Bruce Greene, Megan and Eliza (a month or so one summer), Tim Evans and Elizabeth Johnson, Bill Blaisdell, Diane Nettles, Siva (from Italy - a nanny), Abigail De Witt (studio), Ruth Ostrenga, Randall Rountree and Bethany Scott, and Theresa Müller (from South Africa).

This is the story of the Colonel McDowell/Laurel Cove property through September 5, 1993. I have slides of the rooms before Becky left, during and after renovation.

NOTES

1. Ruby Moody and Louise Toness, "About Celo Community," *The Interpreter*, July 15, 1950.
2. Bill Sharp, "The Valley on the Roof of North Carolina," *The State* 20 (1953).
3. Hugh Sidey, "A Time of Trouble in Toe Valley," *Life* (April, 1957).
4. Letter of Arthelia Brooks to family (LF), July 14, 1948.
5. LF, January 1949.
6. LF, February 11, 1949.
7. LF, February 18, 1949.
8. Grantly Dick-Read, *Childbirth Without Fear: The Original Approach to Childbirth*. Currently available in its 5th ed. (New York: Harper Collins, 1987).
9. Letter of Sunny Davidson to Arthelia Brooks, 1981.
10. Ibid.
11. Letter of Midge Smith Wyman to Arthelia Brooks, January 29, 1981.
12. Ibid.
13. David S. Wyman, *The Abandonment of the Jews*. (New York: Pantheon Books, 1984).
14. Letter of Peace Pilgrim to Arthelia Brooks, January 31, 1981.
15. Letter of Midge Smith Wyman to Arthelia Brooks, December 8, 1992.
16. Letter of Peace Pilgrim (Mildred Ryder) to Arthelia Brooks, January 31, 1981.
17. Arthelia Brooks, *A Diary of Arle's Illness*, (unpublished, entry of April 2, 1951).
18. LF, February, 1952.
19. LF, March 21, 1952.
20 LF, January 24, 1953.
21. LF, April 1, 1953.
22. LF, May 28, 1953.
23. LF, June 26, 1953.
24. Card of Arthelia Brooks to family, July 1, 1953.
25. Card of Arthelia Brooks to family, July 5, 1953.
26. LF, March 21, 1954.
27. LF, June 2, 1959.
28. LF, May 16, 1971.

Hertig I

Grandma Susan Hertig
9-17-1872
12-26-53
P. 4

Grandpa Christian Hertig
1-17-1869
10-12-56
P. 4

Hertig home Alpena, W.Va.

Uncle Godfrey and Grandpa

Willis and Willis Jr. at Grandma's (Buster)

Willis, Jr. and Lucille 7-4-92

Dorothy Ann and Helen Hertig at Grandma's

Hertig II

Clifford, Alecia, Lula ("Biddy") and Esther Burns
P. 9

Carl Christian (Bill) and Dolly Hertig
6-65
P. 10

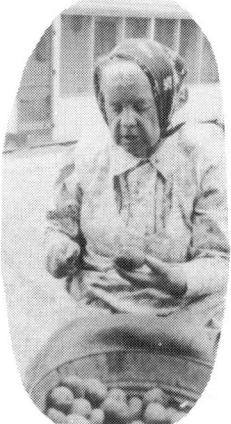

Mrs Ratzer at Hertig home

Marvin Schmidlen and friend

Alpena school
P. 10

Hillearys I

Hillearys II

Lucille ← and Bill Mulligan 2-11-87

Mom 80th Birthday 11-22-76

Harold and Ruth Parcell ↓ 3-65

Edward, Eleanor and Keith ↓ Hilleary 6-65

↑ Tom and Olive Jackson 10-69

The seven ↓ Hillearys 1941

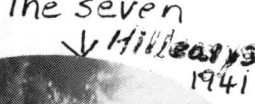

Hillearys III

Five sisters home
(Mill Creek, W.Va.)
1944

Mom with Lucille home from service in Army Nurses Corps
1946

Fred, Edith,(Paula), Lucille, Hazel, Roy.
1946
Edward, Ruth and Olive

Hilleary six at Freds funeral
3-65

Hilleary six in W. Va. 7-92

Uncle Willis with Hillearys
7-4-1992

Hillearys IV

↗ Son Dale and Oma Quay
7-4-90

Fred's family with Cadillac at Celo ↑
1964

↗ Edith and Fred's family
Herbert, Carol, Edith, Susan and Morna Lee
(after Fred's funeral)

Arthelia and Fred's children from top → Paula, Marla, Morna Lee, Dena, Susan, Carol and Herbert

Susan and Megan Perry →
7-4-87

← Ruth Parcell and family in Missouri
7-90

Hilleary V

Gayle and Hilleary Quay
11-7-87

Oma, Marla, Joshua Quay, and Arthelia 9-9-90

Rosemary Brosnan, Patricia and Otis Watts

Rebecca and Brayton Long on the ferry
8-23-92

Walter, Rebecca and Pamela Jackson

Terry Long

Pamela's boys, Becky's girls and Olive!
8-27-92

Hilleary VI

Eleanor, Edward and Keith - family reunion in Mo. 7-4-90

Arthelia and daughters — 75th Birthday - Higgins M.C. 2-11-90

Dick & Carol Shaffer and Morna Lee Green Family Reunion at High Pastures 7-3-87

Olive, Lucille, Oma, Arthelia and Edith

at Lucille's apt. Venice Fl. 3-14-94

Births

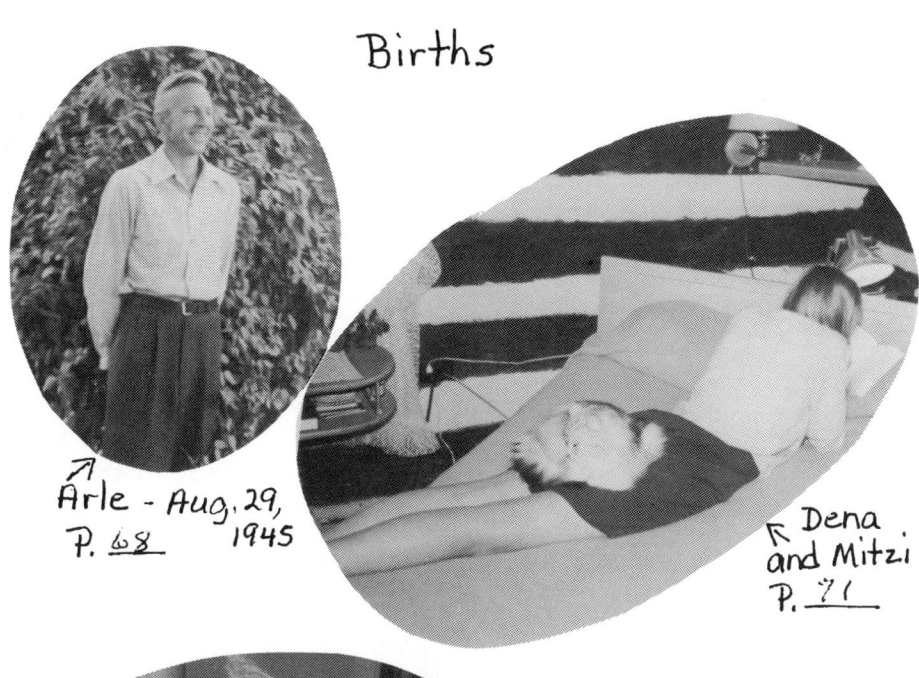

Arle - Aug. 29, 1945
P. 68

Dena and Mitzi
P. 71

Four generations - Robbie
P. 72

Stubbs - Sandy, Jonathan, Jamie and Jim
P. 75

three generations - Jeremy
P. 73

CHILDREN

BIRTHS

Paula — 1945

During the early months of my pregnancy with Paula, Arle and I were living in Arle's hometown, and I was working at Mr. Leonard's photo studio in San Marcos, Texas. Elva, my sister-in-law, worked in the darkroom developing the pictures. My job was at the desk, giving all the well-worn reasons (excuses?) why pictures were not ready when promised. Dr. Williams, the Brooks family's doctor, had his office in the same block. When I went for my prenatal monthly checkups a nurse took my blood pressure, pulse and temperature, then the doctor would come and say "I see you're doing fine," and that was it. Altogether not more than fifteen minutes. Along about the fourth monthly visit I said, "Dr. Williams, do you know how long it takes me to earn this office call fee? About two days!" He didn't charge me anymore until the delivery fee.

From the second month I promised Arle that the baby would be born on his birthday. I talked frequently — and, I hoped, persuasively — to the fetus to help me make the promise come true. I quit working at the studio at seven months. Mrs. Gibson, our next-door neighbor, wanted to know why. I said, "To get ready for this baby due in two months." She said, "If you have a baby in there it must be standing straight up." I never wore maternity clothes.

Around mid-June I told Dr. Williams that I had promised the baby for Arle's birthday on the twenty-eighth of August. He said, "Young lady, who do you think you are, Almighty God? This baby is not due until the second week in September."

Nevertheless, on the morning of August 28 I *heaved* myself up from the two-inch-thick pad on the floor of "Apartment A" (the remodeled chicken coop), as I had done each morning for the past nine months, and made preparations to have the baby. We called Dr. Williams about suppertime and he came out and stayed. Paula was born in the middle room of the Brooks home at 11:45 P.M. *on her father's birthday!* We named her Paula. [The story of her naming is told in the Tragedy section, later in this book. For her Christmas gift 1991 I painted a picture of her birthplace on a sweatshirt. "This old house where I was born - X marks the room." The house itself still exists, but it has been moved up the road toward Wimberly, Texas.]

Maryla / Marla — 1947

The first six months of this pregnancy was spent at the Brudercoop in Philadelphia, a cooperative housing arrangement for about eight or ten young employed adults. Arle was still working with AFSC. For the Christmas holidays, 1946–47, we went to my family's home near Mill Creek, West Virginia. Since we planned to become part of the intentional community at nearby Riverton, with Harry and Jean Wolfe, we decided that Paula and I should go live in the extra house on the Riverton property until Arle returned from Philadelphia in February. It snowed almost the whole month of February. The Wolfes began to worry about having to deliver our baby since there was no doctor within miles; so when Arle did get back around the last of February, they made plans to take us back to my parents' home. There was no fear of slipping off the road because the snow, which had been continuously thrown off the road by the snowplow, was higher than the car on either side. When we got to the house I breathed a sigh of relief, thinking, "Now if we're snowbound, my sister who's a nurse can help deliver the baby." But she did not like that idea, so my brother spent the next day rigging a snowplow in front of his truck and he took me and Arle to my Aunt Marie's in Elkins, fifteen miles away. "Now, you're only four blocks from the hospital. You can walk," they told me.

I was expecting the baby the first of March because I knew exactly when it was conceived: in the Brudercoop I had met with too many delays on my way to the bathroom with a douche bag under my robe. Days and then weeks went by. My other aunt in town called every day and I had to say, "No baby yet." Unlike the "deceiving" figure I had with Paula, I now felt I looked like an elephant — especially since I had to walk by a full-length mirror in Aunt Marie's hall a dozen times a day.

By the middle of March it wasn't just my problem — *all* the babies in the whole valley were way overdue. The maternity ward had been empty for two weeks, and doctors were beginning to become concerned.

On Sunday evening the sixteenth of March, I *did* walk those four blocks to the hospital and the baby came about one-thirty the next morning — and not only mine but many others were coming thick and fast. Seven and a half hours after Marla's birth, I was still begging for someone to bring my baby to me. By Thursday, not only the maternity ward, but the women's ward was filled as well. The nurses were so overwhelmed we couldn't even get a drink of water. Finally I got up to wait on myself and others. One of the young mothers asked a nurse if she could get up. "Who is your doctor?" "So and so." "No, he won't let you get up." "But Mrs. Brooks is up." "She didn't ask me."

Arle and I had had plenty of time during the two weeks of waiting to think about names for the baby. In a news magazine we saw a notice that the famous pianist Maryla Jonas was to be in concert at Carnegie Hall. We decided that Maryla was a *different* name, if the baby was a girl we'd give her that name. It was a girl.

After everything had settled down, the mothers — many of them for the first time — were discussing how far they had gone in school before they quit to get married. Most had not finished high school. I decided I would not volunteer any information, but they didn't let me get by. "How many years did *you* go to school, Mrs. Brooks?" "I went eighteen years, but I feel I am prepared to take care of my children if anything should happen to my husband." They all admitted they would be helpless. Little did I know how soon it would be necessary for me to assume full responsibility for the girls.

When Maryla was less than two months old we moved to North Carolina. Several years later I read a story in *Reader's Digest* about Maryla Jonas, and the tragic events in her life. She had witnessed the death of many family members at the hands of the Nazis, had somehow managed to escape to America, but vowed she would never play the piano again. She was visiting a sister in a South American city where a famous pianist was to give a concert. The sister arranged for Maryla to listen to the man rehearse. Then he asked her to play so he could check the acoustics. She sat down and played for hours. The Carnegie Hall concert we had read about was her first since leaving Europe.

I was so pleased that we had named our child for such a noble person that I wrote to tell her so in care of *Reader's Digest*. She answered, sent an eight-by-ten-inch photograph of herself and a silver plate engraved, "To Maryla Brooks from Maryla Jonas." Because people wanted to pronounce the name Mary'-la instead of Ma-re'-la, when Maryla was in high school she had the spelling officially changed to Marla.

Dena — 1949

We had lived at Celo about a year and a half when I became pregnant the third time. Since the hospital birth with Marla was not a pleasant experience I did not want to repeat it. I went for my prenatal care to the health center in Celo Community and told Dr. Ohle I planned to have the baby at home. He agreed to do the delivery.

Early in the pregnancy a book came to my attention, I think it was published in England, titled *Childbirth Without Fear*.[1] I read it and followed closely the suggestions for diet and exercise, and the plans for a home delivery. I became so confident that when the time was drawing near I even prayed that I could deliver the baby myself.

After a day when I had cleaned house like mad and baked cookies, I thought that was the usual sign of imminent delivery. I prepared my bed and all the necessary equipment to receive the baby in the front room, away from where Arle was sleeping. I went to bed and began to have some pains, but it was raining so hard that I delayed calling Arle because I knew he had a ten-minute walk to Dr. Ohle's home. Finally I thought I'd better call him. He had Cora Belle Hunter, who was staying in the block cabin nearby, to come stay with me while he went for the doctor. He got back before the doctor, and so was there when I got up thinking I needed to pee when I suddenly realized it was the baby coming. I had the blanket ready, and received it from a kneeling position. I wiped its face, it cried, and I said, "It's a girl!" (Cora Belle said later, "you were beatified when you announced her birth.")

At that point the doctor arrived, cut the cord and finished the job. He said, "Well, Tillie, all I can say is that, as a real mountain woman, you should have been out chopping wood when this happened."

She was born about two-thirty in the morning, on August 21, 1949. We named her Dena for a Brazilian mission worker who had visited in my parents' home during the summer of 1943 — a co-worker of my classmate, Sarah Bennett, who also served many years in Brazil. Dina Rizzi, spelled her name with an *i* pronounced *e*, but I changed it to an *e* to simplify things for Dena. Marla's experience had already taught me how unusual spellings of names can cause problems . . . (I visited Sarah frequently, until she died in 1993 at the Brooks-Howell Home. I often read her letters from, and wrote letters to, Dina.)

After about two weeks I went to the health center to pay Dr. Ohle for the delivery.

"How much do I owe you, Elpenor?"

"Well, let's see, I think you got a length of hose for your enema bottle. I guess that was about a dollar."

"Okay, but what for the delivery?"

"Nothing. You did all the work before I got there."

"You're kidding! You made a house call in the middle of the night!"

I tell Dena that she really came cheap, because one dollar is all he would accept.

Kittens of Mitzi, the Cat

Dena went to Arthur Morgan School for her eighth grade work (1962–63). I kept students in exchange for her tuition. Sometime during the early part of the school year, Dena and Marla rescued a kitten that "those *mean* boys" had dunked in motor oil. They brought it home and cleaned it up and named it Mitzi, and Mitzi and Dena became great friends. Often when I came home from work Dena would be reading on my bed, lying on her tummy propped up on her elbows, with Mitzi asleep on her thighs.

Part of the summer schedule of the Church and Community Workers in the Western North Carolina conference was to train college students to work with youth and children in our small membership churches. In 1963, summer training was held at Lake Junaluska. They permitted me to bring my three girls for the five-day session.

We had a problem. Mitzi was due to have kittens that week. We asked the neighbor's children to feed her and hoped for the best. The kittens came the day we got home; and Mitzi demonstrated that she was an inexperienced first-time mother! She had them on *top of the hamper* in the bathroom — six of them. She didn't have space to feed that many, so I drowned two and the next morning a third was dead. She raised the other three and we gave them away; but Mitzi was not well. She had jumped up and down, trying to keep the kittens on the hamper, so many times that she had apparently injured herself internally. She hemorrhaged quite often. I had her spayed, but that did not stop the bleeding. One morning she didn't come for her food. I decided to work in the garden awhile to see if she would come. She did! With a pitiful *meow* she fell at my feet. She was covered with blood, dirt and leaves. I picked her up and carried her to the front porch and called Marla. We cleaned her up, told her how much we loved her, how beautiful she was, and prayed that God would not let this lovely cat die. I also fixed my patent medicine that I gave the girls — whatever was wrong with them — brewer's yeast and honey in hot water, and got it down her throat with an eye dropper. Our neighbor, Minnie, came by and I asked for her remedy. She suggested Knox gelatin, so I got that down her, too. In an hour she seemed fine and was never sick after that. We were never sure what cured her: the brewer's yeast, Knox gelatin, telling her of our love or the prayers. Perhaps all combined.

Mitzi was a gray Persian, a truly beautiful cat. If we had guests she loved to stroll through the room and sit on top of the piano to receive the praise and admiration from those in the room.

She liked to sleep upstairs in the daytime. One day Marla teased her by opening the door a little bit and then closing it. When she finally opened it enough for her to go in, before she went, she went *yeow* and nipped her on the ankle.

I went to Kentucky in the fall of 1968. I think it was the next fall when Marla called, crying, "Something's terribly wrong with Mitzi!" I told her to take her to the vet. Marla drove Mitzi all the way to Marion, an hour away on our mountain roads. Mitzi had been shot in the hip, and the bullet was still there. Since she was seven years old, they decided to put her to sleep. Marla buried her in our pet graveyard, at the edge of the woods by the east garden. A friend of Mitzi's, the little black Spaniel, sat by the grave several hours. I have always hoped that the hunter who shot Mitzi mistook her for a gray squirrel. It was squirrel season, her tail *was* bushy and gray, and she loved to shinny up a tree.

Robbie and Jeremy

The summer before I went to Kentucky, Marla's husband, Charles Lang, was in Vietnam, so she was home with me when her first son, Robbie, was born July 5, 1968, in the Burnsville hospital. I took her for the delivery. I had tried to share with her the *Childbirth Without Fear* ideas.

Her room was in front of the nursing desk. While I was waiting there I realized it was also next to the delivery room. There was a door between the two rooms, and the door had a keyhole that I used to good advantage. I heard Dr. Webb say, "Marla, are you sure you don't want a sedative?"

"No, I've come this far, I don't want to miss the end."

"Okay, I think one more good push and we've made it." And then —

"Marla, it's a fine big boy!"

I dashed out to the desk. "It's a boy, It's a boy."

"How do *you* know that?" the nurses wanted to know.

About that time Marla was wheeled out looking like, "Well, *that* was no big deal."

I think all three of her boys were ten months old when they were born. Derek Hoover was born in the Spruce Pine hospital on November 24, 1969 and Jamie Hoover was born at Memorial Mission hospital in Asheville on October 3, 1973.

My great-grandson, Jeremy, was born to Robbie and his wife in a Norfolk, Virginia, hospital January 13, 1991. I called Robbie recently to ask what it cost to have a baby these days, compared with Dena's "dollar delivery." Robbie said close to five thousand dollars. The prenatal care was fifteen hundred. Health care *really* needs reforming!!

CHILD REARING

I was thirty and a half years old when Paula, my first child, was born. By the time I was thirty-five, all three were "underfoot." While raising young children, I never did *fully* adjust to the way my plans for the day would so often be rearranged with no notice. In my previous fourteen years of working with adults, of course there were times when someone became ill or died or the agenda for the week had to be changed for some other reason. But child rearing requires constant adjustment of plans — daily, or oftentimes hourly adjustments, which, for me, required cultivating a new, and a much greater, kind of patience.

Fortunately for me, except for the four weeks I worked at the Moody's summer camp, I was able to be home with my children until the month before Arle died in 1953 (when Paula was almost eight, Marla was six, and Dena was almost four). Much of the time before Arle's death, there were other people at Laurel Cove who helped care for the girls. Both the girls and I were even-tempered, so there were no problems of pitching fits in grocery stores or malls. They were raised where cooperation was the norm, so they did not develop the "gimmes." (Their comment when the new Sears Wish Book came was "When can we cut out the people?", not "I want this and this and this..." They used the cut-outs to represent our neighbors, the CCI families, when they played paper dolls.) I was grateful that my girls were not prone to these particular misbehaviors because they tend to drive me crazy. But don't let me give you the impression they never misbehaved. That certainly was not the case!

For example, late on a winter afternoon when Paula was about five, Marla was three, and Dena was barely walking, I told the girls I needed to help their daddy saw wood. They didn't want to be left alone. It was late afternoon and they were tired. Their protests were loud and tearful, especially Paula's. We were really low on wood, though, and I had promised Arle I'd help. Hating to leave them in that frame of mind, I made some suggestions about creative things they could do, and went to help Arle. We were within hearing distance, and in sight of the house. Once while we rested a bit we thought we heard a strange noise, but went on to finish our task. When I got back to the house an hour later I immediately said, "Why is it so cold in here?" I soon found out. Eight small panes had been knocked out of the windows in the three downstairs rooms, and the three girls were covered up in our bed. Marla said, "Paula got the hammer and hit them." Paula got her bottom spanked, and just to be sure all the guilt was covered, Marla got a few licks, too. We covered the panes with cardboard until we could get to town to buy glass panes, and my better judgment was confirmed: late afternoon was not a good time of day to leave the girls alone. After that day we arranged our woodcutting to be done earlier in the day.

This incident, and other less dramatic ones, taught me that the time from about five o'clock until young children are in bed are usually the "zero hours" for the parents. That is the time when the children hang onto you and whine (which I had no tolerance for) while you're trying to get supper ready. My own stint at this daily challenge has given me some understanding of the frustration that sometimes leads to children being abused. All mothers, I'm sure, feel unable sometimes to deal with these zero hours. Even healthy families are occasionally stressed out enough that one parent or the other cannot handle the whining without wanting to lash out. But I have particular compassion for the isolated young, inexperienced (unwed or otherwise) single mothers living in city slums, with limited financial resources and no one to turn to for help or advice. I wonder how they do as well as they do. Under the *best* of circumstances children are not always "little angels." They are self-centered and demanding, they try your patience and cleverly test your resolve. In essence, this side of rearing children was once summed up by a bachelor, Edward Mickle, who lived at Laurel Cove for two years. He said to me, "I've never understood why Jesus wanted us to become like little children."

I was remembering all this in the late 1970s when I (in my sixties) offered to buy groceries and help a young mother cope with her two boys — five, and two and a half years old. Their father, one of our Lakeland Parish ministers, Jimmy Stubbs, had been called to two weeks of wintertime National Guard duty. Since it was a slow time in my work, I had scheduled hemorrhoid surgery, and I thought we could help each other during my time of healing and her time to parent alone. I suggested I stay with her while Jimmy was away; but the word came back to me that Sandy wasn't sure she wanted me — the children might be a bother if I wasn't feeling well, and she was ashamed to have me hear her yell at the boys. I went to Sandy and said, "I think I can help you. Don't worry about me. If things get too rough, it's only eight miles home." Of course I didn't know that we would be literally snowbound most of the two weeks.

My ingenuity was taxed to the limit, and Sandy needed as much, or more, support than the boys did. She was a person with deep spiritual convictions, but her emotions were of the roller-coaster variety — real highs and lows. (She once said to me, in this context, "Tillie, you are *so* boring!")

I had brought my slide projector and my slides taken in the Far East, in South America, and in many places throughout the United States. I rationed the viewing during our snowbound days; Sandy and I used Maxie Dunham's *The Workbook of Living Prayer*,[2] which I'd also brought, for a spiritual study time together; and I told her many of the experiences I have related in this book. With the boys we sang, read books, played the cat's cradle game (the one where two or more people pass string configurations back and forth until they have a "cradle"), did hand-clapping rhythms, played basketball and (very soft) baseball in the hall — and, of course, there was TV.

It became apparent that Sandy was a mother who said too often, "Your daddy will tend to you when he gets home." That might possibly have worked when he was coming home every night, but this was a two-week absence. I told her, "You can't let a five-year-old get the best of you. You must learn to deal with him yourself." She had the chance to put herself to the test the very next night.

Sandy always had trouble with zero hour, so I tried my best to keep the boys out of the kitchen while Sandy got supper. One evening, when we were all fed and there was a TV program on that the boys enjoyed, we told them that we wanted a half-hour to ourselves to talk. We settled them in front of the TV at 6:00, explaining that after the half-hour Sandy would play ball with them while I washed the dishes. In a few minutes Jonathan came, wanting to play ball. Sandy showed him the clock and explained where the hands would be at six-thirty. At 6:15 he was back again. She said, "Jonathan, if you come one more time, I won't play at all." He came at 6:25, so that was it — no ball. He began to take a fit. Sandy listened for maybe a minute and then said, "Well, I'll just go play ball now." I knew it was hard for her, especially with me there, but I said, "No, Sandy, that's where we make our mistake — not making our word stick." So she sent him to his room, where he began to scream and trash the room. "Go get him," I suggested, "and physically hold him in your lap until he calms down." (I had done that under similar circumstances with Cary McConnell.) I concluded, "Then he can sit in a chair with a book while you and Jamie play ball and I wash the dishes." It worked. Of course, during those two weeks whenever I asked him not to do something he would say, "You're not a daddy. You can't tell me what to do." My reply was kind and constant, "I was both a daddy and a mama to my girls, and I know *how* to be a daddy."

Jamie, the younger child, was much milder-natured. One evening soon after I came, he brought a *Time* magazine to me and said, "What's that?" It was a capital *T*. I said, "That's a *T* for Tillie", and so our five o'clock ritual was begun. Each evening he would back up in front of me, holding the magazine, waiting to be taken up onto my lap. *Time* was designed so that it started each paragraph with a large capital letter, so before the two weeks were up, Jamie could find all the uppercase letters of the alphabet. He later amazed his father by finding the letters on billboards, and by requesting a typewriter so he could use the lowercase letters.

When our two weeks were over Sandy said, "I couldn't have made it without you. I would have called my father and told him to get a helicopter if necessary, but to get me out of there before I went crazy!" (I was saddened to learn from the 1993 *Memphis Conference Journal* that Jim and Sandy have since separated. I don't know the reason, but feel sure it was not because of young children. . . .)

Difficult as it can be to find the balance between discipline and love, young children are also an inspiration. I've often said my most precious possession is my collection, *The Sayings of My Small*

Children. . In fact, I had it in a little fireproof safe in my office in Kentucky until the day some young kids broke in, carried the safe to a creek bank, cracked it open with a rock, and scattered my insurance papers and the *Sayings*. Another child found the insurance papers, but everything else was gone. (The thieves got a couple of silver dollars for their efforts.) Fortunately for me, Paula had made a copy of the *Sayings* sometime earlier, and could replace my lost copy of the booklet.

THE SAYINGS OF MY SMALL CHILDREN
(Summer, 1947 – Fall, 1956)

Summer, 1947:
PAULA (seeing the moon through the pine trees): "Look, Mama, there is the moon peek-a-boo at me!"

Winter, 1948:
PAULA: Peg, why don't you have a baby?
PEG: Oh, I couldn't have a baby because it wouldn't have a daddy.
PAULA: Our daddy is everybody's daddy. He could be your baby's daddy.

1949
August 20:
PAULA (To Mama who was lying down during the beginning stages of labor): "Mama, when is our baby coming?"
MAMA: "Very soon, I hope, Paula."
PAULA: "Maybe our baby will be dead."
MAMA (with heart having skipped a beat): "Oh, honey, we hope not."
PAULA: "But Ruby's died."
MAMA: "I know, dear. Ours *could* be, but we'll just hope it won't be."

August 21 (after the birth of Dena at 2:00 A.M.):
PAULA (feeling of Mama's deflated tummy): "Now, Mama, you can carry *two* buckets of water from the 'pring and it won't be too heavy."
And later, having watched for the first time Thelma changing Dena's diaper: "Marla, it really *is* a girl. It has a bottom just like ours."

September 15:
PAULA: "Mama, my baby died."
MAMA: "Oh, I'm sorry to hear that, dear."
PAULA: "It's all right, Mama, I'm going to get a new one from Sears."

October 1:
PAULA: "Mama, may I eat meat and cheese when I go to Grandma's?"
MAMA: "I guess you may if you really want to, but Daddy had rather you didn't."
PAULA: "Why?"
MAMA: "Because you have to kill animals and that is a hard thing to do, don't you think?"
PAULA: "Yes, but I could eat cheese. You don't have to kill anything to eat cheese and eggs."
MAMA: "Well, not right at the time, but if you keep cows and chickens, sometime they have to be killed."
PAULA: "Well, maybe I won't eat meat."

December 2:
MARLA (to Mama getting supper): "Mama, what can I do for you?"
PAULA (with her doll at her breast, just like Dena): "I burp my baby between the two sides, too."
MAMA: "Oh, you do?"
PAULA: "Yes, but I didn't use to."
MAMA: "Why did you change?"
PAULA: "Well, she seemed to get the 'tummick ache' when I didn't."

December 10:
MAMA (to Paula, who is crying at the least provocation): "Paula, I think you'd best lie down and rest awhile. You must not have had enough sleep."
PAULA: "Oh, I burned my arm and bumped my head. Marla says I can't be Mama, and now she won't call the machine cover a bench."
MARLA (sitting on the machine cover, and insisting that it *is* what it is): "Paula, if I give you this, will you be happy?"

December 14:
PAULA: "What can I do, Mama?"
MAMA: "I guess you can trim some more strings from the edges of these sacks."

PAULA (very importantly trimming them): "We do lots and lots of different things while Marla is taking her nap, don't we, Tillie?"

MARLA (taking her bath and seeing the hammer on the hearth): "Paula cracked her peanut open with a hammer. Wasn't that a funny thing to do?"

MAMA: "Yes, it was."

MARLA: "I 'cink' so, too."

December 16:

MAMA (coming in from hanging clothes, to the room she had just straightened): "Paula, I do believe you can make a room look messy quicker than anyone I've seen."

PAULA (in a very emphatic tone): "Oh, Mama, I'm amazing with you. I don't know what I'm going to do with you!"

December 25 (both having received an identical book on their "chimney" Christmas tree):

PAULA: "Now, Marla, that *is* my book, too!"

MARLA (holding the book): "No, Paula. This one says 'A.T. Marla,' so it's mine! Your's must be someplace else."

December 30:

MAMA: "It's too bad you don't have pockets to put your hankie in when you have a cold."

PAULA (a little later): "Look, Mama, we've fixed our hankie." (They each had them pinned by a corner to the front of their dresses.)

1950

January 6:

MARLA (coming out the back door, seeing me on the porch): "There's my daddy!"

MAMA: "Oh, no, I'm not going to be your daddy. It keeps me busy enough being your mama."

MARLA: "Then you are my friend. You're getting my dinner, aren't you?"

MAMA: "Yes, I'm getting your lunch and I certainly am your friend."

(After the window-breaking episode, told in the Child Rearing section, earlier in this book):

MAMA: "Why did you do it, Paula?"

PAULA: "Because you went out. I told you I would get into something."

MAMA: "Oh my, Mama just doesn't know what to do with a little girl who would do such a thing. But you can't go to nursery school next time. How did you happen to have the wire brush to break the windows?"

PAULA: "I went out to get the hammer, but couldn't find it."

(On the next nursery school day, to Dave as he went by):

PAULA: "I'm not going to nursery school. I didn't get up in time to eat my breakfast and get my things on. And I broke out the windows and Mama has to braid my hair." (It sounded to me as if she sandwiched it in hoping no one would notice — not even her!)

January 20:

PAULA: "Thelma, you know what? Mama's going to keep me."

THELMA: "Why?"

PAULA: "She said if she had a little girl who liked to wash windows, she would keep her. And I like to."

January 26 (planting in the greenhouse and listening to the girls chatter):

MAMA: "Marla, how many children did you say you had?"

MARLA: "Two."

MAMA: "And what did I hear you say their names were?"

MARLA: "Crash and Bang. That's what I call them."

MAMA: "Well, I'll say! I wish I had thought of that!"

February 1:

PAULA: "Oh, these 'chicken pops' do hurt! (Looking at ads in a magazine): We're going to have to get us car."

DADDY: "Why?"

PAULA: "I'm getting tired of walking to nursery school. Mary Jane Reed brings her children."

February 7:

MAMA (coming home from supper meeting at Tylers): "Oh, Daddy, whose hair is this behind the stove?"

DADDY: "Gee, I've been sick all evening. Paula cut Marla's hair and it looks awful." (He was right!)

February 18:

PAULA: "It was very nice of Velma [Grindstaff, age ten)] to come play with us." (She was selling candy for 4-H.)

February 24:

PAULA: "I hate to sleep!" (And truer words she never spoke. From her earliest days she put off the time for sleeping as long as possible. Quite unlike Marla.)

March 12:
PAULA (to Mama, ironing dresses): "Mama, who made these dresses we got for Christmas? Did Cora Belle?"
MAMA: "No, they were factory-made ones."
PAULA (a little later): "Are you through ironing Marla's dress?" (Laying Dena down): "Here, you lay down, you factory-made baby, so I can take my dress for Mama to iron."
MAMA: "I guess it hasn't quite come to that!"

March 13 (talking about Sunny and Bill coming on the nineteenth):
MAMA: "Did you know they are going to drive, Paula?"
PAULA (to Daddy): "I'll be *so* glad to see Sunny and Bill's car, won't you, Daddy?"
DADDY: "I'll be more glad to see Sunny and Bill."
PAULA: "We *could* be glad to see both the car *and* Sunny and Bill."

April 25:
PAULA: "Hello, Tillie."
MAMA: "Hello."
PAULA: "What are you doing?"
MAMA: "I'm cutting this up to make compost to put on my garden so I can grow lots of nice big vegetables."
PAULA: "That's what my husband was doing, 'cept he wasn't cutting cabbage. He was cutting bananas."
MAMA: "Well, I guess every fellow cuts what he has."

April 26:
PAULA: "Would you like to be dead, Mama?"
MAMA: "Well, no, I guess not right now."
PAULA: "Why?"
MAMA: "Because you children are all small and I would like to stay here to take care of you. When you are big girls and can take care of yourselves, then it will be okay."

May 21:
PAULA (to Marla): "Is this your baby?"
MARLA: "Yes."
PAULA: "Is it a boy or a girl?"
MARLA: "She's a boy like me and Dud [Doug Moody]."

May 21:
PAULA (to Daddy): "My husband works in North Carolina and sometimes in the hospital where he takes care of the doctors."

DADDY: "Takes care of the *doctors?*"
PAULA: "Yes, they get sick sometimes."
(Marla, eating supper, burps.)
DADDY: "You'd better quit, you're full!"
PAULA: "No, that's a sign to eat more. She's only half-full, 'cause Mama feeds Dena out of one side and burps her and then feeds her out of the other side."

June 18 (on the rocks in the river for a picnic):
MAMA: "Let's sing for our grace."
LOIS ANN: "Oh, yes. I was going to suggest that."
ALL: "For health and strength and daily food we give you thanks, dear Lord."
PAULA: "The river is always singing, isn't it?"

June 28:
DADDY (showing Marla a few raisins in her bowl and wanting her to count them): "How many raisins are left, Marla?"
MARLA (taking a good look): "Just that many."

July 18:
PAULA: "How tall are you, Midge?"
MIDGE: "I'm five feet five."
PAULA: "No, you're not. Your 65 inches."

July 27:
BILL (calling to Sunny in the garden): "Are you ready to go swimming, sweetheart?"
PAULA: "Mama, why does Bill call Sunny sweetheart, and she calls Bill sweetheart, too? Why don't they call their names that other people call them?"
MAMA: "That's just it. They are married and love each other, so they want to use some name that other people don't use."

August 6:
PAULA (to Daddy): "When is our birthday, Daddy?"
DADDY: "Just three more Sundays and there it will be."
PAULA: "I'll be five. How old will you be?"
DADDY: "Why don't you guess how old Daddy will be?"
PAULA: "You'll be 41." (Arle was as surprised as Midge was when she told her 65 inches and no one had told her. Like the morning she told Dave it was twenty 'til eight and it was exactly that.)

August 22:
MARLA (looking at sunsuits Dena had received for her birthday): "Paula and I want sunsuits, too. We don't have very many sunsuits. In *fact*, we don't have *any* sunsuits!"

August 24 (to those assembled for supper):
PAULA: "I got Dena to sleep twice today."
DICK: "How did you do that, with a hammer?"
PAULA: "No, I used an axe."
LOIS ANN (in an undertone): "Maybe you'll learn, Domer."

November 14:
PAULA: "This is the Bible, isn't it, Mama?"
MAMA: "Yes, and it has some very wonderful stories about people who were trying to know what God is like."
PAULA: "I was looking in here. I thought I might find a picture of God."
MAMA: "No, you won't find that kind of picture."
PAULA: "But there are pictures of Jesus."
MAMA: "Yes, there are pictures of him because we think he was very much like God is."
PAULA: "How *is* God?"
MAMA: "Well, it is pretty hard to explain, but one of the first things we usually think about God is that he loves us. Do you think I love you?"
PAULA: "Yes."
MAMA: "Can you see my love the way you see the fire?"
PAULA: "No."
MAMA: "Then how do you know I love you?"
PAULA: "Because you treat me so nice."
MAMA: "That's true."
PAULA: "But sometimes you spank us, like you did Marla this morning — but that was because she didn't listen."
MAMA: "I'm sure God does a better job of loving us than I do loving you."

1951
(Daddy at a friend's for supper, Mama doing dishes, girls bathing):
MAMA: "What did you girls put in this water?"
PAULA: "I don't know."
MAMA: "Well, I know. It's Calamine lotion."

MARLA: "Yes, Paula put it in." (Paula admits it and gets into the tub. I warn her to keep it out of her eyes and mouth. Mary Ohle said it was poisonous.)
PAULA: "Are you going to bathe Dena in it?"
MAMA: "I guess so."
PAULA: "She might chew the washcloth. Why don't you get clean water?"
MAMA: "I'll watch her closely."
PAULA: "Mama, I'd feel a lot easier about it if you'd get clean water for Dena." (Later, from her bed) "Did you get clean water for Dena?"
MAMA: "Yes, I did, dear. You can go to sleep without worrying."

March 4:
MAMA (to the girls): "Did you know that Midge is going to have a baby this summer?"
MARLA: "Is she? She isn't married, is she?"
MAMA: "Oh, yes she is. Who do you think she married? Dave Wyman, of course."

(Marla and Daddy eating ice cream):
DADDY: "That *was* very good ice cream." (his gone.)
MARLA: "This *is* very good ice cream." (still has some.)

March 20:
MAMA (to Paula): "Smell this piece of material Lucille sent. Doesn't it smell good, just like Lucille?"
PAULA (smelling): "I think it smells like Olive, too."

April 1:
PAULA: "I want to wear my dress to Sunday school. Is it ironed?"
MAMA: "No, dear. I'm sorry. Mama has had too many things to do this morning."
PAULA: "Then why didn't you get up in the middle of the night and iron it?"
MAMA (who had been to CCI meeting the night before): "If I'd done *that* I wouldn't have had any sleep because that's when I went to bed."

May 6:
PAULA (to Daddy): "Does that fruit have any peanut butter in it?"
DADDY: "No."
PAULA: "Then I don't want any."
DADDY: "You may see the day when you have nothing to eat."

PAULA: "How do you know that?"
DADDY: "I don't, but you might."
PAULA: "How can *that* be? Things grow. The rabbits eat, don't they?"

May 12: After Marla came twice to have a knot put in the thread, she came back with a pretty good job of mending the knees of her pants.

June 16:
PAULA: "Oh, Mama, look at the stars the washing machine slopped out." (Soapsuds *did* look like stars . . .)

July 3:
PAULA: (starting to put on her shoes): "Is this the right foot, Mama?"
MAMA: "No, it goes on the other foot."
PAULA: "I *almost* got it right, didn't I, Mama?"
MAMA: "Yes, dear, you only missed it by one foot."

August 28: Arle's and Paula's birthday. She goes to school. He leaves to visit his family in Texas.

September 15 (at the supper table):
CHRISTINE: "Don't you think Ralph is a little hard to get acquainted with? He and Thelma seem to get along fine. I guess she understands him."

MARLA: "Thelma eats supper every night all by herself — with Ralph."

PAULA (sitting on the toilet in the woodshed to Mama, chopping wood): "I think we are going to have to get another daddy. I don't think ours is coming back, and you need someone to cut wood."
MAMA: "I don't know who we'd get."
PAULA: "Oh, just any old man would do."
MAMA: "Maybe for you, but not for me. I'd rather chop wood."

1954

July 1:
PAULA: "That old Mommie. When she goes swimming with us she doesn't even take her bathing suit."

DENA (coming down from the cellar running): "I ran faster than I could."

July 2:

MARLA (who was mad at Paula): "There is nobody good except God, Mama, Velma, Jeannie, Dena, Mommie and me."

1956

October 27:

DENA (after finishing telling me her dream): ". . . and that is as far as I got. My dream put a bookmark in it there."

This is no bookmark. This is the end.

NOTES

1. Grantly Dick-Read, *Childbirth Without Fear: The Original Approach to Childbirth.* Currently available in its 5th ed. (New York: Harper Collins, 1987).
2. Maxie Dunham, *The Workbook on Living Prayer.* Nashville, Tennessee: The Upper Room, 1974).

Toe Valley View

Cary, Tillie, Connie, John McConnell, Dena, Gertrude Hilleary, and Marla 1957

Barbara and David Killian with children
P. 90

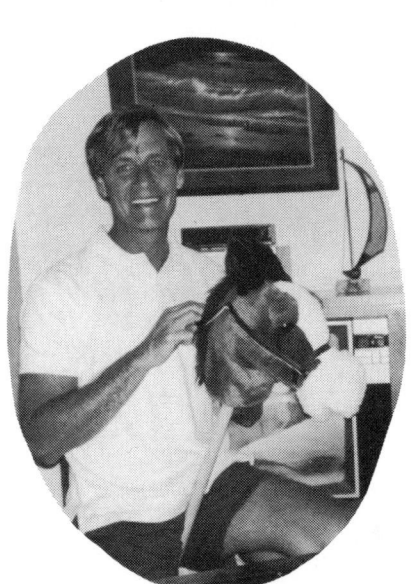

Cary McConnell in Ca.
P. 95

Katie McConnell in Ca.
P. 95

THE *TOE VALLEY VIEW* NEWSPAPER AND WTOE RADIO

John McConnell arrived in Celo Community in the summer of 1955 with his two children, Connie, age nine, and Cary, seven. As far as I know no one knew in advance that they were coming or why. I have the feeling that John had no idea either. They had just drifted in from California after his wife had called it quits. He had no occupation or visible source of income. Their earthly possessions (upon their arrival) were in their car.

I, along with other community members, provided them with housing and food. The next thing I knew, John had persuaded Erling and Louise Toness to join him in starting a weekly newspaper with headquarters in Bakersville despite the fact that there were two papers in the area already — The *Tri-County News* in Spruce Pine and the *Yancey Record* in Burnsville. Perhaps Bakersville felt a bit left out and jealous of the other two towns, and John used that to get support there.

Neither John nor the Tonesses had any capital to begin such a project, but the proof that John was a real "con man" was evidenced by the fact that a building was soon provided in Bakersville to house the office and the second-hand press they moved from Tennessee, and that he had the first paper off press in September. It was named The *Toe Valley View* and *Avery County News* (same news, different name). The linotype operator was Michael Malshuk. In April of 1957, *Life* magazine printed an article, "A Time of Trouble in Toe Valley," that described what happened after a local man "was arrested and charged with attempting to rape a deaf and dumb housewife" and after the *Toe Valley View* printed both the story and an editorial about the hearing. The accused had a politically powerful father and a good mountain lawyer and so he was acquitted. After the acquittal, the linotype operator (Malshuk), was beaten up in Johnson City, the publisher (John McConnell) was slugged, and the editor (Erling Toness) was run off the highway. They finally called a truce.

Erling and Louise Toness worked from the Bakersville office. Louise did writing and editing and Erling worked with the printing press. Though the office was thirty miles from home, on late nights when the paper still wasn't out, the Tonesses could house their family upstairs over the newspaper office.

There was also a *Toe Valley News* office in Spruce Pine, where Ashton Chapman was the writer/editor. Barbara Geouge did secretarial work there. The Tonesses and John McConnell had convinced me that my knowledge of the area (and the people) would be an asset to the paper; so I quit my job with the Methodist women and worked out of the Spruce Pine office delivering papers to Avery County *early* Thursday or Friday morning, depending on the "mood" of the press. I also wrote a column called "People I Meet." I profiled over forty couples or individuals: Mrs. Jane Pennell Baker, William Josiah Baker, Woodward Wawsaw Waulker Braswell, Sam G. Brinkley, James Howard Collins, Mrs. Sallie Craigmiles, Barbara Davenport, Virgil Lusk Edwards, Harding Ellis, Diane English, Mrs. Frank P. Garland, Paul Garland, Simon A. Gragg, Mrs. & Mrs. Luther Harrell, Mrs. Hester Honeycutt, Mr. & Mrs. Troy Howell, Zona Hughes, Robert "Buzz" Jones, Mrs. Laura Pendley Ledford, Joseph Washington Letterman, Mrs. Bobby Lowery, Michael Malshuk, Mrs. Henry Masters, Jr., Raymond McCrary, Mrs. Frank McElwain, Mrs. Winnie Wiseman Peake, Dr. Charles A. Peterson, Mrs. Della Sparks, Julia Sparks, Mrs. Linnie Thompson Stewart, Mrs. Belle Styles, Fred Sullins, Andrew C. Tainter, Sr., Mrs. Anna Rhea Slagle Troutman, David P. Turbyfill, Martha Carpenter Vance, Pearl Webb, Ed and Nancy Whetstine, Mr. and Mrs. Dock Willis, Wilburn Stover Wise, Willie Monroe Wiseman, and Shirley Young. These articles are still available on microfilm at the Spruce Pine library.

In the June, 1958, issue of *National Geographic*, Malcolm Ross did an article, "My Neighbors Hold to Mountain Ways."[1] He had read my columns in the *Toe Valley View* and he used two of them: one on Ed Whetstine[2] and another on Lusk Edwards.[3] (I now live next door to Lusk's daughter, and rent my apartment from his grandson.) Ross' article met with much the same reaction in the local press as Sheppard's book had earlier. He was surprised! He wrote to me soon after his article came out. "Your letter was welcome indeed! It was your column in the *Toe Valley View* that largely gave me the idea of rounding out a story of mountain craftsmen. So I am delighted to have your approval. Seven of the twelve people about whom I wrote have written me with praise and thanks for the article."[4] Bill Sharp in *The State* (May 18, 1957)[5] copied one of my stories from the *Toe Valley View:* about Sam G. Brinkley ("The Longest Beard in the World"[6]).

John McConnell found out that there were plans to start a radio station on Chalk Mountain near Spruce Pine. He was able to persuade the radio station operators to give us time on the air. Supposedly they were to be *paid* for the air time. They (the new station operators) went on the air Christmas day, 1955. The next day I was at the broadcast station from 9:00 to 10:00 A.M. with the *Toe Valley View Hour*. It fell to my lot to do the programming for that hour five days a week. The material covered was quite varied and a good variety of people were interviewed for the articles. On the day the paper came out, I read headlines and interesting articles (during my radio program.) We had people from special agencies and institutions come to speak, such as a counselor from the hospital at Morganton, a young man to help with music appreciation, interviews with older citizens, and skits in which members of our staff participated. John and the staff children usually did the Saturday program.

There were times when I arrived and found the guest for the hour had called in regrets, and I had to do the hour myself. I carried a box of Public Affairs Pamphlets and much devotional material. Once I spent the hour talking about the many roads in the Toe Valley. I had traveled many of them.

I was told that, because I cut the trip time so short, people along my route from my home in Celo Community to WTOE (about 14 miles) would wager that I wouldn't be there to broadcast by 9:00 A.M., but for five mornings a week for five months straight I was there to say, "Good morning. This is Tillie Brooks with the *Toe Valley View Hour*." I had many letters and calls with ideas and words of appreciation — yes, and sometimes with helpful criticism. I shall always be grateful for the friend who reminded me that I said "childern," instead of "children."

I knew I opened myself to criticism when I talked about racial prejudice in a county that bragged "The sun doesn't go down on a nigger in Mitchell County." I said that I would rather send my children into the world with a *grave physical handicap* than with prejudice in their hearts. I also emphasized the harm done to the person *holding* such attitudes, to say nothing of the harm to those against whom they were held. I told the story about my roommate in college that illustrated the point so graphically [the same one told later in this book in the article on the Scarritt Bennett Center]. I did not have to wait long for a reaction from a listener.

My friend, Nuree Hall, had previously called me about her husband Zeb's brother-in-law who lived in the Grassy Creek valley east of Spruce Pine. His name was Will Wiseman. He was a semi-invalid getting up in years and his family was concerned about his "immortal soul." His wife and children were faithful members of the Baptist Church, but he not only had nothing to do with the church or its minister, he held a long-running feud with S.T. Henry, who owned the adjoining farm.

Nuree begged me to go see him because she was sure I could influence him for the good because he listened to the *Toe Valley View Hour* and was so fond of me. I was not that confident.

But another of my paper responsibilities was for subscriptions to the paper. One day when I was calling from names in the phone book, I came to Will's name and called him. He said he would subscribe if I would come out to his house to get the subscription, so the next day I knocked on his door. Apparently no one was home except Will with his male nurse in a ground-floor room. The nurse left us alone.

I took down the information for mailing the paper to him and also a subscription for his brother in the Midwest. He paid me and then he "hit" me about my attitude toward "niggers."

"I am so fond of you," he said. "I'm afraid you're going to ruin yourself in this county. You know it says in the Bible that niggers are not human. In Genesis it says, 'God created every living creature . . . according to their *kind*.' (Gen. 1:21, 24, 25) And then God said, 'Let us make man in our image'(1:26)."

When I protested that the writer of Genesis was talking about animals and things in nature, Will became so angry I was afraid he would have a heart attack.

He said, "Well, I'm not so sure I want to get a paper put out by people who have such ideas."

I said, "Perhaps I shouldn't take your subscription," and offered to return his money. He refused and then calmed down so I could talk to him.

I told him about my experiences with black people during my two years at Scarritt College in Nashville. Many times I walked twenty blocks to hear the Jubilee Singers at Fisk University Chapel on Sunday mornings. I told him about the black children I worked with in Saturday Bible School at Bethlehem Center; about both their parents and the Fisk sociology professor who were helpful in gathering material and giving needed advice for writing my thesis, "The Relationship of Dolls to Race Consciousness and Attitudes." The Baptist Publishing House had my manuscript typed for me free of charge. Finally I reminded him of the story about Alma he had heard me tell on the air — the enormous toll it takes on the health of any person who holds enmity, bitterness, prejudice, and hate in their heart. I said I would pray for him as I drove about the three counties. I kissed the top of his bald head and left.

I was faithful to my promise and *did* pray for Will as I drove around. I think it was his son, Ray, who told me "the rest of the story."

On the Saturday after I had visited him, his male nurse was reading.

"What are you reading?" Will asked.

"My Sunday school lesson."

"Well, read it to me."

He finished that lesson and stopped.

"Don't stop. Read me some more."

In God's perfect timing, the pastor of their church came by and Will asked him to baptize him, declaring he had no bad feelings toward anyone in the world — not even S.T. Henry! — and accepted Christ as his savior.

Soon after he went into a coma and died.

There were times when I wondered if I had been unfaithful to *my* call from God when I quit my job with the Methodist Women and followed this "con man" in that unlikely undertaking. It helped to have letters from listeners whose lives had been blessed by the radio program. Grover Graham's letter was especially helpful. After hearing the program a month or so, he wrote to say he had come to Spruce Pine to serve churches hoping to work with me, only to be disappointed — and critical — when I left the church to be involved with the paper and radio. He conceded that I may have reached more people in a week than his preaching ever did. He served the Kona and perhaps other small churches. He may have been semi-retired.

It was evident that the program was meaningful to the listeners and valuable to the radio station because they kept us on for the one hour a day, six days a week, for five months — and we *never* paid for *any* of the airtime. After thirty-seven years I still meet people who when they hear my voice, say, "Oh, I enjoyed hearing you on WTOE!"

A very special listener friend was Troy Howell in Newdale. He called to ask me to come to see him — perhaps to give me a subscription to our paper. Mr. Howell *loved* to talk. He especially loved poetry, so I visited him more than once because it was such a joy to be with him.

In April, 1956, I wrote to my family that we had over a thousand subscriptions. I have already described how this venture was started on not even a shoestring. And with the unreliability of the press, money for staff salaries was in *extremely* short supply. I was working without any dependable salary. My children never went hungry because I raised a good garden, and we did get some groceries in exchange for advertising. But there was the morning that Marla showed me her shoes with the soles coming off. I said, "Oh, dear Lord, where will I get money to buy new shoes?"

As I drove from home to the radio station that morning, Troy Howell flagged me down on the straight stretch going through Newdale (at least 100 yards from his home). He handed me a five dollar bill saying, "The Lord told me this morning that you needed this." I bought Marla a pair of shoes.

In a letter to my family in early 1957 I wrote, "Though many of the problems that beset us with the paper seem to be behind us, it continues to be nip and tuck. I sometimes wish we'd have to fold up and get it over with — we live in such a constant state of crisis."[7]

During the time that this state of affairs existed, I listened to Joe Petree's prayer before the offering at Celo Methodist Church. In part, he said, "We thank you, dear God, that you have provided so generously that we may now return a portion to you." I had this silent conversation with God:

"I'm sorry that I don't have anything to give."

You have a dollar in your purse.

"But that is for the girls' lunch tomorrow."

Put it in the collection plate. So I did. When the service was over, Joe started to get in his car. He turned, came to mine, and handed me a twenty dollar bill.

"Tommy Tyson sent me this last week and said to use it wherever the Lord directed. He just now told me to give it to you."

I am convinced that the *giving* of the dollar opened the way for the *receiving* of the twenty. I am a *firm believer* in tithing to my church and then giving an additional five to six percent to charitable causes.

In August of 1957, Robert Early, the minister of the Spruce Pine Methodist Church, probably aware that the newspaper was not providing the income I needed to support my family, came to me with a job offer. They lacked a teacher for the fifth grade at Spruce Pine Elementary School. Would I consider the offer? I decided to try, even though I had never had any specific teacher training. With an M.A. degree I could teach on an emergency A certificate. So I deserted the *Toe Valley View* ship and taught fifth grade for three years.

In a letter to my family in 1958 I wrote, "John is no longer with the paper,"[8] and by April of that year he and the children were back in California, and John was off on another scheme — the "Star of Hope" and, later, "A Minute for Peace." Even though I have called John a "con man," I must admit it was always for a good cause, and never for his own financial gain — which is probably why Mary Lou left him. I still hear from Connie once or twice a year. She has changed her name to Coronella Keiper and is a devout follower of Jesus. Cary and I have talked on the phone recently. He also sent snapshots of him and his daughter, Katie.

The Tonesses held on to the paper a couple more months, then gave up and moved to California.

I went back to work for the Methodist women in September, 1960. Now it was a legitimate part of my duties to visit my friend, Troy Howell. I visited him periodically — even after he had a stroke in 1963 that left him unable to speak and in bed most of the time. It was so sad to see him make such *frustrating* attempts to communicate. Some time during his illness, he was able to let his family know that when he died he wanted me to have a part in his funeral service. He died in December, 1967, and the sons whom I know best, Woodrow and Ray, remembered their father's request. They asked me to help with his service — and even offered a $20 gratuity. Participating in Troy's funeral, in some sense, added a touch of finality to my *Toe Valley View*/WTOE two-year episode.

NOTES

1. Malcolm Ross, "My Neighbors Hold to Mountain Ways," *National Geographic* (June, 1958).
2. Arthelia H. Brooks, date of this article in the *Toe Valley View* not available.
3. Arthelia H. Brooks, date of this article in the *Toe Valley View* not available..
4. Letter of Malcolm Ross to Arthelia Brooks, July 6, 1958.
5. Bill Sharp, name of this article unavailable, *The State* vol # (May 18, 1957).
6. Arthelia H. Brooks, "The Longest Beard in the World," *Toe Valley View*, date not available.
7. Letter of Arthelia Brooks to family (LF), April 23, 1957.
8. LF, February 17, 1958.

People

Paula, Wendal, Dave and Frances
← 4-22-85
P. 145

Lydia Holman →
P. 101

P. 133 →
↖ Alvin and Frances Jones, Nora and Tillie Windom UMC
7-67

Estelle White
← 12-24-85
P. 137

Friends II

"Kay" & Chuck
 sitting
White Inn
N.Y
8-1-90

Muriel
Clark -
My
apt.
1-22-94

Jean Quinn -
my apt. 7-13-91

Dorothy Robinson and her mother "Katy" McDaniel
7-31-92

Section II
PEOPLE

LYDIA HOLMAN

INTRODUCTION

The Toe River Valley in the eighteen hundreds was sparsely populated and practically unknown to the lowlanders. Only the hardiest undertook to penetrate its rugged terrain; the last westward migration passed through about 1850. The valley then remained virtually isolated for the next fifty years, until the coming of the railroad and the discovery of mineral wealth opened up the area.

In the 1890s there were a few resorts there. For example, there was the Cloudland Hotel on the summit of Roan Mountain, accessible from the railroad in Tennessee; and apparently a kind of resort community in Ledger, the community settled before Bakersville or Spruce Pine in Mitchell County.

So at this time, when the Toe River Valley was just beginning to yawn and stretch from her long sleep of isolation, my friend, Lydia Holman, stepped briskly and efficiently into the picture. The day was December 25, 1899, and the timing was perfect! The slight frame of this five-foot-four-inch woman did not convey the truth of what she was: a woman whom people would soon come to know and remember as one with a keen resourceful mind, unheard-of courage and initiative, a will to work, an endless capacity for self-sacrifice, an unshakable faith in the inherent worth and goodness of ordinary people, and a great compassion for those in need. The valley needed such a woman — such a nurse!

She came to care for a typhoid patient for two years, and stayed for fifty — because she saw the great need for what she could give and because she fell in love with the people.

Eleanor W. Allen, chairperson of Miss Lydia Holman's Boston Committee,* wrote shortly before Lydia's death, "How I wish she

---

*One of the things that allowed Lydia Holman to accomplish as much as she did was her ability to cultivate financial backing committees — mainly up North. The Boston Committee (formed in 1914) was the committee that

could have assembled her papers before she was taken ill. Over and over again she told me she intended to do this when she 'retired.' Now it's too late! [Lydia was bedridden, and unable even to feed herself.] She was very reticent about herself. I was never able in all the half-century of knowing her to find out any details. She would never tell her age, and I do not know who her parents were or where she lived as a child."[1]

I'm sure it would have helped *me* a great deal to have received her "assembled papers", which she had promised that her great-nephew, Jack Harris, would give to me after her death for the purpose of writing her story. But when she died, I was teaching fifth grade in Spruce Pine, North Carolina, and no longer writing for the newspaper that had initiated my interviews with her. I did not make the effort to obtain this additional material. But I did hold on to the material about Miss Holman that I already had, never completely letting go of my plan to publish, in some form, her life story. It is those materials that I've used in this article.

My main sources, other than my interviews with Miss Holman, were the yearly reports published by the Boston Committee about her work in Mitchell County. They were called *The Friendly Nurse*, and the thirteen copies I had were dated between the years of 1914 and 1947. I also received some valuable help from the letters of Lydia's first cousin once removed, Mildred Holman Williams, and other relatives, including Clyde Holman, and Thomas Holman Latwick. Mr. Latwick had spent a winter with Lydia at Altapass, North Carolina. Some of the information in these sources is somewhat contradictory, but it is the best information I could find.

The interviews started in February or March of 1956, when I was trying to decide on the next personality to write up for my "People I Meet" column in the *Toe Valley View*. Ashton Chapman, on our writing staff, suggested writing about Lydia Holman. He had heard that Zeb Hall had been to Miss Holman's on business recently, and could tell me what the situation was. I called Zeb, and he was pretty discouraging. Lydia's dog had taken a chunk out of his pants leg and a small bite from his heel. The dog was tied in the woodshed guarding the door to the kitchen, and it was most difficult to get Miss Holman to hear a visitor, so getting by the dog

---

remained viable until her death, and it published a yearly report about her efforts, *The Friendly Nurse*. This annual report kept her committee's supporters informed, and was aimed at encouraging continued giving.

was not easy. Not having any great fear of dogs, I decided I would risk a visit. I found the situation as Zeb had described it, talked the dog into letting me walk by, went into the kitchen and called. Miss Holman came and was surprised to see me there. "You must be someone special if that dog let you get by without even barking," she said. So we were off to a good start. (She later admitted that Chris liked women much better than men.) The interviews are used in all three parts of this article.

EARLY YEARS

Thomas Holman Latwick wrote, "Lydia Holman's parents died when she was a child. My grandfather, John Holman [her uncle], went from his home in Pennsylvania's Schuylkill County to Rhode Island and brought her home, along with her brother and sister. John Holman's brother, Phil, took the sister to raise."[2]

Mildred Holman Williams gave this version, "Lydia was one of five children — one brother, Bob, and three sisters. (Perhaps Bob never married and died young.) Edith's first married name was Fox, and her second married name was Van Deneker. Another sister, Elisabeth, married a Bailey and lived in Philadelphia. Still another sister whose name I have not been able to discover was the fifth child.

"Lydia's mother was the sister of my grandfather, John R. His father's name was John Rawse or Raus Holman, born in 1842 in Land's End, Cornwall, England. Lydia's mother came to America with her four siblings, John R., Joseph, Philip, and Harriet, and their father died en route and was buried at sea. The mother settled at Tamaqua, Pennsylvania.

"Lydia Holman's right name was Kazey or Casey. When my grandfather, John Holman, went up to Rhode Island to bring the five orphans down to Tamaqua, they took the name, Holman, since their mother's name was Holman. Dad [Fred Holman] is quite sure they were all born in Rhode Island."[3]

Perhaps the "other sister" that Mrs. Williams could not account for was the one who died in 1953, while living with Lydia at Altapass. That unnamed sister would have been the mother of the Chicago niece who was listed as a survivor in Lydia's obituary, and who also was the mother of Jack Harris, Miss Lydia's great-nephew. [Obituary is printed at the end of this article.]

While I do have in my notes that Miss Holman told me that she was born in Tamaqua and that her parents died when she was seven years old, I think it is understandable that since she experienced such a "mixed-up" childhood, the facts about her family during that childhood might not be recollected the same by the siblings and other relatives. I am satisfied that the above account is as accurate as one is likely to get.

A traumatic event in her mid- to late-teens gave a new direction to Lydia's life. She had to go to Will's Eye Clinic for an operation. While both her eyes were bandaged, she touched a cold, iron bed frame. It startled her so much that she began to cry. This apparently caused her left eye to become infected and resulted in permanent blindness in that eye. But she received such tender, loving care while recuperating that she decided what she really wanted to do with her life was to be a nurse.

Miss Holman told me that George W. Childs sponsored her education for one and a half years at Children's Hospital in Philadelphia. "Doctors gave service there before they went into Philadelphia General Hospital to intern," she said. She entered Philadelphia General Hospital January 7, 1890, and she graduated in January, 1892. The following statements were on her records: "Miss Holman promises to be a great credit, is a thoroughly good nurse and a great comfort. She's thoroughly reliable and always cheerful."[4]

While she was in training at Philadelphia General, she was the only nurse who would care for a Chinese patient who had leprosy, Miss Holman told me.

At some time soon after graduation, Miss Holman worked at Henry Street Settlement House in New York City where there were a lot of foreigners. It was there, she felt, that she learned social service skills and how to deal with welfare problems.

Miss Holman served in the Spanish American War, as well, which took place between April and December of 1898. She was stationed at Camp Hamilton, outside Lexington, Kentucky. They had five hundred typhoid fever patients, she remembered.

After the war she was helping Dr. Harvey Shoemaker, who was on the teaching staff of the University of Pennsylvania Medical School according to Dr. C.F. Lambert.[5] Lydia said that Dr. Shoemaker had twenty patients under his care. Lydia was helping him when she was asked to go to Ledger, North Carolina to care for Mrs. Julia Josephine Ervine who had a summer home there and had contracted typhoid fever. Mrs. Ervine had served as president of

Wellesley College from 1895 to 1899 and may have been the sister of Dr. Shoemaker.

Lydia recalled her first trip to North Carolina quite vividly. She arrived in Marion on December 24, 1899, and did not want to stay there alone. She learned there was a Negro man named Crum in the area who drove a three-seated hack, so she asked him to take her and her luggage to Ledger. He said, "Mam, NOBODY goes up in them mountains this time of year." Nevertheless, he soon found himself on the way. About thirteen miles out of Marion, near Gillespie Gap, an axle broke, and they spent the night with Mrs. Hyams (or Mrs Yancey). Meanwhile the axle was repaired, and they started out at five the next morning, arriving at 10:00 A.M. at Ledger on Christmas day, 1899. Lydia was with Mrs. Ervine for about a year and a half, until Mrs. Ervine recuperated and moved to Paris where she lived until her death. Mr. Wing bought her home in Ledger.

An excerpt from *North Carolina History of Nursing*, picks up the story: "Lydia Holman was sent to Ledger in 1900 to nurse a patient with typhoid fever. During the patient's long illness and recovery, Miss Holman made a study of the living conditions of the people in that area and found their living conditions lacking in many respects. She became attached to the mountain folk and felt that she could be of help to them in combating disease and in teaching hygiene and dietetics.

"After she returned to Philadelphia, many letters were received from the people of Mitchell County urging her to come back to them. Miss Holman felt this to be her duty. She availed herself of the opportunities open to nurses for advanced study in slum work and treatment of children's diseases and returned to Ledger in July, 1902, as an independent worker."[6]

She was now ready to begin the work that she never left thereafter, except for short business trips. The *N.C. History* continues:

"For thirty-seven years she has labored among the people of Mitchell County helping to reduce the number of maternal deaths and checking the spread of pellagra as well as many other diseases."[7]

"During the years from 1902 to 1911, Lydia rented a house in Ledger for forty dollars ($40) a year and worked in a friendly, informal way among the people, teaching by word and example the need for sanitary living conditions, personal hygiene, use of a safe water supply and properly cooked foods. She also warned about the danger of the use of patent medicines, tobacco, whiskey and snuff for little children."[8]

SERVING AS A NURSE IN MITCHELL COUNTY

What was Mitchell County like in 1899?

Dr. Charles Peterson, who was quite elderly when I spoke to him in the winter of 1956, told me, "Spruce Pine was a mud puddle when I came to Ledger in 1900. In 1906 the place where my office is (in Spruce Pine) was in corn. It was the railroad that changed that."

By the time that Miss Holman moved from Ledger to Altapass in 1911, the local railroad had been connected to Johnson City, Tennessee, and also to Spartanburg, South Carolina, by way of Huntdale, Spruce Pine, Altapass, and Marion, North Carolina. Miss Holman was housed temporarily in a remodeled construction shack used in the building of the Carolina, Clinchfield, & Ohio Railroad.[9]

"The railroad company had given fifteen acres [of Altapass land] in a deed of trust on the condition that a health, welfare and educational center be conducted. The deed read that, after Miss Holman's death or if her work ceased, the land and buildings were to revert to the railroad (which is now the Holston Land Corporation). I have a copy of the deed of trust."[10]

Land is only a beginning, though. It took the Boston Committee to raise the money necessary to erect the infirmary. It is still in Altapass today. Miss Holman had an old barn remodeled to be a small library.

One Holman Association was formed in 1911 "to promote rural nursing, hygiene, and social service wherever an opportunity could be found throughout the United States, Miss Holman being established at Station no. 1 at Altapass."[11]

"The town is named Altapass because it is at the highest point on the CC&O railroad. Here the extra engines are left after hauling trains up the steep grades on either side: here freight crews stop over in the railroad boarding house: and here bootleggers are making life miserable for everybody.

"In 1913 the Holman Association disbanded. There were earlier committees that helped with Miss Holman's work. The first was formed in Baltimore under the direction of Dr. William H. Welch of Johns Hopkins University. This was dissolved after a few years as were others in Philadelphia and Brooklyn, New York."[12]

The most influential and faithful committee was the one started in Boston in 1914. "The first year's budget was $1,805, and for 1929, one of the peak years, the budget was for $6,945. This money was raised from as many as 150 contributing members."[13]

Miss Holman must have had some of her own resources, because the yearly reports definitely state that she received no salary. There are references to individuals and causes to which she contributed. Perhaps she had a pension from the Spanish American War or a family inheritance. This whole area of finance is one she considered a private matter. She commented to me once, "I think people don't like it when I don't tell them my private business."

One of the first projects of the Boston group was to raise money to build a ten-bed infirmary. It was started in 1918 and completed in 1920 at a cost of about twelve thousand dollars.

Lydia told me that sometime after she moved to Altapass, "I said to Will Wiseman, 'Why don't you go down to Raleigh and tell them we need a fair up here?'" It became the Toe River Fair in 1914, but strangely enough they never asked Miss Holman to participate until ten years later when she set up a health exhibit.

Miss Arizona Hughes, an eighty-five-year-old (retired) teacher from Spear, visited Mrs. S.T. Henry in 1962. When asked what she knew of Miss Holman, Miss Hughes said, "I did not know Miss Holman personally, but I saw her every year at the Toe River Fair because I liked to go up to the building where she had a place for women and children to rest and stay if they wanted to. She had made a nice playground for little children with sliding boards and swings. In those days the Toe River Fair was the only big entertainment people had, and everybody went. They had as many as four or five thousand people, somebody told me."

Miss Gladys Pardee, a trained nurse who volunteered to work at Altapass with Miss Holman for almost two years, further elaborated on the health exhibit itself in an issue of *The Friendly Nurse*. "We had two rooms in a building right in the center of the grounds. . . . Sometimes we would have seven or eight babies under a year old at the same time. One afternoon a mother deposited her three-week-old twins with us. . . . We had posters on various health subjects, suggested outfits for boys and girls and babies. The 'Witches' House of Woe' showed trash in the yard, no window panes, and a witch serving food forbidden for children The 'Fairy's House of Health' was, of course, promoting ideas exactly opposite to those represented by this actual environment all around the health display."[14]

In the same report, some of Miss Holman's community involvement is noted. "She was elected chairman of the school committee, and through her efforts an appropriation was secured for a new four-room school house. . . . She drew up a petition for the construction of a good road between Spruce Pine and Altapass (four miles) and for the railroad company to move a steel bridge, free of charge to the community, from Spruce Pine to the ford across the Toe River near the hospital."[15] A new bridge was scheduled to be built at Spruce Pine. Miss Holman gave as her reason for requesting the bridge, "Babies down here come in a hurry, and when the river is up, they remain on the other side (from the hospital)."[16]

One of the crying needs that had drawn Miss Holman back to Mitchell County in 1902 was the plight of women and children. This remained her chief concern. On May 11, 1924, Miss Carolyn Conant Van Blarcom of the American Child Health Association, in an interview in the *New York Times* entitled "Toll of Child-birth Greater Than That of Wars," said:

"One of the most wonderful and successful experiments in alleviating distress and averting disaster in maternity cases, as well as in other instances of sickness and disease, is conducted by Miss Lydia Holman, a registered nurse, down in the mountains of North Carolina, with headquarters in the small village of Altapass . . . while she ministers to the physical needs of every man, woman, and child for miles . . . around; the lives she has saved by her prenatal and postnatal care represent one of the most encouraging signposts of what intelligence and care can do."[17]

Miss Holman told me, "Dr. Fletcher in Asheville, chairman of the N.C. Medical Board, gave me my letter of certification [to minister care in lieu of a doctor]. Many people tried to call me 'Doctor.' In fact, one doctor brought me before the court for practicing medicine without a license. The Judge said, 'Gentlemen of the Jury, what we need is a few more Miss Holmans. Case dismissed.'"

In interviews with Mitchell County residents in 1956, Mrs. C.O. Harrison told me: "We lived in the first house in Spruce Pine, and Miss Holman has certainly been a friend to our family. She made arrangements for mother to go to Baltimore for treatment. . . . I think when she first came there wasn't even a doctor here. She has helped a lot of people. We have always loved her."

Charles Mae Sproles stated, "I always thought of Miss Holman as the soul of kindness. When I taught at Altapass she was so helpful."

Mrs. Carrie Edwards at Ledger remembered, "[When I was a child] I had a sore on my head. Dr. Smith and Dr. Butt had been treating me. They gave up. They had been fighting Dr. Holman — because we always called her Dr. Holman.

"Miss Holman said it was gangrene. On Friday she sent word to put a starch poultice on it. Sunday she came and *really* cleaned it out. I'll never forget how it hurt! Mama held me while she did it. She came back several times and dressed it. She charged $7.00 and took it out in feed for her horse. Before Miss Holman came [on Sunday] it burned like fire. Mama would come at all hours of the night and put cold buttermilk poultices on it.

"I saw Miss Holman a few years ago, and I went up to her and told her who I was. She remembered me and said, 'I'm so glad to see that you have a beautiful head of hair. I've wondered all these years if hair grew back on your head.'

"When I was growing up, I used to say that I wanted to be a nurse like Dr. Holman."

Dr. Hilda Sheriff served at the hospital in Altapass from June to December of 1926, and her aunt helped with the housekeeping there. They had to leave in order for Dr. Sheriff to return to Philadelphia General Hospital for her internship. In the 1926–27 *Friendly Nurse*, Dr. Lambert is mentioned. A little girl in the infirmary with a fractured leg was counting the days until Christmas.

"When asked what would make her well, she said thoughtfully, 'You and Dr. Lambert are making me well, but I could get *weller faster* if I had a mama doll.'"

That report also noted that Miss Holman had directed the firefighters when the Altapass Inn burned in May of 1925, and she housed the Inn guests in the infirmary. Also, during this period she was serving as Justice of the Peace.

One of Miss Holman's most memorable programs was providing Christmas gifts for all the schoolchildren in Mitchell County. She wrote in 1928, "we managed to get 3,000 gifts for 42 or more schools."[18] Teachers supplied lists showing the name, age, and sex of each child in their classrooms.

Harvey G. Miller, who for many years wrote "The Pigeon Roost News" for the *Tri-County News*, noted in his column after Miss Holman's death in 1960: "It is said she played the role of Santa Claus to school children for more than 40 years. She would walk the roads in her nearby mountains . . . and give the gifts. Since Pigeon Roost was about 35 miles away, she never did deliver the gifts there personally, but we will always remember how she gladdened our young hearts as we played with the toys she sent us."[19]

Mrs. Henry also told me a story about a Miller column she'd read, as background for putting the cold, snowy winter of 1959–1960 into perspective. That was the year I was teaching fifth grade in Spruce Pine, and traveling back and forth from South Toe to Spruce Pine was a challenge, to say the least. Mrs. Henry said, "There was a particularly severe winter back in 1926 or so. I personally know of one family who were all sick at once, and who were isolated by the snow. Miss Holman wasn't deterred by the weather or by how it affected the roads, which weren't that great in good weather! She managed to ride her horse out there and tend to them. Without her they would have died, for sure."[20]

By 1928, Miss Holman had lost her faithful companion and helper, the horse named Dorothy, who died in October, 1928, at age *thirty-two*. She got another horse, but began to make her rounds in a Ford. The kind of roads (or lack thereof) involved in her travels would certainly have shortened the life of a "mechanical beast." Miss Holman was instrumental in getting the Red Cross organized in Spruce Pine in 1928. Later, Miss Katherine Myers (for ten years the field representative with the American Red Cross Public Health Nursing Service in the Carolinas), wrote to Miss Holman: "I shall always be interested to hear how things are going with you and your work. You have helped advance the cause of better health for Mitchell County beyond the power of words to express, and more than we can expect anybody on this earth to give credit to a 'mere nurse.'"[21]

Miss Holman was able to interest doctors in holding clinics at the hospital for tonsils, teeth and eyes. Two hundred children from the schools came to an eye clinic conducted by Dr. H.H. Briggs from Asheville.[22]

In the 1933 *Friendly Nurse* report, it is evident that the depression had hit. "Day after day men came to the door of the little infirmary begging for work at $1.00, 75 or even 50 cents a day. Or failing that, they asked to be allowed to chop wood, mend fences or roads in return for a pair of shoes or warm clothing for their children."[23]

Miss Holman believed it gave people dignity to give something in return for what they received. This belief of Miss Holman's is probably what prompted the kind of negative comment I got from eighty-four-year-old Mr. Willard Vance when I interviewed him in 1957: "She had all these clothes and things and didn't give them to people. She'd have people come in and scrub floors or wash walls and do other hard work — then she'd give them some clothes to pay for it. . . . She used to have children dress in their raggediest and dirtiest clothes and come to school on a certain day, and she'd take their pictures. Then another day they'd wear their best. She'd send the pictures up north to show what *she'd* done for the poor mountain children. . . . I bought a dog from her and found that it ate chickens. She gave me back the $10.00 I paid for the dog. She sold it to another man, and he shot it. She was really mad at the man for not bringing it back. Another dog she had died. She dug a decent grave and buried it. I never knew her to show that much concern for a human being."

In order to raise the money she needed for her work, she probably did paint a pretty sad picture. The 1942 *Friendly Nurse* has *eight* pictures, and they do show the worst and none of the best. This tactic for fundraising hurt people's pride — and it got her in trouble in the early days with papers like the short-lived Toe Valley *Hornet* and *Yellow Jacket*, causing her, as late as the 1950s, to forbid the *Tri-County News* or our paper, *The Toe Valley View*, to print anything about her while she was living.

Sue Wiseman Norman expressed to me another source of misunderstanding; "If she was ever *really close* to anyone I never knew about it. I don't know what church she would say she belonged to, but she never went to church here."

Remembering some of the things she said to me, I can believe she may not have had many close friends. She admitted that she did not tell people her business — or confide in them. In the third part of this story she gives her reasons for her behavior in regard to church and funerals (that she never attended).

To balance the negative attitudes of some toward Miss Holman, I'll include Ray Wiseman's positive one: "One of my first memories of Miss Holman was when I was going to Wiseman School. Every year she would have all the teachers send a list of the pupils' names, and each one got a toy. If they were needy, they got warm clothes. I remember that year I got a fire engine pulled by two white horses and a black one. It would *really go*! That was the happiest Christmas I had had to that time. I'm sure Miss Holman was sincere and conscientious in everything she did."

Despite differences with some, her work didn't stop. "This year Miss Holman has two fine helpers, one a graduate nurse with three years additional training in obstetrics and mid-wifery, and the other a practical nurse. In addition to maternity and emergency cases treated in the infirmary, Miss Holman has carried on her health work in homes and schools. . . . She made examinations in 22 rural schools, discovering 380 (defective) eye cases, 174 with bad tonsils, and 420 with skin disorders. . . . She also supervises 56 mid-wives (whom she trained) who do much of the postnatal work in remote places. She is trying to impress on mothers of huge families that it is wrong to bring into the world children that they can not feed, clothe, or educate."[24]

Miss Holman wrote, "The 'library,' a barn which has been made into a library, is increasingly useful. . . . Teachers come and select books suitable for supplementary reading for their grades. These books are loaned in lots of 25 to 100. . . . Magazines are sent to the prison convict camp at Spruce Pine. Two community libraries have been started — one at Little Switzerland and another at Gouge's Creek."[25]

"Last winter was a terrific one — below zero temperatures and snow twenty feet deep in some places. . . . An epidemic of flu followed, and Miss Holman barely escaped pneumonia.

"She has clothed this year 910 children, 34 women, and 22 men — receiving in return some bit of service or farm products, as there is little or no money in the mountains. Her present helper is a Scotch woman, Miss MacGill, who is trained in mid-wifery as well as in public health and school nursing.

"The Holman library . . . is open every day except Sunday from 9–12 and 2–5. A New England woman, Mrs. Mabel Alden, is in charge, . . . having given her services for over a year.

"The National Library Association, through its state branch, asked Miss Holman to place books in a camp for 64 colored convicts near Altapass . . . a geography book and dictionary were among the books loaned."[26]

The report for 1938 itemizes the services rendered and adds the note: "The state health officer for North Carolina writes: 'I am glad to report that what Miss Holman has done for the people of Mitchell County is outstanding. She has rendered a marvelous service in what we term a maternity and infancy program. . . . 4,000 children were made happy at Christmas.'"[27]

Mrs. Henry sent me a clipping from the *Tri-County News*, dated December 21, 1961, in which it is noted that the TVA had commended two rain gauge observers for twenty-five years of service. Mrs. Henry commented, "This is just a reminder that Miss Holman kept the U.S. Government rain gauge at Altapass. She had the distinction of measuring the heaviest rainfall in United States in the

1916 flood. The amount was 22.22 inches in twenty-four hours." [The story of how we checked this measurement for accuracy is at the end of the Laughrun-Ray article, later in this book.]

By 1942, Lydia Holman had organized Home Nursing and First Aid classes for women and given defense and recruiting information to men about to be called to the services.

"She has carried on valiantly . . . in spite of additional problems and duties brought on by the war. . . . Her vegetable garden was planted this year as a demonstration 'Victory Garden,' . . . Milk from her goats has greatly helped certain types of stomach trouble, and the animals are borrowed from time to time by the neighbors and passed from one family to another."[28]

"Some of Miss Holman's 'first babies' are now leaders in that community. . . . Her great need is still for electric power. Lines have been extended to Spruce Pine but not to Altapass. The French Broad Electric Membership Corporation wrote recently that they are greatly handicapped still by lack of materials and workmen and are disappointed at their inability to bring a rural district line to her section, but are hoping to succeed by the first of the year 1947. . . . Miss Holman has just been elected as an honorary member of the American Legion Auxiliary."[29]

PERSONAL INTERVIEWS WITH MISS LYDIA HOLMAN

When I told Miss Holman the nature of my first visit, she explained that during the early years of her work in Mitchell County she had received such adverse publicity that in recent years she had not given anyone permission to write anything about her. Now she would be willing to provide me with any information she could provide plus give the yearly reports of her work issued by the Northern committees that supported her work. She also agreed to instruct her great-nephew, Jack Harris, to supply me with any further material I could use — after her death.

I kept a log of my visits. I went again on April 17, 1956. Her first comment was, "I've thought of you every day since you were here. I wouldn't know you if I met you on the street because my eyes are so bad, but I liked the atmosphere you brought into my living room."

Miss Holman was not feeling well that afternoon. Her friend, Mrs. Lambert, (whose home was where the Bakersville Motel now is) had been to see her that morning to tell her that Mr. Lambert's mother had died. Mrs. Lambert had wanted to come the next day to help Miss Holman to dress so Miss Holman could attend the funeral, which Miss Holman had emphatically refused to do. "I told Mrs Lambert that even it was my own sister, I wouldn't go."

Then Miss Holman continued, "I've never been to a funeral in all my life. Many people thought it was a little queer that I didn't have a funeral when my sister died in 1952. But I had asked her before she died what she wanted done about a funeral, and she said she had always been able to go directly to God with her prayers without any preacher as a go-between; so she guessed she'd make it through this, too. I buried her out there." She pointed out the spot in her yard.

Miss Holman said she wanted me to take her to Asheville to do some shopping and to get her affairs in order. She also wanted to have a woman she knew massage her back and shoulder. She explained that once a dog got frightened in an electric storm and scared her horse. She had been thrown to the ground, and her shoulder had given her trouble ever since. In addition, Miss Holman said that she was now having trouble with her ears as a result of their having been frost bitten so often in past winters. She felt that her circulation must be getting poor because this was the first winter her ears had really bothered her. When I got ready to go, I said, "Miss Holman, I know you were not feeling well today. I hope I've not tired you." She replied, "On, no, you have inspired me."

On May 8, 1956, I visited Miss Holman again. Her greeting was, "Oh, you must have known that I wanted you to come. I started to write you a card last night. I want you to see spring with me." Then she took me all around her place and showed me both the wild and the tame flowers. Her joy at my visit reminded me of the time she had said, "I wish I could keep you with me all the time, and I don't feel that way about many people."

When I told her that her dog, Chris, had come up and rubbed his head against me, she said, "Yes, he knows there is something special about you — something that shines out from you. I am animal enough to feel it, too."

I asked Miss Holman when she wanted me to take her to Asheville. She said it was going to be cold for nine more days because Jason's mother had heard it thunder on the seventeenth of February so Miss Holman could not take off her winter clothes until the seventeenth of May. She didn't want to take any chance of getting pneumonia before she had her affairs in order. She said,

"About the only thing that is ready is my grave. I have bought the plot. It is in the new municipal cemetery in Grassy Creek."

We were talking about reasons for the adverse publicity she had received. I suggested to Miss Holman that one of the chief causes may have been that she did not attend any church. She agreed. She said, "When I first came, I did go to church some, but I couldn't agree with what they said, so it seemed like living a lie to go to church and pretend I did. There was one preacher friend who used to reprimand me every Sunday for working in my flowers and making sick calls instead of going to church. The common belief is that one cannot be religious without going to church. I am a member of the Swedenborgian Church in Philadelphia. When I was seventeen, I visited every different church group — even the Greek — to see which one I could worship with in sincerity. My grandmother belonged to the Church of England, and we did lean toward the Episcopal Church. My sister went to the Methodist Episcopal Church."

"When I came to this county," Miss Holman continued, "they had only four months of school. My folks said, 'You are just wasting your time down there. You'll never be able to make a dent in meeting the needs of that section.'" But I said, 'Well, I have to invest my life somewhere, and I intend to invest it right here.' I tried to get the people up there to see that it was only education, and a chance, that these people needed to develop into the kind of people that the nation could be proud of. And my faith has been rewarded. The boys and girls have gone out from here and taken their places in the professions with the best of them."

Later she said, "Some time ago I sent word to Dr. (Melvin) Webb to come and see if he could give my dog some penicillin or something to get well. He said he certainly would come because he would never forget that the greatest thrill of his childhood was the Christmas present I was responsible for. He wished he could find something that would thrill him that much again."

In speaking of her death, Miss Holman said, "I'll just go to sleep and not wake up. It is a habit in our family — we are levelheaded that way."

She expressed concern about the current segregation issue. She could remember hearing her father (really, her Uncle John) and her Uncle Phil discussing the Civil War (in which they had both fought) and her father saying, "If we had been more patient and thought a little slower, we need not have fought the Civil War." (I love that phrase, "— thought a little slower.")

That same day she told me that her parents died when she was seven. She said she often went to bed distraught after hearing stories about World War II that Jasper (the man-helper on her place in Altapass) would tell her. She kept wondering why we couldn't all learn to live together.

The visits continued over the next year, and Miss Holman's health continued to deteriorate. The children and I paid Miss Holman a little visit on May 13, 1957. She was very feeble — hardly able to make it back from the barn where she went to show the girls her horse, Ginger. She said she went to see Ginger every day.

Myrta Davis, Wendal Bull, and I visited the property again in September, 1957, but I think we did not see Miss Holman because we didn't know the state of her health and did not want to disturb her.

After a stroke, Miss Holman was taken to the Oteen Veterans' Hospital January 7, 1958. She was eligible as a Veteran army nurse of the Spanish American War.

Sometime in 1959, I visited Miss Holman in the hospital at Oteen. As I recall, she was unable to speak, but conscious and able to recognize me. I made no notes on that visit.

FINIS

Miss Eleanor W. Allen (chairperson of the Boston Committee) wrote me to say, "I myself visited Altapass four times: once in the early days of our interest — 1916, and the last time in 1953 when Lydia Holman had begun to lose the strength of her eyesight and hearing. I stayed at that time with Mrs. Frank Arnold who has been more than good to Miss Holman for many years.

"Miss Holman lived and worked first in Ledger, and the last I heard was that she still owned the house she occupied there. Another person who might help you is Dr. Lambert of Winston-Salem. He was one of her 'babies,' and his mother was a long-time friend of Miss Holman. He saw her at the hospital last fall and wrote to me.

"All the members of the Brooklyn and Philadelphia Committees have died, and there are only four of us left on the Boston Committee — and one is bedridden, and another is in the hospital. It seems incredible that so many years have gone by."[30]

In a letter to Mrs. S.T. Henry Miss Allen wrote, "At the request of Mrs. Turner in Charlotte, I am mailing you a copy of the letter I sent to all the friends of Miss Lydia Holman who helped to support her work in Mitchell County. . . . Mrs. Arnold has kept me in touch with Miss Holman's condition since she was stricken, and I hear occasionally from Dr. Lambert, also. He tells me she is receiving excellent care but has to be fed and cannot speak. I couldn't bear to have her just fade away without explaining the situation to her many friends here in Boston."[31]

In the above-mentioned letter, which she entitled "The Friendly Nurse — Finis," and which was dated a month earlier, Miss Allen said in part: "She [Miss Holman]) is nearing ninety, and her health has been failing since 1955, when a stroke made hospitalization imperative. It was possible to have her admitted to the Veterans Administration Hospital . . . She is a patient there now, apparently conscious, but unable to speak. . . . Our committee feels strongly that such a dedicated life of service to others, with no thought of self, should not end without some word of recognition and appreciation. Her work will be her monument. . . . without your help, her success would have been impossible."[32]

On my behalf, Mrs. S.T. Henry had written to Dr. C.F. Lambert for information about Miss Holman's early years. Dr. Lambert gave one bit of information I did not have previously. "The first doctor there [at the Altapass infirmary] was a Dr. Tyler who later moved to Greenville, S.C." He also said, "I saw her a few weeks ago and feel she may die at any minute. I do not understand how she has lived as long as she has in such a condition."[33]

Obituary

Miss Lydia Holman of Altapass died Thursday, Feb. 25, [1960], at age 92. . . . There is no way to set a value on Miss Holman's work. Many, many people lived who would have died but for her ministrations.

Funeral services for Lydia Holman were held at Altapass Baptist Church Saturday, Feb. 27, 1960, at 2 P.M. with Rev. E.W. McMurray of Winston-Salem officiating. Burial was in Memorial Cemetery, Spruce Pine.

Pallbearers were Deward Hefner, Lee Medford, Colonel Garland, Ernest Hefner, George Pitman, Lewis Biggerstaff, and Rex McKinney.

Survivors are one niece, Mrs. Lydia Harris of Chicago, three great-nieces of Chicago, and one great-nephew, Jack Harris of Altapass.[34]

**

I was not informed of Miss Holman's death until after she was buried. The last letter from Eleanor Allen said, "I assume there will be a notice in the *Tri-County-News* about the death of Miss Lydia Holman that occurred yesterday. This event will surely absolve you from your promise to Miss Holman to publish nothing about her until her death. I do hope you will be able to carry out your plan. You may be interested to know that we have deposited the reports of her work made over the 50 years with the Women's Archives of Radcliffe College, which is delighted to have them."[35]

I feel so blessed that even though it was at the end of her ministry, I had the good fortune to meet this remarkable woman; and I know personally at least one 'baby' that was born in the infirmary at Altapass — Mary Alice Young Holder, the youngest sister of my long-time friend, Gladys Young, had that distinction.

Now, Miss Lydia, it has been over thirty three years since your death; but at last, with my best effort, my attempt to keep my promise to tell your story is finished. It has taken so long that I feel certain that Miss Allen has joined the other deceased committee members, and I cannot send her a copy of the story that she had hoped to see. Perhaps in the economy of the universe, in some way that I cannot fathom, both Miss Allen and you, Miss Lydia, know that I have kept faith, that I have completed the assignment.

— *Arthelia Brooks, September 14, 1993*

NOTES

1. Letter of Eleanor W. Allen to Arthelia Brooks, June 9, 1959.
2. Letter of Thomas Holman Latwick to Arthelia Brooks, May 1959.
3. Letter of Mildred Holman Williams to Arthelia Brooks, May 27, 1959.
4. Letter of Margaret M. Jackson, Director, School of Nursing, Philadelphia General Hospital, to Arthelia Brooks, May 25, 1956.
5. Undated letter of Dr. C.F. Lambert to Arthelia Brooks, c. 1956.
6. Vivian M. Culver, R.N., Executive Secretary of North Carolina Board of Nurse Registration and Nursing Education, quoting in 1956 to Arthelia Brooks from a book entitled *The North Carolina History of Nursing*. published in 1938. Page numbers not available.
7. Ibid.
8. *The Friendly Nurse*. (1913–1914).
9. Ibid.
10. Letter of Eleanor W. Allen to Arthelia Brooks, June 9, 1959.

11. *The Friendly Nurse.* (1913–1914).
12. Letter of Eleanor W. Allen to Arthelia Brooks, June 9, 1959.
13. Ibid.
14. *The Friendly Nurse.* (1924–1925).
15. Ibid.
16. Ibid.
17. Quoted in *The Friendly Nurse.* (1924–1925).
18. *The Friendly Nurse.* (1928–1929).
19. *Tri-County News*, March 10, 1960,.
20. Unknown issue of *Tri-County News.*
21. Quoted in *The Friendly Nurse*, (1928–1929).
22. *The Friendly Nurse*, (1928–1929).
23. *The Friendly Nurse*, (1933).
24. *The Friendly Nurse*, (1934).
25. *Friendly Nurse*, year of issue unavailable.
26. *The Friendly Nurse*, (1936).
27. *The Friendly Nurse*, (1938).
28. *The Friendly Nurse*, (1942).
29. *The Friendly Nurse*, (1946).
30. Letter of Eleanor W. Allen to Arthelia Brooks, June 9, 1959.
31. Letter of Eleanor W. Allen to Mrs. S.T. Henry, April 22, 1959.
32. Letter of Eleanor W. Allen, entitled *The Friendly Nurse — Finis*, to supporters of the Boston Committee, March, 1959.
33. Undated letter of Dr. C.F. Lambert to Mrs. S.T. Henry.
34. *Tri-County News*, March 3, 1960.
35. Letter of Eleanor W. Allen to Arthelia Brooks,, February 26, 1960.

DAVID SALSTROM

David Salstrom was born July 10, 1916, in the small Minnesota town of Wilmont. He never had a mother's care from the age of three, and when his mother died of TB when he was five and a half, he went to live with his maternal grandparents and maiden aunt in St. Paul. His father was vice-president of a bank in Worthington. Because people were so frightened of TB, his father was fired from his job at the bank when his wife became ill. The father was left with five children when his wife died.

David continued to live with his grandparents and aunt all through high school and his early working years — until he went to Bass Lake Farm, a cooperative enterprise undertaken by a small group of pacifists upon the entrance of the United States into World War II.

Instead of registering for the draft, David applied for, and was granted, conscientious objector status and served in Civilian Public Service camps set up by the U.S. government (but largely supported by the peace churches). The camps where David worked were in Michigan, Oregon, Washington, North Dakota, and Tennessee. Unlike many conscripted conscientious objectors, he appreciated this opportunity for an alternative to military service, grateful for the chance to do constructive work in the nation's service instead of being imprisoned. After the war David returned to Bass Lake Farm in Minnesota. Arle Brooks visited there in the summer of 1945, and the two men found they had many common interests, including their mutual interest in intentional community.

When Rev. Elliot Marston, one of the founders of the tiny Bass Lake Farm enterprise, died in the polio epidemic the next year, and it seemed necessary to sell the farm to provide a little help for that founder's widow and children, David was ready to look for another community. He and Arle Brooks decided they would accept an invitation to try out an enterprise in Riverton, West Virginia, begun by Harry and Jean Wolfe. Dave was there working on the Wolfe farm in West Virginia while I was living in one of the Wolfe family's houses, and Arle was finishing his contract with the American Friends Service Committee in Philadelphia. [See chapter on births, earlier in this book.] Arle joined baby Paula and me, and in March we went to visit my family and then to the hospital for Marla to be born (March 17) in Elkins, West Virginia.

By that time David had decided the arrangement at the Wolfe farm in West Virginia would not work for him, and the fact that they planned to raise beef cattle to support the community did not fit in with Arle's vegetarian convictions. David left to visit Jim Perry's group at Sky Valley, North Carolina, but this did not meet his expectations either. Arle decided on Celo Community in North Carolina, and David came to the Celo Community in the fall of 1947 after we had arrived there in May.

David lived in the log house with our family, slept in the room over the kitchen, and supported himself with a new (to him) enterprise, knitting wool socks, patterned and plain, on a machine developed early in the twentieth century. I embroidered the socks, finished them from off-the-machine shape to wearable condition by closing up the toes, and packed them for shipping. We worked for J. Philip Neal who taught us the craft and marketed the product from his home in northeastern United States. I recall that we did one order of knee-length argyle socks for the stage show, *Brigadoon*.

David had his meals with us. One memorable morning when we were eating breakfast I could not seem to feed oatmeal to eight-month-old Marla fast enough. David said, "Why don't you give *her* the spoon and let her feed herself?" I gave her the spoon, and we sat with open-mouth amazement as she finished the cereal herself without getting food *anywhere* but in her mouth.

David moved to a nearby cabin built by the Foor family in the fall of 1948 and did some of the machine knitting as well as running a little tutoring school for community children — fourth- and fifth-grade academic subjects in the morning and in the afternoon an art class for third, fourth, and fifth grades.

Margaret Calbeck, who lived in our house, worked with Dave in the knitting enterprise and met Philip Neal when he came for a supervisory visit to the knitting enterprise in 1948. They married in October 1953.

When Douglas and Ruby Moody started Camp Celo for elementary school-aged children in 1949, David worked there — first as a volunteer and later as a partner and member of the staff — doing gardening, tent counseling, and working with the children doing nature study and teaching arts and crafts.

In March, 1951, I wrote, "Dave Salstrom is still very much our bachelor boy, and I, for one, never expect him to be otherwise."[1] But I had not counted on Margaret Taylor who came that very summer with her two sons, Robert and John Paul. Margaret was a Camp Celo counselor and led some of the musical activities. She liked it so much that she applied for a staff position for the summer of 1953. Resigning her music-teaching job in Greensboro, she moved into my tenant cabin on the hill, got a job teaching music at South Toe Elementary School. She helped with the school's bookkeeping records, as well, though on a volunteer basis. Because of cafeteria money mismanagement (with which she had nothing to do), both she and the principal, Colonel Bennett, were fired in May. Margaret got a job in the Spruce Pine schools for the 1953–54 term.

During this time Margaret talked with me often about her love for David and the certainty she felt that he loved her too. It took a while for him to realize it, but he finally did, and they were married in our front room on Arle and Paula's birthday, August 28, 1954. Dave and Margaret went to the Brüderhof in Pennsylvania soon after their marriage, but they stayed only five months. Dave didn't like it there.

They returned to Celo Community and lived in the house originally built by Horace Reed, and David was in partnership with Philip Nordstrom in the cabinetmaking and carpentry business. They enclosed one end of my back porch and made it into a bathroom and finished the building of the Celo Methodist Church in 1955.

Bob and Dorothy Barrus, having worked at Camp Celo, were persuaded to take it over for the 1955 season after the Moody family went to the Brüderhof in 1954. David and Margaret continued to work at Camp Celo in the summer, along with their other jobs.

Having worked with David at Camp Celo, and sung with him at a wider-community production of *Messiah*, Margaret had become aware of David's great potential and urged him to further his education. He had no college education other than a couple of courses in accounting at the University of Minnesota. In 1956 they moved to Berea, Kentucky, where Dave spent four years getting his B.A. degree at Berea College. Margaret was always able to find work teaching public school music, both chorus and orchestra — she played a variety of instruments, including the violin, trumpet, and kettle drums besides her main instrument, piano.

Berea just whetted Dave's appetite for learning; so in 1960, Dave and Margaret went to Kent State University where Dave had a graduate assistantship in Elementary Education. He took a competitive test for a scholarship and received so much financial assistance from a scholarship (more than he had ever earned from working at one of his previous jobs) that he was able to complete his master's and Ph.D. work without teaching at the same time, except when the family needed extra money to keep the sons in college and then graduate school, too. Margaret was always able to find work teaching music. Other financial help came, too, from Margaret's uncle, so Margaret managed to work on her own graduate work until she received her master's degree in Music Education. Margaret also took advanced work in piano, her major instrument.

From 1965 to 1968, David taught prospective teachers how to teach science and mathematics at Baldwin-Wallace College in Berea, Ohio, and he continued in that work at Lock Haven State University in Pennsylvania. Teachers returning for advanced graduate work told Dave that one of the main problems they had in their public school teaching was with discipline, especially in junior high school. So he turned his major practical efforts and study to that subject — classroom management and the maintaining of discipline in junior high school. He did his major master's thesis and his doctoral thesis on aspects of that subject.

At some point during these years, though the effects were not noticeable or troublesome until it was too late for remedial surgery, Margaret developed a tumor on the brain. They tried to investigate every avenue that offered hope of a cure, even in desperate hope trying a trip to the Philippines; but Margaret passed away February 5, 1973.

After school was out in May, 1974, David returned to Camp Celo in North Carolina where he had worked before, as he said, "to get my feet on the ground."

His friend and former business partner, Phil Neal, told Dave that he knew a woman he wanted him to meet. So Dave went to the Friends Meeting in Asheville and met Frances Lindsley. They were married August 31 of that year. They returned to Lock Haven where David continued his teaching, and Frances took up where Margaret had left off, playing piano and violin in the college orchestra and teaching private lessons in their home.

David retired in 1978 and they returned to Celo and built a new home where the first Reed house had burned, and where David now lives.

When I returned to Yancey County in May 1985, David called right away to encourage me to join the Yancey County Ministerial Association as the most viable organization to which I should give my time and effort. They had encouraged and nurtured Reconciliation House and Prison Ministries into being, as well as backing other local causes needing the support of capable, caring people. It was at this group that I first met Frances.

Even though Dave was retired, he and Frances gave of their time and finances liberally to Celo Community, the wider community and even helping persons from other countries who were in distress. David met with leaders of the black community and with local merchants to encourage employment of some of the black youth. Cashiers at local grocery stores bear witness to their efforts. David has also given untold hours as a volunteer tutor at the prison camp, a ministry that has meant much to him. There is the prospect, now, of it being closed and merged with other facilities in the state.

Before Christmas in 1984, David and Frances went to St. Paul Minnesota — the house where he grew up with his grandmother — to be with his sister, Jessie, in her last illness. When she died in January they stayed to settle her estate.

I had several opportunities to be with David and Frances — was invited to their home for a meal, and learned to appreciate and love this second wife as I had the first. So in a limited way I shared David's sorrow when Frances, too, was a victim of cancer and died September 6, 1988. David is not bitter about the loss of these three important women in his life (his two wives and his sister); he has said, "I feel fortunate to have had the joy of sharing my life with these exceptional women."

When David was left alone again after Frances' death I said to him, "David, we have been friends for forty-one years. Please don't sit at home and be lonely. We can do some things together that will help both of us." One of our first joint outings was the fiftieth anniversary of French Broad Electric Membership Corporation held in the Marshall High School in 1990. One of the features was a health fair. We went through the whole process, ending with a cholesterol check. I thought mine was pretty good — 180; but when they said David's was 79 I thought he was dying — but *no* that was *remarkably good*!

He has taken care of his health. He was born with a shallow hip joint that causes him to limp, but he does not let it deter him — he even belongs to a hiking club. When I told him about shoveling snow after the "storm of the century," he chastised me, "You should have called me. I'm as strong as a horse."

The problem David has to deal with is not with his body, but with his mind — remembering the *now* things of his daily life, like appointments or what he has just been told. He works at it valiantly and I think succeeds to a remarkable degree.

On February 6, 1993, he was to come to my home for dinner and a movie afterward. When I couldn't reach him at home all day, I knew something had come up, so I invited Marla to eat with me. Afterward we thought we should call to be sure he was okay. He had gone hiking with the club and failed to look at his calendar when he got home. He was *so* apologetic. "What can I do to make it up to you?" he asked. My reply was, "You can take me out to a movie and supper for my birthday next Thursday. We'll meet at 3:00 P.M. at the junction of 19E and 197."

On my birthday I had unexpected company — Charles Teems, whom I hadn't seen for twenty-five years. He had been one of the boys in the prison camp when I held services there in the late fifties. He had entered the Baptist ministry and later brought his wife and two daughters to see me.

After we ate lunch I suddenly remembered that Thursday was David's afternoon at the prison camp, and I had meant to remind him of his date with me. I called his home, but he was already gone. I went to our meeting place at 3:00. At 3:25 he had not come. Since there was a phone handy I called the prison camp. "Yes, David Salstrom has been here, but he's already left — wait, I see him going through the parking lot."

"If you think you can catch him, please tell him that Tillie Brooks is waiting for him in front of Burleson Tire." She got the word to him. In about fifteen minutes he arrived — again *most* apologetic! "You are so patient and helpful to me. You are my *best* friend!" he said.

I guess the feeling is mutual. I consider him my best friend. He is the one I would go to first if I needed help financially, or had a problem or a joy I wanted to share. He is *such* a tender, compassionate man! You've got to love someone who marks special occasions by sending flowers. One card he sent in September of 1993 said, "Dear Arthelia, Blessings, dear friend, you have been and are the brightest scene on my horizon. Love, David." The bouquet of flowers *was* most special — in fact were still pretty when the next arrangement arrived.

Dave left the area in January of 1994 to live near the home of the son of his first wife (John). Dave is now living in a retirement home in Golden Valley, Minnesota.

NOTES

1. Letter of Arthelia Brooks to family, March 1951.

FRANCIS BALLEW

I visited Francis Ballew in the rest home in July of 1993. He was in bed, and I was told he does not get up. I thought he looked pretty good. His hands are all drawn up with arthritis. He did not remember me. Once I thought there was a flicker of recognition when I mentioned that he had visited our family at the log house in Celo many times.

In a letter to my family back in 1947 I found this note about Francis: "We have a friend, a local man, who isn't considered too bright by most of the people around here, but Arle and I have been nice to him, and he pays a call quite often. He talked his sister into letting him bring us some apples when we had none to use, and they certainly tasted mighty fine. The man's name is Francis Ballew. Friday he came and wanted me to type two letters for him. When they were finished, dinner was ready, so of course I asked him to stay, and since then my opinion of his IQ has gone up considerably because he thought it was about the best cooking he had eaten in a long while (*smile,* as Arle's friend used to say in his letters). He is so anxious for Arle and me to visit him and his sister."[1]

The letters I wrote for him were always to young girls, and those staying with us the summer of 1950 were not very comfortable in his presence. They felt he undressed them with his eyes. As my own girls got older, they felt the same way. He came about two weeks after Arle died in July, 1953, and asked me to marry him. I explained to him that I was not looking for a husband, but I would always be his friend. He accepted that and continued to visit periodically through the years until I left for Kentucky in 1968.

I felt there was a certain refinement about Francis. Even though his clothes did not look fresh, I don't remember any body odor, and if he was carrying writing paper (or chewing gum for Marla) — anything special — it was always carefully wrapped in clean paper. More than once he brought me wild blackberries. He knew where to find the biggest, juiciest and sweetest ones. There was *no* trash in them, and they were always covered by a big poplar leaf. He also brought me a wildflower, which he said grew in only one place — on the other side of Seven Mile Ridge. He called it a heart plant. I put it in my wildflower garden, but I think it didn't live.

Once when he was visiting after Arle died, we were sitting in the front room of the log home. He said, "I like this room. It *feels* good."

I said, "Yes, Francis, Dena would say it has *good vibes*. Many memorable things happened here — John and Reva Griffith spent their honeymoon here, Dave Salstrom machine-knit socks here, and Peg Neal spent her first days in Celo here. Dena was born here, and so was the first child of Lois Ann and Dick Domer. Dave Salstrom and Margaret Taylor were married here. In this room Arle and I had such good times reading and talking after the children were in bed. I'm glad Arle did not die in this room. Yes, it does have a special, warm glow. I am glad you can feel it."

In visits with Francis since that one in September of 1993, I have found he remembers what has been said in previous visits. I *also* found he has *not* lost the characteristic that the girls in the fifties and sixties found so disconcerting. As I shook his hand (crippled with arthritis), he said I looked like I was fourteen and tried to pull me down to hug me. I had to say again, "Francis, I am still *only* your friend."

When I told a friend about this visit, he said, "Well, there is life in the old boy yet."

NOTES

1. Letter of Arthelia Brooks to family (LF), September 3, 1947.

JUANITA PRESNELL
MITZI PRESNELL SHOOK

About mid-afternoon on a Friday, probably in 1954, Joe Petree, pastor of the Newdale charge, came to my office in the basement of the building across from the old hospital in Burnsville with a rather strange request — Would I take one of his parishioners home with me for the weekend? She had burned her home to the ground and in some way had burned herself in the process. She was so distraught that the hospital was having difficulty managing her. Her husband and his family were certain she should be committed to the mental hospital in Morganton, but nothing could be done until Monday.

Joe had done some counseling with the family because of marital problems due to the husband's drinking. He assured me that the girls and I would be in no danger. I had never seen or heard about her before, but I took her home with me and let her talk through that long weekend.

I learned that Juanita Presnell was *not* a mountain native, that she had two young sons before she married Clarence, and that together they had a daughter, Mitzi, about two years old. I soon determined that she was *no* candidate for a mental institution, but was a very intelligent though emotionally disturbed woman. I suspected that a big part of her problem was a lack of ability to adjust to mountain ways. She was frustrated with Clarence's drinking, and in conflict with his family and the community in general.

I took her back to Newdale on Monday morning. Soon after, I heard that since their home was burned, they moved to Marion; and I had no further word about the family during the years before I moved to Kentucky in September, 1968.

While in Kentucky, I subscribed to the *Yancey Journal* in order to keep up with happenings in Yancey County. I began to see items copied from the Marion paper about the high achievement and many honors bestowed on Mitzi Presnell. Finally there was a long quote from a report she had made to the service organization that had sent her to Europe as their representative.

Even though I had not kept up with the family, I never lost interest in them. I was so pleased to hear about the good things happening to them after the distress they had experienced earlier. I sat down and wrote to Juanita to say how proud she must be of Mitzi's accomplishments. I sent the letter in care of the Marion paper but did not know if she received it because there was no reply. Then I retired and returned to Yancey County in the spring of 1985, but don't remember having heard anything about the Presnell family.

The Saturday before Easter, 1990, I had a call from Vance's Florist asking for directions to my home to deliver a corsage. I said I would pick it up as I went to church the next morning. That way I had a *whole day* to live in suspense — trying to guess who had sent it.

If I'd had a *year*, I still would not have come up with the answer. The card read, "Yancey Zoe Presnell (baby) and Mitzi Anita Presnell." I suppose I called a relative here to get her married name and address in order to send a gracious thank you.

In subsequent correspondence I found she was a lawyer and married to Terry Shook, also a lawyer. They lived in Charlotte and had an additional daughter, Holly. Mitzi's parents and brothers had all done well. Apparently her mother had told her about the weekend spent with me thirty-six years ago, and she had no doubt read the congratulatory letter I had written. The corsage was Mitzi's expression of appreciation to me.

BEA THOMAS

About a year after I started to work in Yancey County in 1953, I was supposed to visit a Mrs. Bea Thomas in the Cane Branch section of Micaville. I knocked on a door and called to the family living upstairs. The woman who answered said she was Bea Thomas. I must have had the name wrong, or there was another person with that name, because this was not the one I was looking for; but perhaps she was the one I was meant to find.

I found a young mother who was recovering from nervous exhaustion and depression. She had a God-given insight that doing something creative would hasten the healing process. She brought out a picture of Mt. Celo in the snow on a square of cardboard. She had used black and white house paint and had made the brush by chewing the end of a twig. I was so impressed! I thought that anyone who could produce something of beauty with such crude materials certainly deserved something better. By some means I put out a call to the Methodist women of this conference. A society in High Point answered with a set of oil paints and many different sizes of canvas panels, and Bea began to paint in earnest — mostly self-taught.

Later she came out and sat on the hillside and painted a large picture of my log home; the picture hung in my living room until I moved to Kentucky.

After the painting came poetry, and through the years since then I have rejoiced each time I saw a picture or poem in the local papers. In this week's *Yancey Journal* (March 10, 1993), there was a painting of an old church and a poem, "This Old Church," patterned after the song, *This Old House*, which I have on tape. Her great faith shines through all her poetry.

ALVIN G. JONES

Alvin was the pastor of the Newdale charge from 1965–1967. He came into the WNC conference from the Baptist church with no seminary training, though he had attended Fruitland, a small school for Baptist ministers near Hendersonville, North Carolina. He was always defensive about his lack of education; and the fact that I had a master's degree made it difficult for us to work together. His grammar left something to be desired, and this sometimes embarrassed him.

Alvin preached a special graduation sermon at Celo church for those in my daughter Dena's class in 1967. My older daughters, Paula and Marla, were home for the occasion. During the sermon they had a hard time keeping their giggling quiet while Brother Jones referred, several times during his talk, to "the flatform of life" on which the graduates stood at this time in their lives. I asked my daughters afterward if "flatform" had kept them from *hearing what he said*. Despite his misuse of one word, his sermon was very meaningful!

The year before that sermon, Alvin had prayed a prayer of protection for Paula before she left for D.C. His prayer had been so powerful that I was able to wave good-bye to Paula feeling that no evil could touch her. She later told me about waiting for a bus on a D.C. corner when an older black man joined her there. Two men on a nearby utility pole stopped their work to watch. A young couple in a car slowed down. The man asked Paula, "Do you have any money?" She said, "No, I have my bus tickets so I don't carry any money!" The man said, "Well, I can give you some if you need it." About that time the young couple had driven around the block and stopped to check on her. "Are you okay?" they asked. "Yes," Paula assured them, and the couple left. The utility men, too, went back to their work.

Paula, it seemed had taken my advice. "Don't take unnecessary risks," I'd told her, "but always try to think and expect the best from people. Don't live in fear. I would rather see you dead than to know you live every hour in fear." When she told me the story of that encounter, I was proud of her reaction. And I was also convinced that Alvin's prayer had shielded her.

I never heard Brother Jones preach on a Sunday, without feeling I should be a better person. He was a real evangelist. He went into the highways and byways to bring people to Christ; but most of the time they were not nurtured in the church, and so they drifted away. I could have helped there, but the education barrier stood in the way.

I probably never told Alvin how much I appreciated his effectiveness as a minister, so I'll say it here. If I had to choose between a minister with degrees and one with a vital experience with Christ, I would choose the latter. But from my experience with Alvin, I learned how difficult it was to work closely with someone who had such a defensive attitude about his lack of education. Fortunately, those circumstances were not a part of the working relationship with the other ministers through the years.

ESTELLE WHITE

In early December 1993 I thought I was near the end of my narrative for this book, but suddenly I became aware (again) of being surrounded by gifts from Estelle White and I felt that she deserves a tribute to her memory from me.

I met Estelle when she came to Lakeland Wesley Village in the spring of 1983 from her home in Louisville. She wanted to be near her only child, Theo Marie Tuck, who lived twenty-three miles away, near Murray, Kentucky. It soon became evident that they were unable to spend much time together with any degree of satisfaction to either of them.

If Estelle became ill, Theo would come and take her to the doctor. She would also clean house for her periodically. Once, she tried taking Estelle home for a few days' visit, but as I remember, the visit was not very pleasant for either of them. *One hour* was more than they could usually spend together and get along. I had some insight into why this was so.

Theo (named for her father) must have been a throwback to a pioneer grandmother. Her main interest was horses — she'd rather shovel horse manure than dress up and go to a fancy party. She also loved dogs, so that is what she and her husband, Tommy, had on their place. Their lifestyle was as foreign as it could be to someone like Estelle.

The things that were important to Estelle were family money, the prestige of belonging to the elite society of Louisville, and cherishing family antiques. She gave Theo some heirlooms several different times in her life, each time hoping that Theo would forever hold them dear. But Theo simply had other interests.

Estelle heard that there was to be an auction at the Galt House in Louisville, held by Tiffany's of New York and Christie's of London. Because of the importance of both the auctioneers and the owners of the items to be sold, the advance advertising was elaborate. Possessions of former Vice-President Alben Barkley (1949–1953), whose home was in Paducah, were going to be auctioned, and also items from a very wealthy woman in Louisville whom Estelle had known. Estelle decided to attend.

Once there, Estelle was devastated to learn that some of the antiques she had given to Theo were scheduled to be sold as well! I'm sure Theo had no idea her mother would care as much as she did, or that she would make the trip to Louisville to attend the auction. But I think it was this incident that put a touch of finality to the hopes Estelle had of a close relationship with her daughter, and so she turned to me as a substitute for the object of her affections.

A class-conscious person like Estelle, was certainly out of her element living in a HUD rent-assisted facility such as Lakeland Wesley Village. There was a range of income at LWV, down to some whose rent was fully paid because they had no income at all. A few actually arrived with no furniture to put in their apartments.

Estelle's feeling of superiority was not overt, but it didn't take long for the other residents to sense her disdain. She made no effort to develop friendships with anyone but me and my sister-in-law, Hazel Rose, who lived at the Village. In her mind, as resident manager, I qualified for membership in a social class worth relating to. There came a day I clearly remember, when we all were waiting for the mail to arrive. I noticed her shoe was untied, and, worried that she would trip, I knelt down to fix it for her. She expressed amazement that a person "of my position" would stoop down to do such a thing in the reception area with half of the residents present to see. I hadn't thought much about it until she reacted that way. Suddenly I felt sorry for her, stuck so deep in her own rigid definitions. From that day I vowed to help minimize her self-imposed isolation.

Estelle was arthritic. Sometimes she used a cane, but usually she got around quite well. She wore tie oxfords and pants; she didn't own a dress. After the first few months, I began taking her to most of her doctor and dentist appointments, as I did for the other residents. (This was a task I assumed as part of my job, though is wasn't formally in my job description.)

Even though Estelle had been brought up in the Catholic church, she decided to go with Hazel and me to the small Union Ridge UMC, where I often taught the adult Sunday school class. Once she said she saw an aura about my head as I taught. Estelle loved the people in this little church, and said she got more of her questions about God and salvation answered there than in all her years of attending the Catholic schools and listening to sermons at mass.

During the year and a half that Estelle lived at Lakeland Wesley Village, she gave me a wide range of things: a stereo set, a pottery vase, a necklace, a barnyard mobile she'd made, a lace bedspread, a brass-covered inkwell, an antique coffee grinder lamp, some pink rugs, a shower curtain for my bathroom, a three-by-eight-foot blue rug, a black iron bull paperweight, a "wire tree" she made, some special jewelry, and a Seiko wristwatch. She also did an oil painting from a photo I'd taken of my Celo log home.

In October, 1984, Estelle decided she should return to Louisville where she could be near her doctors and other conveniences. She found what she wanted at The 800, an apartment hotel in the center of town that had a grocery store, restaurant and laundry facilities, all in the same building.

During the Easter holidays of 1985, Hazel and I drove to Louisville to visit. And a few months later, I retired in May and returned to Burnsville, North Carolina, to live. I thought about Estelle's tale of the wonderful time she'd once had with her husband in Gatlinburg, and of her expressed wish to see the mountains again. At the height of the foliage display in October, I drove to get her and bring her back through the mountains for a visit. We spent one night at Jenny Wiley State Park, and then continued on to my home in the North Carolina mountains. Marla and I took her up for a drive along a section of the Blue Ridge Parkway; and since she did not appear well enough for a bus trip home, I drove her to Charlotte to get a nonstop flight back to Louisville. I hope it brought her joy. From that time on, she was in and out of the hospital regularly.

Estelle's subsequent phone calls were so frequent and long, that my girls bought me a phone I didn't have to hold to my ear. It was apparent that she was ailing, and that she was very lonely, so at Christmastime I packed some food, decorations and gifts, and went to spend the holiday with her. On Christmas Eve I bundled her up in her wheelchair, and took her to midnight mass at the Episcopal church across the street from her hotel. On Christmas morning we opened the gifts. Theo had left a gift when she'd come by on Thanksgiving, some fancy kinds of tea, because she would be out-of-state on vacation at Christmas. No calls came on Christmas day. I think it was that Christmas that Estelle gave me a stadium coat that she'd hardly ever worn, and that I later gave to Marla. I fixed our solitary dinner from the food I'd brought from Burnsville.

Early in 1986 she called from the hospital and asked me to come. I got there on a Tuesday and found her dressed to go home! She wanted me to persuade her doctor that I would care for her. I went along with her wish; her doctor discharged her, and I stayed until Friday. It was then that I came to understand from how she treated me, why she had trouble keeping a nurse. Her attitude plainly said, "I am paying you by the hour, and therefore I'm due your undivided attention." From that time on, she had nurses around the clock whenever she was not in the hospital.

Estelle did not pay me for my time that week, but she did add two thousand dollars to the four thousand she had already put in a ready-access savings account for me after she'd returned to Louisville in 1984. (She had a goal to finish it to ten thousand so the interest would help me in my retirement years.) She also gave me many things as gifts, in particular from her china closet, a cut glass bowl, two saltcellars, carving set rest, a bottle stopper, a "chocolate" set (covered pitcher, six cups and saucers), eight glasses, which she called finger bowls, that would play the notes of the musical scale, a French leaded, bevelled-glass mirror (which I gave to Marla), a spring-operated pendulum clock made in France in 1889 with a hand-painted china face (on which I've spent a hundred dollars for repair). My favorite is a red glass hand-painted pickle jar in a metal frame with metal tongs to remove the pickles. Estelle had a need to give back for my time and attention, and I felt it necessary to let her.

I made one more trip to Louisville in November, 1986, after Theo called to say Estelle was quite ill and in the hospital. I wanted to visit her one last time because I knew I would *not* make the trip to her funeral. On that last visit she said she would instruct her lawyer to finish my savings account to her ten thousand dollar goal, but she was too ill to carry through on her promise. I visited Estelle daily, and slept at Estelle's apartment. While I was there, Estelle's alcoholic sister called me and accused me of visiting "to get what she's got." I was upset, and I talked about the call with Elizabeth, a close friend of Estelle. Elizabeth said, "Please don't pay any attention to her. She's afraid she won't get anything. If Estelle gave you every material thing she has, it would not repay you for what you've meant to her."

Even though I've never been too interested in antiques, I do appreciate the things Estelle gave me. On one occasion she said she wanted them cherished and she was sure they meant nothing to Theo, that Theo would only auction them again as she had before. The practical things, both the items and the savings account, she gave because she loved me and she knew my finances were slim; she wanted to help take care of me. In her memory I do cherish my clock, pickle jar, and chocolate set. I've tried to give the other items to younger people who seem able to care for them.

Estelle died in January 1987. Her nurse (whom I begged to stay with her even though she was most difficult to please) called to say she was one of thirteen at Estelle's funeral. I don't clearly remember Theo calling me after the funeral, but my friend Gladys Young says I did mention a thank-you call from Theo.

The car I drive today is yet another reminder of Estelle's concern for me. Instead of paying interest, I took money from my ready-access account to pay for it.

There is *no way* I can ever forget you, Estelle!!

Laughruns/Rays and Jacks Creek

Elizabeth Silvers, Winnie Lou Ray, Mildred Ray and Lem Anglin at Lunch at Mildreds 3-78 P.386

Ike and Lena Laughrun with Mildred Ray 3-78 P.144

Robbie Hoover with Gretchen Cort at her 5th birthday party 6-86 P.171

Glenn and Velma Ray P.147

Henry Ray P.150

Tillie, Ethel and Luke Laughrun 70th Wedding aniv. 10-3-93 P.158

Tillie with Mack and Dorothy Ray dinner at Ray's 4-10-94

LAUGHRUNS / RAYS

Even though the title of this article says Laughruns / Rays, I want to start with Augustus T. (Gus) Hensley. He was the father of Lena Laughrun and Mildred Ray, and two other daughters, Marguerite and Evelyn, whom he and his wife reared in one of the oldest houses still standing in Yancey County: the two-story house on Possum Trot Creek, off Highway 19E near Bald Creek.

In his later years Gus lived alternately with Lena and Mildred, where I came to know him. He was a very intelligent man. The history of Higgins Memorial UM church[1] notes that he once wrote a biography of David Proffitt, the head of one of the early families in the county.

I remember Mr. Gus especially because during the two years I knew him, his was the first Christmas greeting I received. (This year, 1993, my first card came from Esther Banks, the first fellow classmate I met at Scarritt College in the fall of 1938.) Mr. Hensley died December 2, 1962, and Mildred remembers that I did the eulogy at his service.

Between the years 1953–1955 my Church and Community office was across the hall from Helen Phoenix's beauty shop, in the basement of the building now used by the *Yancey Journal*. Quite frequently Lena would call in the morning and invite me to lunch. That was how I came to know her husband, Ike Laughrun, and his mother, Loula Laughrun, who lived with them. Loula was a most remarkable woman. With one leg off at the knee she raised nine children!

Paul, Ike's brother, told me that Loula probably had a form of cancer, but they didn't know much about cancer in those days. The doctor just knew that the bone was all "honeycombed" and would break if she walked on it; so he recommended amputation, which was done. Paul commented, "That was before I was born."[2]

About ten o'clock on April 5, 1955, Ike called me at work to say, "We feel pretty certain that mother is dying. Will you come up and be with us?" I went to the Laughrun home and found that the Higgins Memorial church pastor, Worth Royals, was also there. He stayed until after lunch. I was glad I had nothing urgent on my agenda, so I was able to stay until Mother Laughrun breathed her last about midafternoon.

From the summer of 1955 until the fall of 1960, I was not in Burnsville, but when I began to work with the Methodist church again, the Laughrun invitations to lunch resumed. I remember the Laughruns had my daughters and me as guests one New Year's day. At other times there were gifts from Ike's prolific vegetable garden, and one day I went home to the log house to find Ike had put a copper hood over my cookstove.

I moved to Kentucky in September, 1968. Ike and Lena came to see me in October, and brought Mildred. Before I could visit him in his last illness, Ike died on March 19, 1983. Rev. Don Shuman conducted his funeral.

I returned to Burnsville to live after my second retirement in May, 1985, and so was privileged to help Mildred and Lena celebrate several July birthdays and attend the Mildred Ray Circle with them before Lena died on February 1, 1991. Rev. Robert Scott conducted Lena's funeral, and Rev. Ralph Jacks combined a short eulogy with his prayer. (Ralph should publish the eulogies he has done for Higgins members.)

Kenneth, Ike's son, has not only continued his father's business, Laughrun's Heating and Sheetmetal, here in Burnsville, but also Ike's habit of doing favors. This spring when I needed a roof to cover my hummingbird feeder, he and his helper, Billy Joe Silver, designed a clever Oriental-looking one similar to a metal chimney cap. I was sorry, though, that I'd mentioned the stove-hood gift to them, because Kenneth wouldn't charge me for the roof.

Probably the first in a long line of Rays who have figured prominently in my life was Winnie Lou. The Higgins Memorial Methodist church was named for her family, and she was the first person I met from that church when she came to my husband's funeral on July 7, 1953. Hers was another home where I ate many lunches, both informal and formal. I also attended many Bible study groups with her. Those of us who met in the pastor's study after I retired here will remember that we always saved the big black easy chair for Winnie Lou, who was usually a little late. Her husband, Troy, had sometimes been our Route Five mail carrier when I lived in the log house in Celo Community. After Winnie Lou died on March 11, 1987, her home was bought by Rush Wray's daughter, Mary Louise Connor, to house a museum in memory of her own father, Rush T. Wray, who died July 23, 1985. The old filling station, once run by Hobart Ray, below the house on West Main Street and across from Pollard's Drugstore, was to be renovated for a welcome center. At present, there is little movement toward completion of these projects.

I never knew Troy and Winnie Lou's son, Ronnie, but the two girls, Charlotte and Lewellyn, are still counted among my friends. On October 18, 1993, I spent the night in Asheville with Charlotte and her husband, Roger Derrough, and spoke to her women's circle the next morning about some Church and Community Worker projects. Lewellyn and her husband, Roger Estep, have recently built a home (for vacationing and retirement) on the mountain above my daughter Marla's home on Green Mountain Drive just outside Burnsville. The Estep home is on Easy Street. Their daughter, Tammy, is a United Methodist minister.

Since the early 1960s until this present time, when cold weather comes, I sleep under Chatham blankets. They were given to me by Zula (Wilson) Ray, who is eighty-seven and who lives in Pensacola with her husband, Theo, an eighty-eight-year-old amputee. When she gave them to me she said that each year her family was generously supplied with these blankets when the executives of the company that made them in Elkin, North Carolina, came to bear hunt with her famous grandfather, Big Tom Wilson. Big Tom was one of Dr. Elisha Mitchell's guides when Mitchell was surveying and measuring the mountain that now bears his name. The company in Elkin, incidentally, was started by my friend Betty Motsinger's maternal grandfather. Betty says that now, in 1993, the executives come to fish.

Zula and Theo have a son, Bobby Ray, who lives nearby and who has three grown children. Zula has relatives that I felt pretty close to in the Pensacola Methodist church. Since I returned to the county in 1985, I saw her sister, Pereda Bagwell and her son Gilmer at the Burnsville hospital a few times before she died, May 27, 1991. The other sister, Emma Hensley, and her family evoke very special memories. Her grandchildren, Norma Jean and Harrison Metcalf (along with Emily Hensley's Robema and Jimmie) were the mainstays of the youth group at Pensacola. Kathleen was the daughter who lived nearest to Emma, and she was very devoted. Her husband Byrd had been admitted as a minister in the WNC conference but could not itinerate because Kathleen felt she couldn't leave her mother. When Emma had to be hospitalized with cancer, Kathleen hardly left her room.

On the morning of June 27, 1966, Zula called me at my office in Burnsville. She said, "Tillie, we are at our wits end. Emma is in such a terrible condition! She's eaten up with the cancer, and the odor in the room is unbearable. She is ready to go, but Kathleen won't let her." I said, "Well, let's pray that she will release her." And we did.

That afternoon the county youth were to have an overnight camp-out under the big tree at my house. Byrd and his two young ones were there. In late afternoon, Byrd got the call that Emma had died. Later, when I visited Kathleen to let her talk about her mother and the day she'd died, she said, "I was standing in her room looking out the window, when suddenly a great feeling of peace came over me and I said, "'Lord, I can give her up if she can just go peacefully,' and she went that way." Her hour at the window was when we had prayed for Kathleen, so not only was Emma free, but so was Kathleen, and Byrd became able to serve Methodist churches in the WNC conference. Byrd died December 2, 1987. I attended his funeral at the Holcombe Brothers chapel. It was good to see Kathleen, Norma and Harrison again.

Ruby Ray Hensley, sister of Roy and James Ray, and of Ruth Sholes, for many years had a florist shop on West Main Street, where Something Special is now. Ruby was also a member of that very meaningful morning Bible study group in the pastor's office I mentioned earlier. I shall never forget the day she said, "I want to stand up (and she stood) and say 'I think Harold Anglin is the finest man in this town.'" That morning I had passed Harold walking from his home to the square, and had said much the same thing in my heart, because he had been unselfishly caring for his invalid brother, Joseph, for many years. Mildred Ray, who kept in phone contact with Joseph, said "Amen" to Ruby's accolade. Anyone who has known Ruby in recent years will also remember her public statement, "My daddy was a *Baptist*, but he was *good* man." I could also vouch for that because I visited the family both when they lived on Bolen's Creek and then on Academy Street in Burnsville where Ruby now lives.

Of all the Rays I've known, I guess I've been closest to Mildred. As with Winnie Lou, I have eaten many lunches with her — alone and with other guests. She was ninety on July 4, 1993, and I've often said to her that she looks much the same as she did in her fifties and sixties. I wonder if she thinks what I do when friends say something like that to me. I always *think*, "I guess I've always looked old," but of course I *say* thank you and try to consider it the compliment it is intended to be.

Mildred and I have been in a lot of prayer/study groups together, first at Mrs. Fred Proffitt's, and then at the church, when I moved back to Burnsville in 1985. She has been such a help to me in writing this narrative. I've called on her good memory to supply many facts. She was flexible enough to adjust her lifestyle when her son James retired, at age sixty-five, and came to live with her. (Now *his* schedule had to be met, not the one she followed when living alone for twenty-three years.) She has been an inspiration to me through the years. I can't quite conceive of life here without Mildred. I'm glad she's in good health. Her husband, Hobart, died on November 11, 1967. She says I did his eulogy.

When I retired and returned to Yancey County, I decided I wanted to do some volunteer work outside the church. The Mountain Friends program required one to commit for a year to spend four hours weekly with an at-risk young person. My girl was Carolyn Scott. Her father was in prison, but I thought she was a pretty stable girl. It was my second volunteer choice that involved another Ray. In the fall of 1985 I took hospice training. My first patient was Glenn Ray. Kay Aldridge went with me for the initial visit about nine o'clock in the morning. We couldn't see him at that time, and he died that evening, November 15, 1985. I went to the funeral home and later visited with his widow, Velma. I felt sure that she would get through the grief process with a minimum of trouble because she was a woman with deep faith, a supportive family and church, and she was a strong woman. My second hospice patient was someone Velma knew because she'd played the guitar and sung at Nettie's Baptist church on Baker's Creek. I *did* get to visit with Merle and Nettie Mae Edwards several times over a couple of months before Merle died. Even though Nettie is a much smaller woman physically than Velma, I knew she possessed the same strengths. I call them my "hospice widows" and their friendships mean a lot to me. We had dinner together recently, and then attended the annual Hospice Memorial Service. Also shared a Christmas lunch at my home.

Velma's husband was Frank Ray's first cousin. Frank and

Maude lived in the white house above Green Mountain Baptist church on Green Mountain Drive. After Velma told me they were kinfolk, I was especially careful to wave to them — especially Frank, as I drove back and forth to Marla's. One day I stopped for a short visit. When later I didn't see anyone for a long time, I called Velma to ask about them. She said Frank had died in October 1991 and Maude was in the Yancey Nursing Center. In December, 1993, I added her to the list of patients I visited there. She is a delightful person to know. She told me she was eighty-five, but she certainly didn't look that old. (Of course, age stereotypes don't seem to fit people here in the mountains.) She also told me she was a registered nurse, and had worked as a charge nurse on the second shift at the new rest home that was built in Burnsville.

In *Stories 'Neath the Roan*[3] Maude told of her experience as a midwife in Yancey County after she was sixty-five, and planning to retire. She was called to a home to deliver a baby where they had seven-year-old twins. This delivery was also twins, and the month was February. Maude delivered two more sets of twins to this family, two years apart, and also in February. She finally advised the husband to stay away from his wife in the month of May! In the book Maude said, "I think that is one experience worth telling." I agree, so I wanted to tell it again. On my first visit with Maude she mentioned that Grace Banks was her daughter.

I associate Grace Ray Banks with the tiny building on the west side of the square, where I bought my license plates the last eight years before I went to Kentucky. The little building served as the office for the Yancey Merchants Association, where Grace worked for twenty-three years beginning in 1961. That same year she helped them organize a bona fide Chamber of Commerce. She served as secretary/treasurer of the Chamber, essentially as a volunteer. They established a credit bureau as part of their services. The Merchants Association decided, also in 1961, to add a service that would be helpful to the people of the county and bring in some much-needed funds. Previously the nearest N.C. Tag Agency office had been in Spruce Pine, but now an office was opened in Burnsville. Grace estimates that in 1961 from twenty-five hundred to three thousand plates were issued, and they got eleven cents for each transaction. In 1992, Hazel Huskins estimated that between seventeen and eighteen thousand stickers were sold, and the Merchant's Association got ninety-two cents for each transaction. (Grace and I were curious about the increase.)

Grace now works for the Division of Motor Vehicles as hearing officer for the seventeen western North Carolina counties. This involves trying to work with individuals who have lost their licenses to drive because of lapsed insurance policies. She told me that she is able to clear more cases in Yancey County than in any of the others. She thinks these mountain people really *are* easier to deal with. Grace plans to retire March 31, 1994.

For twenty-nine years, 1943–1972, the friendly faces at Ray Bros. Grocery were Roy and Julia Ray, James and Billie Marie Ray. Their first store was a little red-front building on West Main Street, near where the Hill Top Restaurant is now. Then they built a larger building at the back side of the present Post Office parking lot. When it burned in 1972, they decided not to rebuild because BiLo had already come to Burnsville. Julia told me that it was a daily afternoon gathering place — especially for the women — to exchange news of the day, both good and bad. I wonder how many families could say as Marla once did, "We would have gone hungry if they hadn't let us charge groceries." (Of course I always paid the bills later.) I mentioned Marla's statement to Grace Banks and she said, "I can identify with that! When we were living on Jake's ninety-seven-dollar-a-month G.I. bill income, we had to spend most of it for the groceries they'd let us charge, and if I needed two dollars for medicine, they'd give me the cash and put it on my bill."

Roy and Julia Ray's children, Norman and Judy, left the county to make their homes in Tennessee. James Ray died on January 20, 1986, but Billie Marie Ray and their twins, Jimmy and Jeanne, are here and fully involved in the life of Higgins Memorial and the community.

It would be interesting to know how many members of Higgins Memorial church have joined because of the interest, concern and invitation of Mack and Dorothy Ray. Dorothy taught home economics at East Yancey High School for eighteen years, and then for five more at Mountain Heritage. I think my girls did not take any of her classes, but feel sure her influence on her students was far-reaching. Mack worked with the Farmers Home Administration, a federal loan agency, from 1939. In 1940 he transferred to an office in Yancey County, and worked there until he retired in 1965. In 1951 he was called to Washington, D.C., to receive a distinguished service award. In all the United States, his was the only office that had collected a hundred percent of their loans. This says as much about the caliber of the people in the county as it does about Mack. In 1953 he received the Carnegie Award for saving the lives of two swimmers, along with another man, at Vilano Beach in St. Augustine, Florida. He also has a Purple Heart. Both Mack and Dorothy Ray have helped with the rearing and education of their four granddaughters.

One can find these two supporting any good cause at Higgins Memorial, or in the county. (Mack has already promised to sell ten copies of this book!) [Their daughter, Carolyn, is one of the people mentioned in my article entitled "Younger Friends," later in this book.]

Dorothy Ray Westall and her first cousin, Gladys Chase Coletta, were granddaughters of Garret D. and Elizabeth Bierchfield Ray. Their years of work with the children of Higgins Memorial is legendary. I remember best the creative dramatic programs Gladys gave for the Mildred Ray Circle. Dorothy's and Gladys' homes were included in one of the annual home tours, organized to raise money for the Parkway Playhouse. I served as a hostess on the tour, three different years. One house I hostessed was the little house Rush Wray built for his daughter, Mary Louise. Dorothy's home is on North Main Street, just off the square, and Gladys' is next to the Nu-Wray Inn, right on the square. Both are filled with antiques. Dorothy's father, was Judge Bis Ray, and Gladys's father was Dr. William Chase. The land for the Higgins Memorial Methodist church was given by Dorothy's father, and the right-of-way for Avery Street was given later by her mother.

The family for which the Nu-Wray Inn is named spell their name differently from the Rays, but it is pronounced the same. The summer that I worked at the desk of the Nu-Wray Inn (1958) I had a chance to get to know Rush and Jane Wray. Rush had a special interest in cultural things, and gave much time and effort to get the Parkway Playhouse under way. I was especially glad to have worked there before the matriarch of the family, Miss Julia Wray, died at the age of ninety-six on October 16, 1966. Mary Louise Wray Connor is in the process of selling the property (including the house) to the present innkeepers, Chris and Pam Strickland, who have changed the spelling of the inn to NuWray Inn.

The last Ray that I wish to include here is Henry Ray, who has no Yancey County ancestors, and is not a close personal acquaintance of mine. But he has made a very specific contribution to this book.

When David Salstrom typed the article on Lydia Holman, in which Mrs. S.T. Henry told me that Lydia had the distinction of reporting the highest rainfall in the United States in a twenty-four hour period, the 22.22 inches mentioned earlier in this book, David said, "You must have that wrong. That's impossible! *Four* inches is a lot of rain to fall in twenty-four hours." I said, "Well, I'll have Marla look it up." She works at the National Climatic Data Center in Asheville. She recruited Henry Ray, whom we call our weather guru, to do the research, and she soon came back with several pages of printed data. The area report was done by John S. Bowen, but Lydia had read the gauge at Altapass. From 2:00 P.M., July 15, 1916 until the same hour on the sixteenth: 22.22 inches had fallen. Only 2.38 inches were recorded during that same time period at Asheville. Henry was sure that record had since been broken, and he later gave me this information: the record has been broken five times since 1916, the latest at Alvin, Texas, July 25–26, 1979. The amount was an estimated 43 inches — probably a byproduct of a hurricane.

NOTES

1. Lloyd R. Bailey, Sr., *A History of the Methodist Church in the Toe River Valley*, ed. by Rev. Donald Lee Shuman (Burnsville, NC: Higgins Memorial United Methodist Church, 1986).
2. Conversation between Paul Laughrun and Arthelia H. Brooks, February 23, 1994.
3. Blue Ridge Reading Team, "Yancey County Midwife," *Stories 'Neath the Roan*, (Burnsville, NC: 1993), pp. 52–53. Published courtesy of a grant from the Community Foundation of Western North Carolina.

MEMORIES FROM JACK'S CREEK

I am amazed to discover how many memorable experiences I've had involving people on Jack's Creek. Of course I originally met most of them at the UM Boring's Chapel church that was on the Bald Creek charge with Pensacola when I was working with the Methodist churches in Yancey County. I was acquainted with all the ministers there from 1953* until 1968, except Darrell Parris, who served 1958–1960 when I taught school in Spruce Pine; I was especially close to Don and Joretta Noblitt and Thomas and Carol Weeks. The Methodist Church sold Boring's Chapel to local Free Will Baptists in 1970, and they have continued services, using the same name of Boring's Chapel, changing only the name of the denomination.

In his history of the Toe Valley Methodist churches, Lloyd Bailey said I "helped keep the church alive for the elderly women members."** I did so mostly by visiting people, and by seeing that their needs were met.

One of the people I visited was Annie Byrd. One night when it was icy, she went out to shut up her chickens and she fell hard. Annie was elderly, but not particularly frail. She managed to crawl into a shed, but couldn't make it back to the house. It got down to fifteen degrees that night, and she wasn't wearing her coat. The shed contained no straw. The next morning, the neighbor who checked on her regularly found her disoriented and unable to stand. He took her to the hospital, then notified me. Her hip was broken, and her hypothermia was severe. I went to see her and was there when she died the next day, January 12, 1954.

---

*See Lloyd R. Bailey, Sr., *A History of the Methodist Church in the Toe River Valley*, ed. by Rev. Donald Lee Shuman (Burnsville, NC: Higgins Memorial United Methodist Church, 1986), p. 59–60.

**Ibid., p. 259.

I regularly visited Lloyd Bailey's grandmother, Lillie Bailey, and his father, Glenn. After Lillie died, someone said to me, "Glenn Bailey wanted me to ask you if you're interested in dating." I never bothered to see if it was true; I was too busy to have time for dating.

Quite often I visited Phyllis Bailey's mother, Georgia Honeycutt Peterson, who was blind. She listened to the *Toe Valley View Hour* on WTOE radio. One of my cherished possessions is a letter this dear blind lady wrote to me about how much she enjoyed that hour. She died July 26, 1956. (The letters I received from listeners are another elusive collection "someplace safe" where I cannot find it.] I believe Miss Georgia was Madge Fout's aunt. I always thought Madge's mother was one of the most beautiful ladies I'd ever seen. I doubly hate shingles for what it did to her.

Luella Honeycutt was one of my closest personal friends, probably because she was a fellow native West Virginian. In the early sixties, her physically handicapped sister, Sarah Hipkins, lived with her. From her youth she couldn't walk and her hands were drawn up with arthritis. They had no wheelchairs when Sarah was young, so she learned how to get around in a *rocking chair* — not only in the house, but outside. She did all the braiding of her sister's hair, and told me she had shelled roomfuls of peas and capped an uncountable number of strawberries. Now she was in the Burnsville hospital.

One day, after many visits, I said, "Well, how are you making it today, Sarah?" She answered, "I'm in a lot of pain. I could have gone home to the Lord last night, but Luella wouldn't let me." I decided something should be done, and that I should return to the hospital after the youth meeting in Pensacola I had scheduled. When I arrived, Luella was asleep on a cot in the room, and the nurse said that yes, Sarah was dying. I sat there and prayed for some time — until Luella awakened and saw me. "Oh, Tillie, she's dying," she cried, and she grabbed Sarah's hands and began calling to her. "Sarah, Sarah, you can't die. You can't leave me. Sarah, Sarah!" I went to her and said, "Luella, why do you want to see her suffer another day? She's said she wants to go. Why don't you just release her?" Luella let go of Sarah's hands. A beautiful smile came over Sarah's face, and she was free at last. I took Luella home, and put her to bed. Sarah died on October 8, 1964.

Phoebe McKinney lived on lower Jack's Creek (Horton Hill). I had bought a quarter of beef from her and she was kind enough to let me pay for it in three monthly payments. When I went to make the last payment, I asked if she would like to go with me to see some slides I planned to show at Boring's Chapel. She thought it would be too much trouble for me to bring her back, too far out of my way. I assured her I wouldn't mind. She said, "Okay, let me throw on another dress." As I watched her change, I saw a large dark spot on the side of her leg. "How in the world did you get that big bruise on your leg?" I asked. She stopped brushing her hair, looked down and said, "Oh, that's no bruise, that's dried cow manure." She brushed it off, and then finished brushing her hair. I drove with my war windows open, and the people at church gave her a wide berth! It was Phoebe, too, who invited the Women's Society to her home for the monthly meeting, and met us with a raggedy apron on, an old felt hat on her head, and no shoes on her feet. We all acted as though this was quite normal hostess behavior, so she soon took off the hat and apron and put on her shoes. Her home was in good order, and refreshments were prepared. Her granddaughter, Maxine Westbrook, agreed with me that she was a "character," and that she enjoyed the role. She was pretty stingy, but did see that all four of her children were educated beyond the local schools.

Claudine Peterson, later Mrs. Jim Arrowood, was cited in Lloyd Bailey's remembrances about his early years in the Boring's Chapel church. "Madge Bailey (Mrs. John Byrd) playing the piano; Sinclair Conley (a seminary graduate) teaching the adult class in the far-right-hand corner; Claudine Peterson (Mrs. Jim Arrowood) teaching the children in the near-left corner and presenting a Christmas program. Vacation Church School was held in the summers."*

Claudine helped me with Vacation Church School one summer, but mostly I knew her from her attendance at WSCS. I remember we met at her home once. She says she lives in one of the oldest houses in Yancey County — on Gilder's Creek (a tributary of Jack's Creek), below the falls. Claudine was much younger than her husband, Jim, who died on September 10, 1982.

Claudine and I grew close because of problems with her daughter, Louise. Louise had had impacted bowels from early

---

*Ibid., p. 259.

childhood, and her problems continued until she went into the Burnsville hospital for a week, sometime around the age of ten or eleven years old. Dr. W.A.Y. Sargent said there was something unusual wrong but he wasn't sure what it was; he made an appointment for her at Baptist Hospital in Winston-Salem. I took Claudine and Louise down to Winston-Salem for the examination, probably in 1961. Louise ended up having seven operations over the next three years.

After not seeing each other for at least twenty-five years, Louise and I met in Pollards' Drugstore in the summer of 1993, and were pleased that we knew each other. I think no Christmas has passed since 1961 that I have not received a Christmas card from Claudine. Now I see her frequently at Reconciliation House in Burnsville.

Roy and Grace Duncan lived on Cox's Creek, which goes all the way across the mountain to Tennessee. There was very little level land on their place, but by dint of very hard work they made a living from those steep hillsides and sent their daughter Evelyn to college. I know they had plenty to eat because I ate there frequently. Roy's maiden sister, Cartha, lived with them until she died. [This is the same Cartha Duncan who made the rug for me out of dyed hosiery in 1965, mentioned in my Mini-Autobiography article, earlier in this book.] Every spring the Duncans gave me early leaf lettuce from their tobacco bed. James, their son, may not like to be told that I held him on my lap when he was a little boy of seven or eight. He's over six feet now, with two big boys of his own.

Roy and James went to the Methodist Boring's Chapel church, but Grace and Evelyn attended the Baptist church nearby. Grace, however, was an enthusiastic and faithful member of our Methodist women's group; and if I'm not mistaken, Evelyn baked the cake to celebrate my fiftieth birthday at Luella Honeycutt's in 1965.

I went to Kentucky in 1968. When I returned to Yancey County in 1985 I heard that Grace was ill. I called several times and went to see her once before she died on October 24, 1991, but I missed her funeral because I didn't know about it until after she was buried.

While I was working in Kentucky, James had moved to a mobile home near the Duncan home, and was very helpful during Grace's last illness, and a comfort to her. When Roy was diagnosed with cancer, he moved in with James and his family, leaving the old house empty. Despite protests, though, Roy insisted on keeping his truck, and often he'd drive it up to the old house he and Grace had shared. I visited him once and called several times during his last months; and I did go to his funeral, at the Boring's Chapel church. Roy died June 18, 1993.

James' family now attends Ivy Gap Baptist church. I'm still amazed at the number of high caliber people coming from Jack's Creek. The Duncan family is a good example. They work so hard to make a living, and that perseverance results in a strength of character to be simply admired. I am as proud of Roy and Grace's children as if they were my own.

Evelyn and her husband live in Brasstown, North Carolina. She is director of the Child Development Center, where she tries to determine whether preschool mentally handicapped children can be mainstreamed or need special facilities. Her husband is library technician at Tri-County Tech in Murphy, North Carolina. They have two children.

And the hardworking qualities of Roy and Grace still exist in their grandchildren. Recently I saw a carry-out boy at BiLo who reminded me of James. I asked the cashier his last name. "Duncan," she said, which confirmed my suspicion that he was James's boy. I called James to get some answers to my questions. Bradley, the carry-out boy, is a senior making a B average. He has been made student assistant manager at BiLo, and takes extra hours at Mayland Tech to prepare to be a paramedic. Their younger son, Justin, is a freshman and has to work harder for his grades, but he too works — as a cook at Mountain Breeze restaurant. James drives a truck for Ingles.

It was probably 1966 when the mission board sent Toge Fujihira to North Carolina to take promotional pictures. He spent two days and one night with my people, and we drove out to Jack's Creek in search of some good photos.

We found Euphrates McCurry cleaning out a drainage ditch in his overalls with no shirt on, his felt hat, and holding the shovel as he spoke to us — the perfect image of the picturesque mountain farmer. He posed facing the camera, leaning on his shovel handle, and talking to me while Mr. Fujihira took the picture with my back toward the camera. The editor of the Methodist women's magazine decided to use that photo for the June, 1967, cover. The Western North Carolina conference secretary of missions was so pleased to have "one of our own" so honored, that she insisted I leave Bible school or whatever I had on my agenda and come to Lake Junaluska to speak to the women at the annual meeting of the Women's Society of Christian Service. I agreed to go for one morning session.

The secretary introduced me with a triumphant flourish of the just-released magazine, that most of the women had not yet seen. My introductory remark that day was, "Ladies, if you've ever aspired to be a cover girl and have not made it, take heart! If your face can't make it, perhaps your backside will!" When I showed the magazine to Rose McCurry and told her it would be seen by people around the world, she said, "Oh, dear Lord, and Frate in his underwear!" Later his picture appeared on a church bulletin cover by himself — the day I was substituting for the Eddyville (Kentucky) pastor.

The November 1977 flood was well documented by Yancey Graphics in both pictures and story.[1] I was working in Kentucky at the time, but Wendal Bull told me that the early Sunday morning deluge came up and went down so fast that up on the hill above my log house in South Toe, he didn't even see it. He just couldn't understand why our mailbox was filled with sand when he took letters out there on Monday morning. Every bridge in the county was washed out, and the flood did not spare the Jack's Creek community. Because I had taken some training with the Disaster Team that the Methodist church sponsored, I was asked to return from Kentucky for a week in March, 1978, to try to assess how well the needs of affected citizens were being met by recovery agencies. I drove over the whole area and was shocked at the devastation still apparent everywhere. Pensacola and Bolen's Creek were particularly bad.

Luke and Ethel Laughrun lived very close to Jack's Creek, where Gilder's Creek enters the larger creek there. Their son had become aware of the rapidly rising water next to their home in time to get them to an outbuilding on higher ground. All night he waited with them there, and the next morning he felled a tree across the creek to get them to their daughter's home in Burnsville. Their children then cleaned and prepared the home for their return. Amid the mud and disarray they found one item that needed no extra care: Luke's false teeth. They had apparently floated in their plastic cup — along with the water in which they had been put to soak the night before — from the kitchen counter to the top of the freezer on the porch.

I was pleased to help Luke and Ethel celebrate their seventieth wedding anniversary on October 3, 1993, in that same lovely home, with all their family and many friends with them. Ethel died soon after, on December 28, 1993.

***

During the bicentennial year of the Methodist Church, 1984–1985, Lloyd Bailey undertook the task of writing a *History of the Methodist Church in the Toe River Valley*.[2] Don Shuman, pastor of the Higgins Memorial United Methodist Church in Burnsville, was the editor. I returned to Yancey County in May, 1985, as they were finishing the task. I found that Lloyd had included me in the Boring's Chapel segment. "Some assistance was available through a Deaconess who worked primarily through the Women's Circles. I remember in particular Arthelia ("Tillie") Brooks, a wonderful lady who helped keep the church alive for the elderly women members." That was fine. I *had* been especially close to several of the members on Jack's Creek.

But I was not the only CCW in the Toe Valley. Margaret (Peg) Calbeck had done volunteer work, especially with the youth, before she was hired full-time by the Women's Division in March, 1951. She worked until she married Philip Neal in October, 1953. I had started in June of that year and worked until September, 1955. I came back in September, 1960 and worked until September, 1968, when I was transferred to West Kentucky to a resort-type ministry. There were also three women who worked in Avery County — Geraldine Surratt, Martha Jean Henson, and Virginia Miller. When I found there was no mention of any of these in the manuscript of the church's history, I told Don, "This history cannot go to press with such an omission." Consequently, Church and Community Work *was* added. It appears now as number XIX under Miscellaneous.

Ola McCurry, who lived on Patterson Branch, was a member of Boring's Chapel and our women's society. Her husband, Elzie McCurry, was dead, and I think she and her son Travis lived on the homeplace with her father, Clayton McCurry. After her father became ill, she did not have the time to attend either church or the women's society. I visited her in the home after her father was bedridden, and Ola said that late each afternoon it was as though he'd already gone from this life to the next: he would happily greet his wife Ida, and other dear ones who were dead. I decided their pastor should come to see them.

Tommy (Thomas W.) Weeks was serving the Bald Creek charge at the time. His sight was so impaired that he could only read by holding the print very close to one eye, so of course he couldn't drive. His wife, Carol, had the job of taking him to his appointments; and she had four small girls to complicate matters. My admiration and love for both of them was unbounded. To make things easier on Carol, I often took Tommy to call on our families. I called him about Clayton, and said I would pick him up. We arrived at the home early in the afternoon. I held Mr. McCurry's hand while Tommy prayed specifically that this day he would not make the trip "back." Clayton died that evening, and was buried on Labor Day, 1965. Ola died while I was in Kentucky, in February of 1979.

Travis married Florence Fox, a Yancey County Fox from a family of twelve, their daughter, Sheila Woody, told me. I met her where she works at Roses. She has a small daughter, Chelsea Lanay, and a married sister, Kathy Wheeler. It's up to Sheila to uphold the Jack's Creek tradition because her parents now live in Red Hill.

NOTES

1. Yancey Graphics, *Flood Disaster: November 6, 1977*, (Burnsville, NC: Yancey Graphics, 1977).
2. Lloyd R. Bailey, Sr., *A History of the Methodist Church in the Toe River Valley*, ed. by Rev. Donald Lee Shuman (Burnsville, NC: Higgins Memorial United Methodist Church, 1986).

TRAGEDIES

The old Windom Methodist Church was about to reach the end of its usefulness when I worked with the members during the years 1953–55. The tall, white frame building looked rather "un-church-like". Apparently it was the custom around 1900 to have separate doors for men and women in church buildings. The old Celo Methodist Church had this same feature as Windom.

I knew it was about time for a new church when one night I sat in a pew next to the wall and saw it lean away from me during a strong gust of wind. In speaking of that experience with Ed Harris recently he said, "Yes, and the lights hanging from the ceiling also swayed."

When Highway 19E was built by East Yancey High School in 1962, the State Highway Division bought the church property for six thousand five hundred dollars, which was used to help build the new church further up on the hill. The Dumpsters are now where the old church stood.

My chief reasons for remembering this old church are because some of the members have greatly enriched my life, especially Mollie Hensley. She had always wanted to be a missionary, but having the care of her aging parents she did the next best thing — she taught school and worked in her church. My two older daughters had Mollie as their fourth grade teacher at South Toe School. In 1960, her parental responsibilities at an end, she went to teach at an Indian Christian school near Phoenix, Arizona, where she taught until she retired and returned to Windom in 1980. The Sunday before Thanksgiving 1991 the members had a special surprise evening to honor Mollie and Gwen Harris for their years of faithful service to the Windom Methodist Church.

This was all brought to mind because the old Windom Church figured prominently in one of the most memorable nights of my life. It was July 18, 1954. We were having a series of evangelistic services at the church while Joe Petree was the pastor. He had invited Tommy Tyson to do the preaching. Tommy had visited in the

Newdale charge some time before as a Bible teacher/retreat leader. I had attended the meetings and was inspired by his teaching and came to respect and love him very much (as I do to this day. Once the whole Brooks clan spent the night in his home in Goldsboro on our way to the beach — nine of us). However, my regard for Tommy in no way prepared me for what happened that night.

As I listened and watched Tommy in the pulpit as God's spirit inspired his preaching, suddenly I saw a great circle of light surrounding his head and shoulders — just glowing!! All my life I had wondered about the pictures with a halo of light around the head of Jesus and the Holy Family. Now I was seeing it around an ordinary person being used extraordinarily by God. [I have seen this phenomenon six times in the years since — around the heads of four ministers, one laywoman and one layman when they were communicating something especially God-inspired. Many years after I experienced this at the Windom Church I learned that the aura — different colors emanating from a person — can be filmed by the use of Kirlian photography.]

JUDY SHUFORD

But my night of July 18 was not ended yet. As I left the service I felt exalted! Talk about a spiritual high, this was it! As I drove toward Celo I was not sure my wheels were touching the pavement! *Then* I went around the curve at Westall's store and was confronted with parked cars as far as I could see. I stopped and walked up the road to find the cause of this concern. I ended at Bradley and Lucille Shuford's door.

When I went inside and saw the two of them huddled together in front of a casket holding their only child, Judy, I hit a new emotional low. Though I didn't know Bradley or Lucille very well, nine-year-old Judy had been my Paula's classmate and special friend. Paula had visited in the Shuford home, and I knew that Lucille had stayed in bed during most of the pregnancy in order to carry the baby to term; she probably could not have another. All this went through my mind as I joined that heartbreaking scene. I honestly felt I could just as easily have seen one of my own girls in that casket. Later I asked what had happened.

On Thursday evening the sixteenth, Lucille had been sitting at the dining room table, making up the payroll for the men who worked for Bradley. Judy had been sitting in a chair behind her. A sudden clap of thunder frightened her so much that it brought on an asthma attack. She was taken to the hospital, but they were unable to restore normal breathing. She died on Friday, and was buried on Sunday, the nineteenth.

Afterward I visited Lucille many times — even tried to encourage them to adopt a child. They had so much to give. But I suppose no other child could fill the void that Judy had left.

In 1993 Marla took Connie Styles and me to the Shuford's new home farther up the valley to see Lucille's fabulous doll collection. They filled practically every room in the house — must have been more than a thousand (she won't count them). They represented different ages, sizes and races and each one had been lovingly and exquisitely dressed by Lucille herself. She has sold most of them.

DARRELL GIBBS

Darrell was the only child of Edward and Marjorie Gibbs who lived at Celo. She worked as Dr. Ohle's assistant at the Health Center. During the summer months in the mid-sixties Darrell mowed the grass and helped care for the center's grounds. I can remember saying to myself as I saw him working there, "What a very special young man you are, Darrell." It was not just because I saw him willing to work and save money for his college education, but for other admirable things I knew about him. He was an honor student, member of the student council, president of his senior class, and a fine athlete as well.

He was also musically gifted. He probably played the boogie-woogie for his young friends. In fact, I remember hearing him doing just that at Arthur Morgan School, but he also used his talent to play for church services at his Brown's Creek Baptist Church. He was a handsome young man and had a steady girlfriend. It seemed he had everything going for him. That was why it was such a shock to the whole South Toe valley when on Sunday evening, January 7, 1968, he took his own life.

The family had been discussing his college plans. His parents had reminded him once more what an early marriage would do to those plans. While the subject may have been very upsetting to him, that, taken by itself, could in no way account for what happened subsequently.

I visited Marjorie over a period of weeks, trying to help *both* of us understand, WHY?

I finally came to a conclusion that made some sense to me, and I hoped it would to Marjorie. I learned that Darrell had suffered a rather severe head injury during the football season the fall before. To all outward appearances he had not sustained any permanent injury; but a cousin of his said he was subject to debilitating headaches that he never mentioned to his parents. It was my theory that such a headache had caused him to lose control momentarily — just long enough to reach the point of no return.

Darrell's death brought again to my mind Judy's death, over fourteen years before. It seemed like such a cruel twist of fate that these two mothers who were first cousins, should lose their only child before they hardly had a chance to live.

UNNAMED GIRLS

The third tragedy involved a couple (names withheld by request), the parents of three daughters. The eldest lived to the age of twelve and the twins, respectively, to seventeen and twenty-six. A deficiency in the brain prevented the development of the muscular structure of the body, while the skeleton developed almost normally. The result was eventually rather large, utterly helpless children who had to be fed, diapered and have every move made for them.

The twins were born on my birthday, which made them special to me. Lura McMahan helped me keep them at my house for a few days one summer so the parents could make a little trip. Those few days gave me a closer understanding of what their lives — and their parents' lives — must be like.

The girls were aware of what went on around them, and in a limited way could express their displeasure and joy. I know from experience that this was true of the twins. As soon as they heard the voice of someone they knew and loved they let you know. They even recognized my voice when I came on WTOE radio. They were pretty girls, with blue eyes and blonde hair.

Having been involved with the families of the other two tragedies I've mentioned, I tried to think about the burden these parents had to bear. It is certain I would not want *anyone* to go through such traumas. While the swiftness and finality of the first two tragedies would be hard to bear, this third seemed like the hardest of all. The mother described it as "going through hell." The first two sets of parents at least had the memories of normal children for a time, the third??? *Twenty-six years* of constant care! The physical tasks were difficult enough but what about the other aspects? I could only begin to imagine what their thoughts and feelings were during the dark night hours. Did they feel (1) their own bodies had betrayed them, (2) humiliation at having less than perfect children, (3) disappointment that they would never see their girls run and play or achieve normal adulthood, (4) that God, family and friends were not very understanding or helpful, (5) worry about the girls' illnesses, and (6) utterly exhausted from dealing with the hourly and minute-by-minute care of their children?

Whatever their private demons may have been, I never found the home a place of doom and gloom. I loved to go there and so did my girls — even spending nights. The atmosphere in the home was warm and welcoming. I was in Kentucky the last eleven years of the twins' lives, so I don't know how it was those years I was gone; but while I was a periodic visitor I was sure the twins were cared for with patience and love, because they were so joyous.

In all my working years I have not known of a situation that I think would be harder to cope with. The fact that the parents survived is a tribute to their fortitude. Whatever it took, they had it! They deserve our admiration and unbounded praise. The quality of care they gave these girls is a kind of heroism that deserves community recognition and commendation — and the girls deserve their bit of immortality, too, a witness that their lives were not lived in vain because they *are* remembered as being pretty, knowledgeable and happy, responding to their friends with joy.

Emotionally, these tragedies may have affected me more deeply than two that happened to me during my early school days.

During my sophomore year in high school, two of my classmates were playing "Hands up or I'll shoot" with an old revolver in an outbuilding. They thought the gun was unloaded, but one cartridge had remained in the gun, and a young man shot his best friend. We attended the funeral as a class, and that night I had to acknowledge that my phobia with funerals, which I'd hoped had vanished with my childhood, was still with me. I slept with my aunt.

It was my senior year in college when my sorority pledged my close friend Fisher's sister. Fisher had seven brothers, but Paula was his only sister. Fisher and I worked together at the West Virginia state agricultural laboratory. During Easter week when we were going to a night service at a member's home in the country, Paula, who did not know the streetcar tracks were parallel to the highway, was hit by a streetcar. She died two days later.

At the funeral I was heartbroken as I watched Fisher look at his sister for the last time. I said in my heart, "Fisher, this sorority has deprived you of your only sister. I promise that if I ever have a daughter I will put another Paula in this world."

And so it is that my eldest daughter is named Paula.

SOMEONE HAD LISTENED*

When in 1947 I came to the North Carolina mountains in Yancey County I soon became aware that prejudice against "Negroes" (as we called them then) was pretty widespread. (It was not as bad, though, as in the adjoining county where they were known for bragging, "The sun doesn't go down on a nigger in Mitchell County.") In Yancey County there was a small black neighborhood on the edge of Burnsville, with an A.M.E. Zion church and a condemned school. The black elementary schoolchildren were bused forty miles to Negro schools in Asheville. The high school students attended our Methodist Allen High School, also in Asheville.

After more than twelve years of petitions, boycotts, litigation (a couple of cross burnings) and school board meetings, the schools in Yancey County were integrated in September, 1960 — the first county in North Carolina to do so.

When I came back to Church and Community Ministry in 1953 and joined the Celo Methodist Church I made a conscious effort, in a non-aggressive way, to say to all I dealt with — women, Bible school attenders, youth, and members of adult Sunday school classes — that prejudice was not a Christian virtue; and that it was probably more detrimental to the person holding it than to those against whom it was held. In the late sixties, I had some indication that I may have been heard.

A lay speaker from Asheville arrived at Celo Church early; and since the adult Sunday school class met at the back of the sanctuary (behind partly closed folding doors) the man was invited to join us. I was not teaching the class.

I forget how the subject came up, but it was about people of color. The lay speaker said, "You know the Bible says that Negroes

---

*The first part of this article has been submitted for possible publication in the sequel to *Along the Way* (Experiences of Church and Community Workers), published by the Methodist Office of Church and Community Workers, 475 Riverside Drive, Third Floor, New York, NY 10115.

are not human. In Genesis, chapter one, verse twenty-four, God said, 'Let the earth bring forth the living creature *after his kind.*' And then in verse twenty-six, 'Man was created in God's image.'" (KJV)

It was not I who refuted him, but Arcemus Simmons who said, "Oh, no, that is not what the Bible was talking about. It meant the animals, birds and all things in nature. Humans are human, even though they are many different colors."

This was the same Arcemus Simmons who, perhaps about twenty years earlier, had suggested to the pastor of the Celo Methodist church, Joe Petree, that it might be wise to remove the two families from CCI from the church rolls, namely the Philip Nordstroms and Arthelia Brooks. Joe came to tell me, and the very next day I visited the Simmons' home. Only Edna was home, and I think I was able to refute the rumors, or at least explain how the wild rumors about CCI got started.

In an area where, if young people went away to school they didn't come back because work opportunities were so few, it was not hard to understand people questioning the motives of "these people with college degrees" suddenly appearing in their midst.

I think in those early days that Dorothy Thomas, who worked as the area librarian, and I, in my job as a church worker, did much to assure people that CCI had no ulterior motives — just loved the mountains and found it a wholesome place to raise their families.

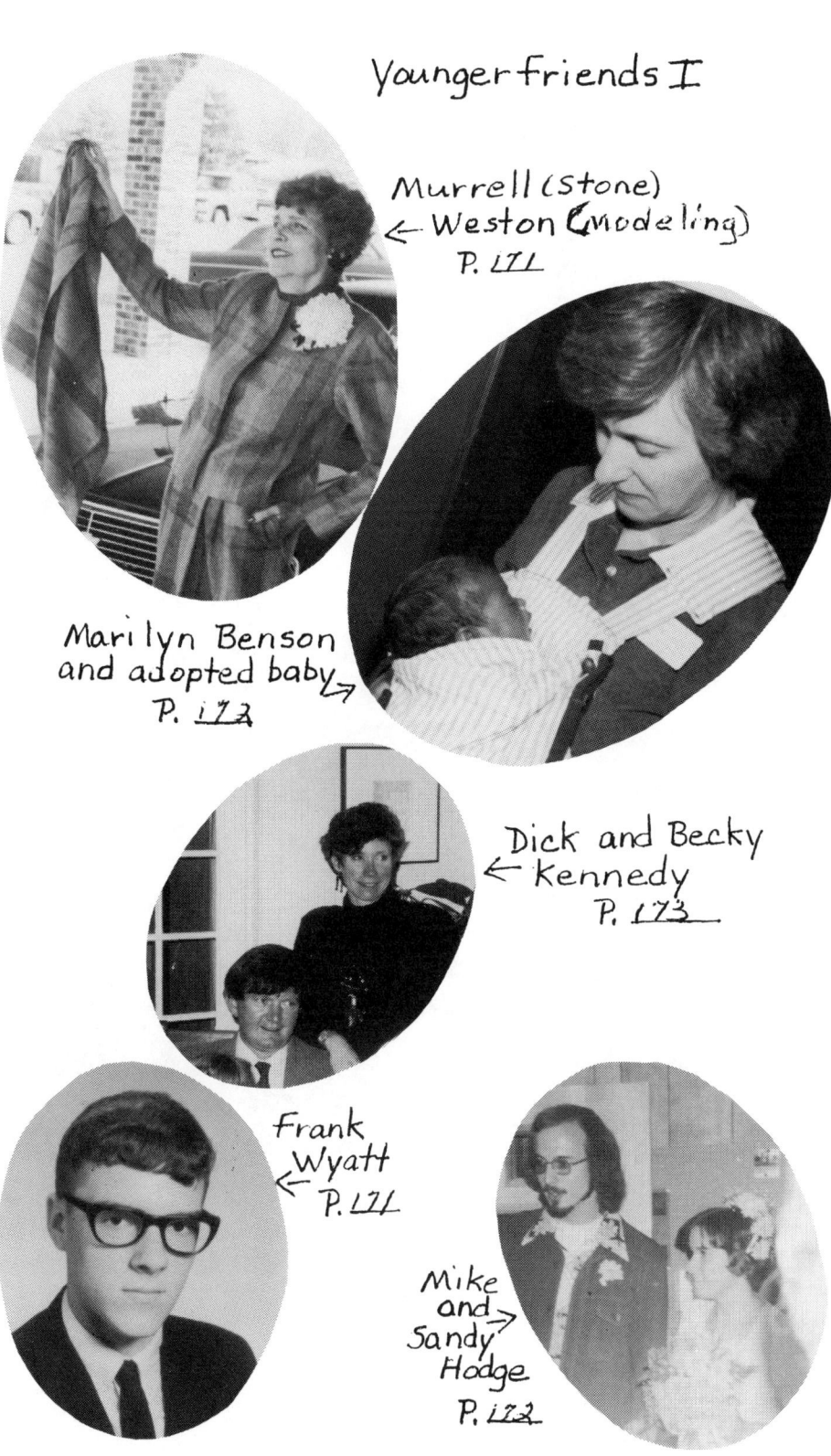

Younger friends I

Murrell (Stone) Weston (modeling) P. 171

Marilyn Benson and adopted baby P. 172

Dick and Becky Kennedy P. 173

Frank Wyatt P. 171

Mike and Sandy Hodge P. 172

YOUNGER FRIENDS

Through my working years many younger people have brought a special blessing to my life. I would like to pay tribute to just a few of them, even though many more could be named.

Murrell Stone Weston. She lived in Big Sandy, West Virginia, one of the four mining communities where Myrta Davis and I worked during my first three years (1940–43) as a rural worker in southern West Virginia. Murrell's sister Emma taught in a one-room school up one of the "hollers." Murrell did get further education, which was somewhat unusual for that place and time. She then married a Methodist minister, and they now live in retirement in Sedona, Arizona. We at least exchange Christmas greetings every year.

Carolyn Ray Cort. She was my pick from the eleven years in Yancey County (1953–55, 1960–68). She is the only child of Mack and Dorothy Ray, and by all odds should have been spoiled, but I remember the comment of the mother of one of Carolyn's childhood friends - "I don't know how any child can be as perfect as Carolyn Ray is — so patient, unselfish and caring." It naturally followed that she should become a pediatrician.

She is married to David Cort, also a doctor, and they live and practice medicine in Burnsville. They have four *very* talented daughters: Lisa, Heidi, Carrie and Gretchen (who has been an "adult" since she was five); the whole family is musically inclined. Lisa is already in college.

Frank Wyatt. Frank was also from my Yancey County years. His parents were Robert and Frances Wyatt, and he was part of the county youth group, along with his brother Robert (Ben, to me), and his sister Joy. Frank helped me in the office — probably with the newsletter we provided for the youth and for Methodist people of the county. When I moved to Kentucky in 1968, I was not in touch with Frank personally, but I did know he served as a minister to independent churches for several years. Now he serves at Liberty Covenant church in Micaville, North Carolina.

I did see Frank at a program at the local high school a couple of years ago, and again at Willard Hill's funeral on October 4, 1993. It was a treat to give him a hug and say, "I loved you so much." He and his wife Janet have two boys. Frank teaches at Asheville-Buncombe Technical Community College.

Sandy Bryan Hodge. Sandy Bryan's family lived near Paducah and went to a little country church where I attended Sandy's wedding to Mike Hodge. Her family let them "do it their way." Mike played the guitar and sang to her the John Denver song, *Follow Me Where I Go.* He also made bread for the reception.

Sandy worked with me both at Grand Rivers in the Louisville conference and with the Lakeland Parish in the Memphis conference. I may have had some influence in Sandy's decision to attend Scarritt College, where she met Mike.

Mike Hodge. Mike is the one who became a Church and Community worker — the core of my church service personnel. From 1972 until 1980 I saw him more often than I did Sandy, especially when we worked on the History Task Force. They live in Nashville now, and have three sons. Mike is no longer a CCW, but now works with an association of forty-three interfaith groups, Tying Nashville Together (TNT), which is a branch of the Industrial Areas Foundation. This spring he called me to request a letter of appreciation for Sandy. She was being ordained at the Tennessee annual conference and was planning to become involved in the hospital chaplaincy.

I saw Mike at the Appreciation Banquet for Church and Community workers at the Brooks-Howell Home on September 16, 1993. I thought he was going to leave without speaking to me; but he was waiting for me in the parking lot, and I got my hug. The Hodges are a creative, dedicated couple.

Marilyn Benson. Marilyn is also a Church and Community worker, and for some unexplained reason has always had a special place in my heart. I told her this as we visited at the Appreciation Banquet in 1993. She has spent many of her working years in my home state of West Virginia; and at the last CCW meeting I attended she — a single woman — had just adopted a tiny baby from India. I was afraid it would not live; but now she showed me a picture of a healthy third grader. This could not have been an easy task, to work and raise the daughter alone.

Laura Wells. Of all the Church and Community workers, I have been closest to Laura. In the early sixties we both served in the Western North Carolina conference, and for several summers joined the other workers to help train college girls to work in our small membership churches. We also were roommates at the West Virginia University during a special week-long workshop for those in ministry in Appalachia. I visited with her several times when she was on the staff of Scarritt College and living in Nashville. One of her great contributions was to the prison ministry in the Tennessee conference. She is now serving her last year before retirement in Martin, Tennessee.

Becky Gray Kennedy. Becky had her pottery shop in our barn in Celo Community, and when Marla moved out of the log house in 1979, Becky moved in, but would let me "visit the house" when I came back for vacations. I learned to love and appreciate her very much. I even felt moved to write a letter to Celo Community on her behalf when her membership was being debated with negative overtones. I felt as though she were an additional daughter. After she married Dick Kennedy and left the log house, when her children Katelin and Ian came along, I considered all of them part of my family. Becky took the part of my former holding containing the structure that had formerly been the barn. It is now her pottery shop and garden space. She also took as part of her holding the building that was first a corn crib and then remodeled to be a little dwelling that we called the crib cabin.

She is a potter *extraordinaire!* Even the smallest of her fanciful figures is modeled with so much expression! I have two angels, a hen, and a bear-whistle. At one of her first shows downstate, a man bought several animal whistles for Christmas gifts — *he said*; but after several years and many more purchases he admitted he had *not* given any of them away, but had finally built a display cabinet for his *collection!*

I don't see Becky Kennedy often, but periodically we get in a good phone conversation.

Robert "Buzz" Scott. My first brief contact with Robert "Buzz" Scott was at the 1988 annual conference at Lake Junaluska. Mildred Ray and I went just for a day — to meet our newly-assigned minister. He squatted down behind the last row of seats in Stuart Auditorium to talk to us. I said we had come to welcome him because I would not be in Burnsville when he came with his family (I would be at Lake Chautauqua for the summer). At once I thought, "I like this man!" And I got a royal greeting from the pulpit on my return to church at the end of August.

Our understanding and appreciation of each other was greatly enhanced through the Wednesday morning study/prayer fellowship that we shared with eight or ten very special church members.

When we were ready to begin our first *Disciple* Bible study course, I was debating whether or not to take on the thirty-four-week commitment. The course, based on a written guidebook,[1] is very structured. It was settled when Buzz *requested* that I join. Those fourteen people will always be in a separate category in my affections. Those in the class were: Robert Scott, Willie Weeks, John and Charlene Austin, John and Melanie Stallings, David and Carolyn Ray, Becky Gillespie, Leon Taylor, Jeanne Tyner, Greg and Tonya Helms and Greer Edmonds. I had to miss the last class to go my sister's.

At my last meeting Becky Gillespie arranged a little party. She had prepared a special "Book of Remembrance" in which each class member wrote a tribute with respect to what I had meant to them during the many sessions. This is part of what Buzz wrote: "When I brought the elements of communion over to you on New Year's Eve, I was acknowledging that you have been as my priest. That is, you have offered absolving grace, gentle wisdom, a guiding light, a loving witness, and an atmosphere of trust. I am grateful to you and inspired by you."

I have loved *all* my ministers. One, Wright Pillow [see the article on western Kentucky experiences, later in this book], would be a close first runner-up to Buzz, but I must admit that Buzz is the *most dear*!

Roy Willie Weeks. I really got to know his wife, Renée, before I knew Willie. She was a part of that very special Wednesday morning study group; and I came to admire the many ways this young couple found to serve. But Willie was one of the fourteen in that first *Disciple* class, and that made the difference! His contribution to my "Book of Remembrance" was unique. He wrote his contribution in a very businesslike way:

To: the Lion of the Tribe of Judah
From: Willie Weeks
Subject: Tillie Brooks

Thank you for placing Tillie Brooks as a member of our Disciple Bible Study group. . . . I feel you have placed her in my path in response to my requests, as a guide on my journey. Tillie has performed this task admirably.

Respectfully,
Willie Weeks

In 1992 Willie had the opportunity to go to Palestine with a group from the WNC conference to get a better understanding of the problems facing Israelis and other residents of the Holy Land, especially Palestinian Christians. It was a real mind-changing experience for Willie! He met Elias Chacour (a Palestinian Christian who lives for peace and reconciliation) who wrote *Blood Brothers*[2] and *We Belong to the Land*.[3] Chacour lectured at Chautauqua, New York, while I was there during the summer of 1993, and I bought and had him autograph the second book. "We are all descendants of Abraham and must learn to live together" is his premise.

Scott Kisker. Scott served as our Duke summer intern for 1990 and 1991 at Higgins Memorial Methodist Church in Burnsville, North Carolina. The members of the congregation were asked to assume some responsibility for feeding the young man; so I dutifully asked him to lunch. It turned out to be a blessing instead of a duty, and so it was repeated several times in the course of the two summers.

We found we had much to talk about — even got into several theological discussions as he expressed interest in knowing what conclusions I had reached "at my advanced age." We did not always agree, but we did agree to disagree.

Three times he has asked me to write references for him. The first was when he applied for a year's study in Germany, the second in preparation for his ordination. The third reference I wrote with some reluctance, because I didn't really think he should go back to Germany for another year, but I had to trust to his leading. This time it was for a position in an English-speaking church.

I have greatly appreciated his two generous (time-wise) visits when he came back to the county.

In the references for him that I've written, and to him personally, I've said that he is the "most *graciously endowed* young minister that I have ever known."

NOTES

1. The current edition of this course is: Richard Byrd Wilkie and Julia Kitchen Wilkie, *Disciple: becoming Disciples through Bible Study* (Nashville: Abingdon Press, 1993).
2. Elias Chacour, *Blood Brothers* (publication information not available.)
3. Elias Chacour and Mary E. Jensen, *We Belong to the Land* (San Francisco: Harper Books, 1992).

West Ky. Years I - Pisgah / Grand Rivers

Beverly Sewell, Louise O'Bryan, Louise Lummus, Margie Mitchuson 7-90

Tom, Mark, Charles, Nancy and Carla Rogers → 10-77 P xx

Ruby and Robert Shaver (Hopkinsville D.S.) with Derek Hoover 7-70

Kuttawa U.M.C.
A.L. Fraser
← Marla, Derek and Tillie

Charles and "Billie" at Ky. Dam 9-69
P 293

christening   house - Grand Rivers

West Ky. Years II

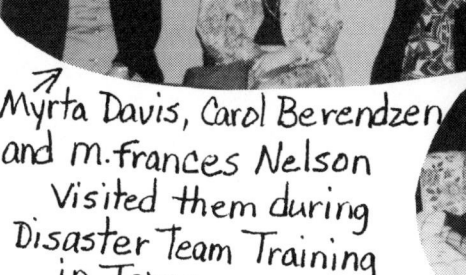

Myrta Davis, Carol Berendzen and M. Frances Nelson Visited them during Disaster Team Training in Texas   1978

Myrta Davis and Tillie   1978

Gail Williams, Tillie, James Hankins, Marvin Judy, Glenn Biddle, William Appleby, Harold McSwain

At Gen. Conf. UMRF Ind. Indiana 4-16-80

Tillie, Ray Wyatt, John Vincent, William Evans, Dossie Wheatley, Roy Stevenson, Walter German
Memphis Conf. UMRF Exec. Comm. 5-14-80

West Ky. Years - III -- C.C. Work

Core Leadership Team C.C.W.
(Tillie chair at time of pic.)

Diane Ramsey, Tillie, Lois Marguart, Laura Wells and Kathryn Mitchem

Betsy Ewing

Ann McKenzie, Kathryn Mitchem and Gladys Campbell 12-72

Roma Cupp, Mary Owen, Alice Cobb, Laura Wells, Tillie, Rhoda Edmeston at Alice's in Nashville

West Ky. Years IV - Lakeland Parish

"Santa" Paul → Pillow

↗ Ruth Kissel, Wright Pillow and Shirley Nimmo P. 185

Hal McSwain and Susan ← Hilleary P. 186 Summer '72(?)

Kermit (candyman) and Dorothy Ellenberger, ↙Sophie Reynolds, Ray and Dorothy Hall at Ellenberger's 5-23-88

West Ky. Years V - Lakeland Parish

Tillie, Nancy Harrington, Wilma Jones, Sue Mitcherson, , Arabella Sowell, Andy. At Arabella's (Union Ridge)
Aurora, Ky. 7-16-92
M.C.

"Bud" and "Lee" Blackie
(Benson and NovaLee) - Lakeland Wesley Village
12-83

Lakland Parish youth Singers
Top Mitch, Ron, Susan, Nancy, Murray, Jeri and Barry
Bottom Jim, Tillie and Fred
9-15-75

West Ky. Years VI – Lakeland Wesley Village

Robert Werle at L.W.V.

Banana tree in Atrium Russell Hall →

Ruby Gregory, Sue Inman and Connie Doering

Opal Jackson, Hazel Rose, and Goldie Boyer 4-'85

Betty Benckendorf 4-'85

West Ky. Years VII - Lakeland Wesley Village

Henry and Lillian Bishop, Martha and "Pete" Tomlin

Minnie Schneider, Harriet Werle, and Ruth Kissel

Harold and Helen Grebel on Roan Mtn. N.C

Ova and Leonard Copeland at Tillie's Burnsville apt.

THE WEST KENTUCKY YEARS

In my thirty-seven years as a working adult the nearest I ever came to being discriminated against as a woman was with the Land Between the Lakes Area Ministry (LBLAM) on the Western Kentucky-Tennessee border. I had served over a year as the Methodist representative on the Council when Gene Branson, the executive secretary of the LBLAM ministry, decided to take another job in Washington, D.C. He asked me if I'd be interested in the part-time position of executive secretary; it seemed right in line with the tourist ministry I was already involved in, so my New York executive, Ralph Nichols, gave his formal approval and I agreed to take the position on.

But when it was brought before the full council the Baptist representative was not so sure his ministers would approve of a woman in that position. Privately he explained to me that for forty years a Baptist minister had traveled the lakes area preaching that "women should be silent in the church" to such an extent that one day it caused problems with a relatively simple transaction. In a church meeting where a woman had written for a transfer of membership, the men couldn't find her name on the books, and were totally puzzled and finally gave up. There was a woman member present at the meeting who knew *why* they could not find her name — she had requested the transfer under her married name. Because "women are to be silent in the church" the woman member had to solve the mystery by telling her husband after they got home. Earl, the Baptist representative, said that things were changing, but he didn't think the ministers he represented were ready for a woman as executive secretary of LBLAM.

Since LBLAM had to depend on the more numerous Baptist ministers to provide leadership for the five campground worship services and for the three TVA chaplaincies that ran from Memorial Day through Labor Day, we had to consider Earl's concern.

The other members decided such prejudice should not be encouraged and set a day for the vote. When the day came, Earl was present despite the advice of his "higher-ups" who suggested he just stay away so he could not be blamed. The vote was unanimous and I served ten years with splendid cooperation from the TVA, state officials and *all* the ministers. It was probably the most satisfactory experience of my working years, and the year after I retired from that position, I helped the new person settle into the job of executive secretary. I was also asked to write a history of the LBLAM.

Even though I am not an ordained minister, I filled in as worship leader and chaplain many times during those ten years. After conducting a service on making moral decisions at TVA Rushing Creek, I received a letter from a Lutheran minister that said: "Of the three Sundays that we participated in worship as a part of the congregation during our vacation, yours was the most meaningful and relevant message. It was an exciting experience and a welcome change for us to know the presence of God in worship without either the formal setting or the liturgy to which we were accustomed. Our sincere thanks to you and your Area Ministry for providing this opportunity to campers like ourselves."

One of the first things I needed to do after I was elected executive secretary of LBLAM council was to consult with the Methodist district superintendents in the three districts surrounding Kentucky and Barkley lakes — two of the districts were in Kentucky, and one in Tennessee.

When I went to see William P. Bailey, the newly appointed superintendent for the Paducah district, he showed me a map and told me of his plan to form a cooperative parish with the churches in Marshall County on the west bank of Kentucky Lake. It sounded good, but would not involve me that much because I was in the Louisville conference on the east side of the lake.

The next year, Bill began to implement his plan. He appointed Joe Piercey, Sr., to the Benton church, Fred French to Calvert City and Mt. Carmel, and Wright Pillow to Briensburg, Maple Spring and Union Ridge. He instructed them to work together to bring Lakeland Parish into existence. Wright was to have the organizing responsibility.

Now to these three capable young ministers on their way up the appointment ladder, this was like a demotion — especially to Wright! We said, "He came kicking and screaming to Kentucky!" To be sent to that little strip of western Kentucky, bordered by the Ohio, Tennessee and Mississippi rivers, that comprised the Paducah district, was much like being sent to the mountains in the Western North Carolina conference. The ministers felt as if they'd been banished to Siberia.

But Bill knew what he was doing. Wright had the knowledge and skill to pull it together. [Through my years of experience in the Methodist church, I've often said, "It will never really fulfill its mission until salaries are equalized and ministers are appointed to the places where their gifts meet the needs instead of where salary brings them status!"]

That year, on the door at my house in Grand Rivers, I kept finding "Kilroy was here" notes, signed by Wright and Fred. Finally we were able to get together at a leisure ministries conference at Lake of the Ozarks in Missouri. They wanted me to join them as a Church and Community worker in the parish venture. I knew at once I wanted to work with these guys, and I was able to persuade my executive, Ralph Nichols (in New York), to change my appointment in the middle of the appointment year. He did so, and I moved across Kentucky Lake to Aurora, Kentucky, the first of June, 1972.

Wright was a superb organizer, and able to inspire people to do things they didn't know they could do. He told me, "Don't ever make the mistake of *asking* for volunteers. You might get the wrong person for the task. First decide who can do the job, and then *you* ask *them*." He was talented and creative — a perfectionist, and one who needed to plan well in advance. He once told me, "Jo (his wife) drives me up a wall when we plan a trip and then the day before I can't see her getting ready. I'm fit to be tied." But he'd then admit that she always had it all together when the time came to leave. With four little children, she knew how to prioritize her tasks, and she still does — for eighteen years Jo has been the coordinator of Risk Management at St. Francis Hospital in Memphis, and during the same eighteen years she saw her children through their turbulent teens and into responsible adulthood. Now her influence will be brought to bear on her six grandchildren.

If a job didn't involve a challenge, Wright didn't want to do it. And the Lakeland parish was one he met head-on. A large building was purchased on Highway 68 with office space, utility kitchen, dining and meeting space for churchwide events. The arts and crafts room was used for such activities as oil painting and rug-hooking (the hard kind where they cut and dye wool from used clothing and develop their own designs). Nova Lee Blackie was the first teacher there. Thelma "Ted" Hardin still carries on.(I took notes in painting class and have since painted about thirty pictures — only one of which was actually done in class. I knew I'd never be a great artist because I couldn't stand having a teacher looking over my shoulder.

Most of the paintings have been given to family and friends — four are hanging in my apartment.) Another room in the building was designed for pottery and ceramics, and still another for a book and craft/gift shop. College students were hired as interns during the summer. [One of them, Sandy Bryan, was profiled in the Younger Friends article, earlier in this book.] One summer they formed a singing group that sang in the campgrounds and they also held a coffee-house ministry in the office building of the old Angle Motel, next to my mobile home in Aurora. Parish children were brought together for Bible school, day camp, and membership training — especially with the four smaller churches: Briensburg, Mt. Carmel, Maple Spring and Union Ridge. The youth were used in many ways: as summer interns, to teach the children, and to help with worship in the campgrounds.

One of the first interns was my niece, Susan Hilleary. Barry Sirls served two, or perhaps three, years there as a summer intern. He later trained for the ministry and served churches in the Memphis conference. When he was the associate minister at South Pleasant Grove, he went out on a limb and asked a *woman* (me) to do the closing night service of Holy Week. He later served as youth director of the largest church in the Paducah district (Broadway). His next appointment was with a church of his own in Tennessee.

While in Tennessee, he came to a realization about his own preferences, which required a complete reorientation of his life. He gave up his ministerial credentials and separated from his family. Barry had grown up in the Maple Spring church in the parish. He met Jerri Lake, also a parish intern, and I was the first to know of their engagement. I went to her home church in Illinois for their wedding and took pictures, and I also took some photos later of their first child. Having had no information about what had happened to Barry, I kept writing to ask for some word of him. I guess the word got to his mother because when he was visiting her this summer, he called me in August of 1993. He told me little about his life except that he lived in Florida, had a challenging job, and was happy. I said to him, "I love you Barry. I wish you would come by to see me." Those of us who love him are still searching for answers to our questions — how and why he gave up so much. I need him to help me understand.

Since this lakes area had many retirees, my main responsibility was with the elderly. Wright and I met with a small committee that tried to interest seniors in organizing. After four months with no response, Wright said, "We'll not waste any more time with Marshall County. We have so many older people in our parish churches, you organize them." A meeting was called, and they accepted my suggested name: Zesta Club. After publicity about our trips, etc., in the county paper, the other seniors got aroused from their lethargy. I was called by the members of the original committee to come to an organizing meeting of the Marshall County Advisory Committee on Aging in 1973. I was elected secretary, and served until I retired (for the second time) in 1985. During those years, senior centers were established in Calvert City, Benton and Hardin, and transportation was provided. At the time it was acknowledged as the most successful senior program in the state of Kentucky.

I served on two committees in the Memphis conference; Wright, because of his expertise in so many areas, must have served on three or four. It seemed to me he was going to Jackson, Tennessee, about every week for a meeting — a round trip journey of over two hundred miles. And he *always* came back with aggravated psoriasis. I finally said, "I wish you would *quit* going to Jackson." Perhaps he needed to hear it from someone, because after I said that he told the council, "I will come only once a month — *you* decide where I'll be of most help." He continued to serve diligently, and after a couple of years in the parish, ministers in the conference were saying to me, "What have you done with Wright up there in Kentucky? He's so much calmer and easy to get along with." I think we did have a good influence on him; but of course Fred French was *so calm* and *agreeable* that it often worked adversely on Wright.

The Lakeland Parish staff also had an influence on a Nazarene minister, Rick Dye, in Benton. He left his church and asked for admission to the Memphis conference. I doubt it was because of any of the minister trying to persuade him to make the change; I certainly didn't do that. I met him when the Zesta Club hired him to drive our bus on a trip to Nashville, ate lunch with him, and was most favorably impressed with the wisdom and deep commitment of this young man. When I heard of his plan to change denominations, I wanted to know why. The Methodist Church gave him room to think for himself, he told me, and he liked the way he saw the parish staff ministering to the needs of the people. And because the Nazarene church is an offshoot of the Methodist church, the organizational structure was familiar to him. (My daughter Paula has found a very caring church home in a Nazarene congregation in Portland, Oregon.)

The parish ministers and I decided we would try to make at least a small crack in the wall of black prejudice around Marshall County. We invited the dynamic young black minister, William W. Morris, to speak to the fifth Sunday service of the parish churches at Calvert City. He was enthusiastically received! Now they should remember with pride that he preached there (like "George Washington slept here"). Rev. Morris later served as a district superintendent and a Tennessee conference council director. I worked with him in a conference he directed for small membership churches at Lake Junaluska. He served the all-white church membership of over a thousand at Gallatin, Tennessee, with great distinction and is now a bishop in the Southeastern Jurisdiction with headquarters in Montgomery, Alabama.[1]

Since that experience at Calvert City went fine, Wright and I decided we would invite Manuel Easley, a dear elderly black man I had met when I directed a conference camp for mentally handicapped adults, for some evangelistic services. He was a counselor, and Wright knew him as a conference minister. The poor man was scared to come to Marshall County, but he said, "I knew you and Wright would protect me." He held Sunday through Wednesday night services and the people loved him!

Preaching was not Wright's forte, but his sermons were always informative. He was first and foremost a teacher, and an enabler. We worked together in harmony for the five years he served in the parish. I did note, though, mostly from his conversations, that in general he did not hold women in very high esteem; so I decided he was at least a borderline male chauvinist. With that in mind, I was most apprehensive when, near the end of the five years, the New York office decided that all Church and Community workers should be evaluated by the director and a lay person in the project where they served. They sent the evaluation sheet, with, I think, twenty areas to be rated from one to five. I made a copy of it and asked Thelma "Ted" Hardin to rate me and not to spare my feelings. Then I rated myself, probably more as I thought Wright would. I was so aware of what I considered his superior abilities in comparison to my own that I rated myself low (even though I had always had confidence in myself). Wright and Kermit Ellenberger had to do the evaluation in my presence with some input from me.

I was so astounded at the final results that I put Wright's figures beside mine and Ted's, and have kept that piece of paper all these years, but it's one more thing that's is "somewhere safe" that I can't find after looking "everywhere". (I can think of three memorable instances when an item *was* found after looking "everywhere": (1) my car keys in an extra pair of shoes I'd carried from the car, (2) my billfold behind the typewriter that was closed-up in my desk's pull-out shelf, and (3) my checkbook with my paid bills in the lower part of my desk. Throughout my whole life losing things that are "nowhere" has been the source of my greatest frustration!) Since I can't give the actual figures, suffice it to say that Wright's rating came out far ahead of either Ted's or mine, and right there I missed my last best chance of being discriminated against as a woman in the workplace!

I have said that spending the last thirteen years of my thirty-two years serving with the Methodist church in the Memphis conference was like icing on the cake. From involvement in the Conference council, camps and the Lakeland parish, and later with my managing the Lakeland Wesley Village, I knew most of the VIPs. (In my 1993 *Memphis Conference Journal* I have starred 147 ministers whose appointments I am still interested in knowing.)

I served a three-year term on the Core Leadership Team of CCW (CLT), the last year as chairperson. I was elected as a lay delegate to the Southeastern Jurisdiction conference at Lake Junaluska in 1980. It was the year to elect bishops. I dutifully voted for our candidate, William P. Bailey. (Secretly I was glad Bill didn't get it. I have often thought it's using poor judgment to elect our most effective ministers to the post. Bill Morris is another case in point. But I *do* hold them in high regard because I know it is because of their outstanding service that they have been elected.)

Also in 1980 I went to General Conference to help our United Methodist Rural Fellowship get their agenda through the legislative process. I had just received a citation for my eight years as treasurer of UMRF. It was presented at Memphis annual conference held in Paducah, and I received a spontaneous standing ovation. I also helped to get a UMRF chapter started in the Memphis conference. The United Methodist Women dedicated their 1980 yearbook to me. That was the year I formally retired from the National Division of the Board of Global Missions.

I think it is evident why this was a high note to retire on. I had experienced many of the changes the denomination had gone through: Rural Worker to Church and Community Worker; Women's Missionary Society to Women's Society of Christian Service and the Wesleyan Service Guild to the present UMW; Union of Methodist Episcopal Church (1939), M.E. Church South, and Methodist Protestant Church to form the Methodist Church in 1939,

The Union of Evangelical United Brethren and Methodist Church in 1968 to form the present-day United Methodist Church.

[As mentioned earlier in this book, I did stay after this retirement to recruit residents for the Lakeland Wesley Village then under construction, and ended up serving as resident manager of the ninety-six apartment complex from July 1981 until May 1985, when I retired for the second, and last, time.]

NOTES

1. "A Black Pastor in a White Church: a Success Story," in *Circuit Rider: A Journal for United Methodist Ministers* (February, 1994).

The Arle and Tillie Brooks Album I

Arle and ←Tillie 6-49

Dena and doll ↓

Lucille with girls ↘ about 1955

↗ Emma and girls - Gertrude's steps P.___

Mabel K. ← Howell and Paula

Tillie's Older Girls I
Paula

graduation dress mom made - log house 1963 ↓

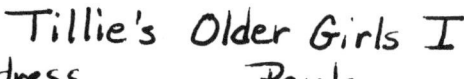

with Warren Vickers at Mom's Styles apt. dressed for class reunion. ↓ 9-2-89

"Glamour" shot ← 10-27-92

with Harold Haley in her apt. on her birthday 8-28-92 ↓

with Jack Kincaid at Hazel's apt. San Marcos, Tx. ↓

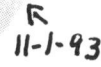 11-1-93

"Tillie's Older Girls II
Marla

Glamour Shot 2-1993

With first "real" boyfriend Gene Roberts

Halloween at Dr. McCalls D.D.S., Mary Bailey, Forrest and Marla

With friend Billy "Bo" Hoyle 1986

early morning storytime with grandson Jeremy - spring '93

Tillie's Older Girls III
Dena

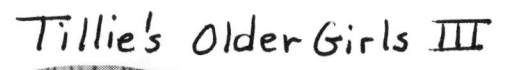

Modeling at American Legion CA → 1992

↗ By Oak Tree at log house 5-61

Mom, Paula, Dena and ← Ed Langowski

May 1978

Peter, Ed and Dena Langowski 4-5-89 →

Irene Stubbe, Dena and Rhoda Civils Irene's apt. Hawthorne, ← CA. 9-4-92

Brooks '92–'93 Reunions

Elva, Hazel, Tillie and Mabel – 7-6-92 my apt.

Brooks daughters – San Marcos, Tx. in front of Elva and Hazel's apt. 10-31-93

Marla, Tillie, Dena and Emi- Higgins mumc 2-11-90

Elva, Tillie and Hazel 10-31-93

Jewel Kincaid

Section III
ARLE BROOKS

BIOGRAPHY OF ERNEST ARLE BROOKS

There is a sense in which one cannot separate the two of us, Arle and me. Arle has been present in much of what I have written, and many aspects of his story have already been told, but this will be an attempt to get deeper insight into the spirit of this man who, in his short forty-four years, has touched the lives of so many — even as he did mine.

It has not been easy to write this portion of my narrative. I suppose that is why it has been left until last. The story will be told with quotations from Arle's letters to me, from his book, *We the Offenders*,[1] an essay of his entitled "Tomorrow is Now," the book published by the American Friends Service Committee entitled *United States of America vs. Arle Brooks*,[2] and from letters written by friends after his death.

Arle was born near Grimes, Oklahoma. His father was Ernest Brooks, of probably mostly English extraction (March 28, 1878 – January 18, 1957). Arle's mother was Mary Wilson (July 7, 1879 – June 24, 1972). Her ancestors were Norwegian/German, and their name was probably changed from Oleson to Wilson when they arrived in this country. Arle's sisters were Elva Marie Brooks Stringer (January 26, 1906 –) and Hazel Lee Brooks Rose, (August 18, 1907 –). The one son was Arle, whose life span was August 28, 1909 to July 6, 1953.

Ernest Brooks had gone with his brother to stake out a homestead in Oklahoma before it became a state. Elva was born while their home was a dug-out, partially under ground. Arle was born after Oklahoma became a state in 1907.

The family returned to Texas in 1910, and Ernest cleared land in South Texas for cotton farming. There were no schools available, so Mary taught the three children at home. In 1915 the family moved to Stockdale where Ernest was overseer for a seven hundred acre cotton farm. In 1920 they moved to San Marcos, and the children entered school — Elva, third grade; Hazel, second; and Arle, first. This was the "Home Place" until Mary sold it around

1971, and divided the proceeds with the three children. (I got a fourth of Arle's share.) The original Brooks house was moved up the road. The girls and I rode by it in November, 1993, when we visited Elva and Hazel in San Marcos.

I met Arle at Scarritt College in March of 1940 when he was recruiting for American Friends Service Committee (AFSC) work camps. Constance Rumbough, who lived in Nashville, came with him. I was called because I was president of the student body, but Arle didn't ask me to arrange for a meeting so he could speak to the students.

I had a letter soon after the visit, that read: "Dear A??? Hilleary . . . Unofficially I would enjoy hearing from you, at least to the extent of knowing how you spell your first name, so I could tell the office about the great person I found at Scarritt — but who may decide against going to our camps."[3]

I had told Arle I would not go to a camp that summer because I had not been home for two years — having worked at a school for children from broken homes between my two years at Scarritt. He gave me his family's address in San Marcos, TX. I *did* write to him.

Arle replied: "Dear Arthelia, Thee [Arle usually used thee and thou — the old Quaker custom] *did* write, didn't thee? [I had asked for some information about him.] . . . You asked for it — I was born in Oklahoma around 30 years ago (hope that will not frighten thee away). Moved to Texas when I was two. Lived on a ranch until I was twelve. Moved to our present place in 1920. Finished high school 1927, attended one year college here (Teachers' College in San Marcos). Went to business college in San Antonio. Completed the course and worked two years for a loan company (loan sharks). The depression relieved me of my job. Went to Texas Christian University, finished in 1935. I attended Chicago University and Chicago Theological Seminary at the same time (1935–1936.) This past fall I was at Pendle Hill [a Quaker school]. That's all my formal education. But I've learned more outside of school than within . . . [Arle was ordained a Disciples of Christ minister.]

"I worked two years (while at T.C.U.) full time, as Intake Supervisor, Texas Transient Bureau; one summer with Daily Vacation School in Wyoming. I worked with Boys Clubs, Chicago West Side (slums) while in Chicago; one year as a Visiting Supervisor, Texas Relief Commission; one year Sr. Assistant, Bureau of Classification, Texas Prison System; 1½ years at Delta Cooperative Farm [a Sherwood Eddy project in Mississippi] where the work was educational, recreational and religious. [He served as the pastor of the group.]

"That's all there is except my dreams. . . . Most of my work has been in the form of social service. . . .

"While studying in Chicago, I became interested in cooperatives. I tried to get poor people who were denied medical care to organize a medical cooperative. The State Medical Association heard of it and put pressure on my boss, the state director . . . to either give up the cooperative [idea] or my job. Stubborn as I am, I gave up my job, took a vacation, then started work at the prison."[4]

Arle left the prison work to go to Delta Cooperative Farm, where he stayed for one and a half years — "until asked to leave because I and three other staff [members] felt the democracy of the farm was being threatened . . . by the dictatorial policy of the director.

"I am enjoying my work with the Service Committee [but] I feel the need for roots in a community where I could grow . . . and help people as a citizen of the community. Perhaps Constance has told you of her plan to buy a farm in southern Mississippi and to allow me to live on it.

"I must confess I have thought of thee too much since I first and last saw thee. A very foolish thing to do, I suppose, but after all thee seemed to be a most wonderful person."[5]

"It was so grand seeing you and being with you and [I] must admit that all the visit was nicer than I dared hope for. You are a very nice person, you know. It seems so much longer than one week since I was with you. Last Sunday about this time we were at Madison College drinking soy milk. 'Scuse me for mentioning it, but a little *chocolate* changes everything."[6]

Constance had us to dinner that night, and Arle became ill during the meal. We thought it was probably the soy milk. (It may have been the beginning of his [fatal] illness.) Arle seemed to recover soon that evening and walked with me to the home where Helen Gage was house-sitting. Since it was a little unusual for Scarritt women to be dating, she was of course curious to meet Arle. She came to the living room in her dressing gown, and they *both* sat there. I looked at my watch a couple of times — and perhaps yawned, but no one moved. Finally I said, "I don't know about you two, but I think it is bedtime for me." Helen excused herself and left, and Arle proposed marriage to me. I refused — the main reason was my promise to the women of the West Virginia conference that I would work at least four years to repay my two-year scholarship to Scarritt. Arle and I agreed that we'd be friends — no strings attached — and if we were both single at the end of four years we could discuss the proposition again.

My first appointment was to Roderfield, West Virginia, a mining town in the Bluefield (West Virginia) District. I wrote to Arle about the circumstances, including that Myrta Davis and I would be furnished a new Ford car. Arle replied, "It is unfortunate that you will have a new car which will certainly not help you in working with the miners or the less fortunate. Too often religion has been or still is closely tied with new cars, large churches, etc. You will do a good job in spite of it, but it is an unfortunate handicap."[7]

During the summer of 1940, before I started work in September, I was with my family in West Virginia from July 24 until July 26. Then, we from the Methodist Episcopal (M.E.) Church, South, were taken to Chicago to be consecrated along with the home and foreign missionaries from the other uniting (1939) Methodist churches. Arle was also in the area, and we visited in the hotel and had an evening in the park on Lake Michigan. It was *so hot* that I didn't tell him I was staying over a few days with Uncle John and Emily, even though I knew he could see me if he knew.

It was August, 1940. War was already going on in Europe, and our Congress was considering conscription. Arle wrote, "Don't forget to write your congressman that you want him to oppose the conscription bill."[8] Then, a little later, he wrote, "The radio just announced the passage of the Peacetime Draft Bill for all males between 21 and 35 which catches me . . .

"Several of us have been thinking of starting a co-op house. . . . We are looking for a large, vacant house with some land around it so that we can exploit the soil for a little food."[9] And then, soon after: "We have found a large house (seven bedrooms) which will house at least twelve people. Rent is $35 a month. Of course coal, gas, lights, and water [must be added.]"[10]

Most of those who lived at the house were pacifists.

In the September fourteenth letter Arle continued, "We will all be caught in the draft. . . . When the time comes, we will take different stands. My own stand — in case you are interested — will be not to register. . . . It is perhaps less understood than other positions which will be taken. I take this stand for several reasons: (1) to have as little to do with the whole affair as possible. I realize that during the past year I have indirectly supported war armaments. I have, however, written and spoken against money being spent for armaments. (2) I question the right of the state to conscript people for any purpose, especially for destructive purposes. (3) I believe that the conscription will hinder the growth of democracy here. (4) My objection to . . . war and violence goes back to my belief that love is the way of life. . . . I want to be free to continue the work which I think is most important.

"Fortunately you do not have to decide . . . but I trust thee will understand my position. I like thee most of all the thees I know."[11]

"Last week I met two men from the Brüderhof in England. They were intelligent men, believers in simple living. Their purpose was to find a new home for their group of three hundred which will have to leave England shortly. Canada refused them entrance; America will not welcome them because they are pacifists and will not sign an oath to defend the country. Paraguay sold them a thousand acres of land for fifty cents an acre. . . . After they reach the port of Paraguay, they will have a thousand miles of land to cross. These two men wore beards, plain clothes. . . . There was a sparkle in their eyes and something about them which told one that these were not fools, only to the extent that they took the sayings of Jesus seriously. This community is open to everyone."[12] (Our friends, Jim and Kore McWhirter were at one time members.)

"I've just discovered that my trial will not come up until January 6. I'm leaving tonight for home in Texas. I can stay only a few days, but it will be worth it to me and to my folks."[13]

The Peace Section of AFSC printed a booklet: *United States of America vs. Arle Brooks- In the District Court of the United States for the Eastern District of Pennsylvania, before Hon. George A. Welsh, Judge.* — *Friday, Jan. 10, 1941: Edward A. Kallick, Esq. for the government; Walter C. Longstreth, Esq. for Arle Brooks.*

> *Judge Welsh:* "I would be very glad, and I am sure others would be glad to hear the reasons that have motivated you in the stand you have taken. I want you to feel free to express yourself in your own way and tell us exactly how you feel about it, if you will, please."
>
> *Arle:* "Yes. I appreciate your sympathetic consideration. My conscience forbade me to register under the Selective Service Training Act of 1940.
>
> "The present wars are the natural product of our economic system and way of living. Preparation for war is easier than going through the painful process of reconstructing our social and economic system and improving our own way of living.
>
> "Wars destroy human lives. Individuals have the right to give their lives for a cause. They have no right to take

the life of another. Wars are futile, destructive, and immoral. Wars have failed to solve the basic problems of the world. Participation in war to settle international and national differences does not do justice to man's intelligence.

"The people of America are filled with fear of an invasion. Are we so morally weak that the power of one man could control one hundred and thirty million free people? Free people cannot be enslaved unless they will it. Are we too lethargic to find a better method for solving international affairs? The people of India have almost won their freedom from Great Britain without firing a shot. They have been willing to give their lives, but have refused to take the lives of the British soldiers.

"Democracy does not mean a blind following of the will of the majority. In a democracy the minority has a right and a duty to follow its ideals. Sometimes the ideals of the minority have eventually been adopted by the majority. Gandhi said, 'We are sunk so low that we fancy that it is our duty and our religion to do what the law lays down.' If man will only realize that it is unmanly to obey an unjust law, no man's tyranny will enslave him . . . It is a superstition and an ungodly thing to believe that an act of a majority binds a minority.

"I believe and have worked for the brotherhood of man which is the highest form of democracy. I have worked with children of the slums in Chicago. I have worked with transients, with relief people and prisoners in the State of Texas, and with sharecroppers in Mississippi.

"Conscription is a denial of the democracy for which I have worked. Under conscription the individual is required blindly to obey his superior officer, even [if] his superior officer is wrong. Hitler could not have waged his wars if the people of Germany had not granted him the power to enslave them. The United States is adopting a system of conscription which may produce tyranny instead of freedom.

"I cannot agree with those who believe that registration is a mere census. Registration is the first and necessary step for conscription. My conscience will not permit me to take that first step.

"As a minister I could have received complete exemption. I felt it my moral duty to do all within my power to protest against conscription which will eventually weaken and destroy democracy. I am not evading the draft. I am opposing it. I am defending democracy.

"Thank you. . . ."

Mr. Longstreth: "Your Honor, Arle was born in Oklahoma in 1909, and his father and his grandfather and his great-grandfather were American citizens.

"At the age of 16 he joined the Christian Church, which is sometimes called the Disciples of Christ. . . .

"And as he has told you, in 1935 he went to Chicago and studied at Chicago Theological Seminary, where he helped to organize the first cooperative dining hall. And as his field work, he worked with the Italian children in the Chicago West Side, which was one of the worst sections of Chicago.

"And then in 1936 he went with the Texas Relief Commission, and he was Visiting Supervisor, having supervision of the case workers in twelve counties in Western Texas.

"In 1937 he was employed by the Texas Prison System as the Senior Assistant in the Bureau of Classification of Prisoners. And the following year he went to the Delta Cooperative Farm in Rhodale, Mississippi, which was organized by Sherwood Eddy for the relief of dispossessed sharecroppers, and he worked there for fifteen months conducting religious services and educational classes, recreational activities, and summer outing camps for boys; he ran the farm newspaper, and he worked in the cooperative store there. And he received no salary during those fifteen months except fifteen cents an hour while he was working at the cooperative store. And in order to live he spent the savings that he had saved up previously and the proceeds from the sale of his automobile because he wanted to render service to his fellow man.

"Then he entered Pendle Hill in the fall of 1939, which is a Quaker school for social and religious study, and as he told you, since February of 1940, he has been working for the American Friends Service Committee.

"Now, Arle is not a draft dodger. He wrote a letter which was received by the Draft Board on the day of registration which set forth his age, his address, and his name and why he could not register. And this Draft Act gave him a choice of either registering or being punished for not registering. And he has elected that latter alternative as a protest against a statute which he feels is evil.

"Arle Brooks has never injured any fellow man, his sole crime is that he is unwilling to enroll himself among those who may be called upon to learn to kill their fellow man. . . .

"Men are won to higher ideals by seeing idealists willing to suffer for their ideal. . . .

"Now, future generations will gauge the degree of civilization that we today have attained, according to the tolerance that we show men that differ from us. . . ."

The Court: "Well, Arle, I know that you have thought over this subject for some time. I am convinced that your action here is not precipitous, and you must in the quiet solitude of your own closet have tried to wrestle with the question as to what you should do. Feeling as you do, that, of course, was a real battle, because a conscientious man — and I believe you to be entirely conscientious — would be torn in a situation of this kind between two loyalties: the loyalty to the Supreme Being that you have been trying to serve for a number of years in a very active, practical way, and loyalty to the Government that gives you physical protection and opportunity even to exercise your right of conscience. . . .

"But America is not normal today, and you must be charitable with the rest of us. Now, here is where you have got to exercise your charity. Those ideals that you have expressed are more deep-rooted in our people than you think. I believe countless millions in the United States feel just as you feel. And I believe right in this court room with this mixed audience we are all of one mind. I think right in the very hearts of all of us here, we are in complete harmony with your objective. And I am not here to pay any compliments or throw any bouquets. *I am going to sentence you; it is hard for me to do it, but it is my duty, and I feel like Pontius Pilate. I have got to obey the law, and that law commands me, and I would obey it if it meant my life.* . . .

"As I said the other day, you cannot, and ought not to argue with a brother man on a matter of conscience. This is your conscience, and it is your duty to obey it, even if it brings physical pain or death, when it comes to a real matter of conscience. . . . and I am going to give you a year and day."[14]

Walter and Emily Longstreth were important in both of our lives. Emily has been mentioned before — and will be again. Walter was the proverbial "Philadelphia lawyer." They lived in an apartment hotel and had no children. Arle was like a son to them. They were two City-of-Brotherly-Love Quakers, who "set out to do good and did well," but they lived *very* simply. When Emily died in 1965, she was a millionaire, but the list of recipients in her will shows how extensive her caring and desire to do good was. I was on that list, along with the Philadelphia Yearly Meeting of Friends, Swarthmore College, AFSC, and several other beneficiaries.

Arle was sent to a new Federal prison in Danbury, Connecticut, along with several other COs.

Charles R. Swift, M.D., who was with Arle the whole time he was at Danbury, wrote: "Arle impressed me as a man of rock-like strength whose conviction, and action growing out of it, would never be shaken. . . . His calm, poise, and quiet reserve (which some mistook for aloofness) attracted men to him — never in droves, but singly or in pairs. Often these were men with a problem to talk over — something had gone wrong at home, and what could they do, or how could they change their work assignment. I remember that Arle patiently wrote letters [for one CO], dictated by an illiterate man.

"Arle suffered more than many of the COs did. Part of this was because he was less gregarious and had fewer social outlets; and part was that he had only the crudest privacy for his reading, reflection, and meditation, but part was due to his sense of his freedom really being taken from him. Arle was never a 'company man' — not that he shirked work either — but he saw little use to strain himself in executing labors [which had no meaning] contrived to 'keep us busy.'"[15]

Charles has described Arle pretty accurately. Arle had written to me about how unhappy he was at Danbury most of the time. He was especially uncomfortable with the activities of the other COs.

Since they were a pretty large group, they went on a hunger strike to get their way. Arle did not like *group pressure*! He felt their actions were often inconsiderate and unloving. I shared his feelings. I remember a time when Scarritt students rode the streetcar to Percy Warner Park several miles out of Nashville, for an evening picnic. The group *took over* with their singing. They did not ask the weary home-going commuters if they'd enjoy being sung to. I managed to take an earlier ride back to the city to avoid being embarrassed.

So neither Arle nor I would feel comfortable in any kind of a public demonstration, even though I may applaud those who feel constrained to do so — certainly those who use nonviolent resistance. I am more in tune with the way the Quaker AFSC has used this nonviolent resistance through several wars and other controversies. I think that, today, RSVP (Rural Southern Voice for Peace) uses the same tactics — listening, understanding, and seeking ways to resolve the conflict without taking sides. The Carter Center in Atlanta and Habitat for Humanity also receive my commendation and financial support, along with Farmland Trust (trying to keep the soil from being paved over) and the many Nature Conservancy groups. I think those are all causes Arle would care about.

My first letter from Danbury did not come until June, 1941, five months after Arle left for prison. "My Dear Tillie," he greeted me. (I don't know how he learned my nickname, but from that time I was Tillie.) The letter said, "I have not forgotten thee, I couldn't. I can write only two letters a week. One usually goes home . . . the other . . . to Naomi Binford at the office [AFSC]. I always remember thy strong convictions, thy dreams and thy strength. . . . How glibly we Christians repeat . . . phrases, which because of lack of testing mean so little. How often have we said, 'Resist not evil, love your enemies, bless them that curse you, do good to them that hate you, and pray for them that despitefully use you.'. . . We have thought of them as sermon material. . . . We cannot love a person and kill him at the same time. Our failure to use non-violence is due partly to the fact that Christians have not sought 'the Kingdom' first but possessions first. It then becomes necessary to defend [the possessions], which to them were more valuable than human lives."[16]

Arle gives his thoughts about war — ". . . we must see the failure of past wars to settle basic problems. . . . Surely if wars were the best possible means of solving our differences we would have reached a higher state of peace after centuries and centuries of warfare. . . . A new method *must* be found. Wars are too destructive, too expensive, and too inhumane to remain the way of settling our differences. . . . People must realize that they can be free, that no tyrant can enslave them unless they will it. . . . Wars are the inevitable product of our present social and economic system. . . . To a certain extent we have to live within and support the system that produces poverty, unemployment and wars. . . . But this we can do: simplify our living (functional poverty), small scale production and small, self-supporting communities, . . . and the only true progress of civilization is that of love, the progress of man and his relations to his neighbors . . . with complete sharing and absorption in the spirit of love — possible through hours of meditation and contemplation."[17]

Arle was paroled to a CPS (Civilian Public Service) camp at Relay, Maryland. His next letter was in July, 1941, "I received my registration card. The warden at Danbury signed my card. I shall send it back to the Selective Service Administration. I do not consider myself registered."[18]

"Life at camp goes on. I am on kitchen duty this week. . . . It will be a long time before we have a peaceful world. People are too concerned about the fullness of their own stomachs to be greatly concerned about building a peaceful world. . . . You would be amazed how we pacifists fuss about the kind and amount of food. We want heavy meals, snacks and drinks between meals. Hours are spent in preparing food so that it will satisfy their sensitive tastes. . . . Before pacifism goes very far we must solve our stomach problems.

"Thee asked about Naomi. . . . We worked together in the Work Camp Section of the Service Committee, but did not know each other very well until late in the fall of last year. I knew that I would not be around so we were silent about our feelings . . . and nothing was said until her first visit to Danbury. Across the wide table we decided to venture out together. . . . We would like to rent or buy a farm and make our living on it. . . . We want to go into a farming community and work and live and do our best to be good neighbors. . . . We hope that other couples will join us and we can be a cell of peace. . . . Constance is on the trail of a farm in Mississippi."[19] I wrote and congratulated them.

Typical of Arle, he did not stop writing to me. His September letter said, "If all goes well, Naomi, Larry Kirkpatrick . . . and I will leave here Saturday, the 27th, to visit Celo, North Carolina. . . . We have been asked to be members of Celo Community. . . . Joseph Lippincott and wife Eleanor are the directors."[20]

"[I] bought a Model A Ford coupe which we hope to turn into a small pick-up, large enough to carry my belongings South with me. It is a wonderful little buggy, a 1930 model with a good motor, all for $40. I'm not sure that even this fits into functional poverty, but I haven't enough imagination to see how I could get started without some kind of transportation . . . since the farm (in Mississippi) is 16 miles from the nearest town."*

"Sturge Steiner, who was in Danbury with me, will be released from camp on the 21st. He plans to get married on that day, and he and his wife, Blossom, will go south with me and stay for a couple or three months.

"I have not told thee . . . but recently Naomi has decided to stay on with the Service Committee. . . . She believes in everything I want to do, but as time drew near for her to change jobs, emotionally she could not do it. I wish that I could make the necessary shift in . . . my plans so that the two of us could work together, but I can't, no more than she can go south. . . . I am very sorry and sometimes wish that I did not have such foolish dreams.

"I heard E. Stanley Jones the other evening in Baltimore. He was very good. Let us work and pray for peace."[21]

"I can't imagine thee with chicken-pox — not at thy age. Of course I don't mean that thee is old, but chicken-pox does belong to the children. Maybe thee has 'become as a little child.'

"Constance has informed me that she may be able to get the farm for $3,000 instead of $3,300. . . . Sturge and Blossom do not feel as I do about shaking ourselves loose from all but essentials . . . [but] it is good to know that they will be along.

"When thee goes to Philadelphia please stay at the Brudercoop. They would love to have thee."[22]

I did stay there and enjoyed meeting the people, especially Naomi.

"Would thee believe that I am taking a short course of six weeks . . . at Kimberton Farms Agricultural School. . . . This is the only school in the country that teaches Bio-Dynamic Farming. . . . We must keep the soil alive and feed the micro-organisms in the soil. . . . The best soil is humus soil. . . . We are learning how to . . . maintain the humus . . . through the use of compost, manure, rotation of crops and aeration of the soil. It is really very wonderful! . . .

"Arthur Morgan, ex-president of Antioch College and chairman of TVA . . . will be at Pendle Hill on the 28th. I want to have a long chat with him, if possible, about community development.

"I hope to arrive at the farm about January 20. . . . There are one main building and four tenant houses and a good barn. . . . I hope one of the tenants will stay next year. He has his own teams and tools. I hope we can rent at least 100 [of the 300] acres to him.

"Farming has become an industry and not a way of life as it should be. . . . I think people should live in small, non-acquisitive communities near the soil, and that life should be simple and creative . . . where our children can grow up knowing some skills for their hands to do and love toward others.

"A mere dream, of course."[23]

I think this has been the philosophy at work in Arthur Morgan School at Celo, North Carolina.

"I arrived at the farm February 10. . . . Life is very simple here, and I like it. It helps my spirit. . . . After finishing the tasks for the day, I cook my one food in a pot over the fire in the fireplace. When the food is ready, I sit in front of the fire with cup and spoon and enjoy the food and the spirit which seems to come from so little thought and bother of getting and serving food. When the cat has had his fill, he curls up on the hearth and we find peace, but *not* loneliness for I know that out there somewhere are all of you, and the Divine in us all brings us together, and distances are nothing."[24]

"I now have my stove up and am ready to try it out . . . I think I shall try out my little hand grist mill I got from Sears . . . see how well Brooks can cook a small batch of cornbread . . . People around here use nothing but white flour and white bread, and I just can't go it.

"I only wish there were many more who felt as I do about the soil and communal living. . . . I laugh sometimes to think of my dream of such a community when in contrast I am living alone with a cat. I now have a banty hen and rooster given to me by a neighbor; [and] two pigs and a mule."[25]

"I'm glad thee is a convention-going Methodist. Three of the four times I have seen thee have been at conventions . . .always in the cities. . . . Thee kinda seems to belong to the hills. . . . Thee still has two more years to work with the church, doesn't thee? I better not wait that long, or I'll be too old to be appreciated.

"There is something real about being so close to the good earth, and I believe man was meant to sweat and toil, to be burned by the summer sun and chilled by the winter wind. Because I love this life so much does not mean I have forgotten those who live in the slums . . . or those who die in useless battle.

"What are thy plans? . . . There is too much joy here for one. I would like for someone to join me. I wish that we knew each other better. There was a time that I knew thee, but time has blurred thee, and then we have not discussed so many things which may matter later. And of course thee may not be at all interested in coming. . . . *Out of the many girls I know there seems to be about two who have the spirit and who may consider such a life*. . . . I was just wondering if thee had ever vaguely thought of coming farther south.

"P.S. Perhaps the above is a little unfair to ask since I do not know my own mind in the matter. But I have thought of thee often and wondered what thy thoughts were of me."[26]

I suppose I was a little unfair to him, and if I had known what later letters revealed, I would have understood; but at the time it seemed quite unflattering to have a vague proposal of marriage as one of *two* prospects. I wrote and told him so. He told me later that my letter was brought to him in the field. He read it and said, "Well, I'll mark *her* off my list!"

He told about the church service he attended, didn't say which. "I am convinced that you can teach a child to believe almost anything, and if that child is kept within that teaching he will reject all truths and hold to that which he was taught.

"Thy last letter certainly marked me as a cold, calculating individual without warmth or understanding of the feelings of another. I would like to marry and have a family, but I know that no woman will ever be my first love, the fulfillment of my dreams. My first calling will always be this search for reality and the building of a community. And should a person ever join me, she will have to be free from the need of too much attention. She must be a seeker after truth so together we can wander through the wilderness. I have so much to learn, so much to discover, so much to master in my own self. I would welcome another to go along with me. She will never be the Good, Love, and Beautiful, but only a partner in the search for them. Until one comes along, I will struggle along alone.

"I think of thee often there with coal dust on people's faces and problems in their souls."[27]

At least I was *not* marked off his list!

Authorities heard Arle was not carrying his draft card. "As matters now stand, I come up for trial in November term of Federal Court in Jackson. The case may be dropped, but it may not. The District Attorney said he saw nothing to keep me out of the penitentiary, and he meant it. He was a good old man, member of the Baptist church. Too bad he isn't a Methodist. I understand they are the salt of the earth."[28]

Arle took the opportunity to go home to see his family and several friends. In his next letter he wrote, "On my way back I stopped at Jackson, and Monday morning I called the District Attorney. I told him that I was on my way to the farm. He told me to go ahead, and they would come after me whenever they wanted me. . . . He did not seem to be in any rush. It may be that they will drop it, or they may be after me before thee gets this. I am prepared for anything. . . . The people here have been wonderful. The F.B.I. agent visited some of my neighbors. As one said, 'I talked until I had tears in my eyes'. . . . I love them all."[29]

Written from the county jail, Jackson, Mississippi: "On Dec. 2, I was sentenced to two years. When we have money we feel independent. . . . Only when we lose our money do we realize that real security lies within ourselves and in cooperation with each other.

"Remember the number of self-help co-ops that sprang up all over the country in the early '30s; [then] when WPA and other agencies began to help . . . most of the co-ops faded out,"[30]

"I understand I shall be transferred to Federal prison sometime before Christmas. The Kingdom of God *is* here *now*! My prayer is that in the midst of the hatred and violence you will find the *Peace of God* which passes all understanding."[31]

He was sent to Texarkana Federal Prison. He had given James (his helper on the farm) his address book and asked him to write and request that we write to his folks. I wrote to them, and so did many of Arle's friends. Arle's sister Elva answered my letter, and so *our* correspondence began.

The above-quoted card, written December 21, 1942, was the last communication I had from Arle until January 9, 1944, but messages were sent back and forth through Elva.

When he heard that I was having health problems, he suggested that his family invite me to see them. [The story of that visit is told in "Texas in August," immediately after this article, later in this book.] It was that August that I visited Arle on my way back from the visit to his family. I remember that I didn't want to take advantage of a man who hadn't seen a woman for a while, but I guess he took my behavior towards him for indifference. When he asked if I would like to be on his mailing list, I said yes, but when four months passed, and I didn't hear, I wrote Elva, "Is he going to write to me or not?" He wrote to Elva, "I wasn't aware that she *really* wanted to hear from me." So the first letter came.

"I guess I am an ungrateful being, not writing thee after so grand a visit with thee so long ago.

"It is our inner spirit that determines our outward affairs. That is why it is so futile to hope that out of all this mess of murder and destruction we will achieve peace."[32] The next letter began, "Dearest Tillie, Tillie, this is a very shallow letter, deliberately so, I should let my correspondent rest from my emphasis on what *I* think. Yet I feel our responsibility is so great — not to save the world but to discover the source of the Power that alone can."[33]

And in February, "Most of us can plan for a better world than we are capable of living in. . . . Would thee write Madison College? I would like all the information they can give (free) on the comparison of soy beans with milk, as to food value, etc. Can we get more nutrition from an acre of soy beans as food or as food for a cow and then *borrow* the milk from the cow. . . . I believe life would be simpler to eat the beans and let the cow enjoy a natural life. *Foolish*, isn't it?"[34]

"I feel like I know thy family. . . . I have thought about thy brother but have hesitated to ask about him, not knowing if anything had happened."[35]

My brother, Fred, served with the Engineers Corps in Italy and returned home safely, but died in 1965 from causes not related to the war.

In Arle's last letter of February, 1944, he questions the advisability of churches and chaplains giving Bibles to soldiers going into war. "Only one thing can happen when they try to take both ways — split personalities . . . many mental breakdowns occur because we have tried to follow God and then destroy our neighbor."[36]

"As to meat for human consumption. We do live off of other life, but it seems to me we may be able to live off the lower forms of life — such as vegetables. . . . I do not eat meat because I feel better by not doing so. . . . I would, however, eat meat to keep from offending others. . . . It is not the effect of what killing and eating has on the animal killed, but the effect it will have on me. I find it hard to kill an animal I have come close to."[37]

I had evidence of that the first fall after we were married when Arle helped his dad butcher a hog. Arle was *physically* ill! I vowed he never should do that again. My mother told me about a runt pig my dad raised, and then it followed him all over the farm like a dog. When it got to be a hog, my mother said, "When are you going to butcher that hog?"

"I think I'll just keep her for a brood sow."

"John, you *know* that she is not good stock."

I think my father sold her.

In the same letter referred to above, Arle said that he did not want to call himself a vegetarian for fear it would foster pride in him; but he was a vegetarian, and a *strict* one — not using any animal products. How can I bake a birthday cake without eggs and milk? We used soya milk by the twenty-pound can, and I experimented and I *did* make an edible cake.

Once when we had been at my home, and the girls had eaten meat and eggs, I explained to them on the way home about Daddy's feelings about those foods, and Paula said, "Well, we could have *fried-a-patoes*, couldn't we?" She had liked grandma's fried potatoes. I didn't usually fry anything.

Arle wrote (looking forward to his release from prison), "My own summer after July 10 [his release date] is not yet planned. Tillie, I do love to hear from thee, and I think our friendship is real and lasting whatever the future holds."[38]

"A new person has been assigned to the hospital, so maybe my work will let up a bit. I have a lot of personal typing and studying to finish before I leave."[39]

"You cannot give truth to another. You may point the way once you have experienced it, but he will not understand until he has experienced it himself. . . . The feeling Love within me is made clear through the way of living of the Society of Brothers (Brüderhof) in Paraguay and other places where persons 'have all things in common.'"[40]

Several times in these sixty-four letters Arle has held up Acts 4:32–35 as the ideal for the community of his dreams.

> Now the whole group of those who believed were of one heart and soul, and no one claimed private ownership of any possessions, but everything they owned was held in common. With great power the apostles gave their testimony to the resurrection of the Lord Jesus, and great grace was upon them all. There was not a needy person among them, for as many as owned lands or houses sold them and brought the proceeds of what was sold. They laid it at the apostles' feet, and it was distributed to each as any had need.[41]

Apparently *that* Christian ideal did not last very long; so what are the hopes for community living. As far as I know the one in Paraguay is still in existence, and also the branch in Farmington, Pennsylvania, where "Pep" Hinkey, Doug and Ruby Moody, and Dick and Lois Ann Domer, still are. Others who were a part of the 1954 exodus from Celo Community did not stay.

Arle knew Clarence and Florence Jordan who started Koinonia Community in Georgia, and that community has succeeded, and

Habitat for Humanity grew out of it. Celo Community, Inc. has grown since I was a part of it. These are the communities most familiar to me. I think all of them have departed from the Acts ideal in a greater or lesser degree in order to survive.

The Shakers took seriously Paul's admonition that it was *no use to marry* because the end of time was coming, and their communities died for lack of new blood. I have visited Shakertown in Kentucky — spent the night and enjoyed the food. Probably disciplined living *does* foster creativity because the Shakers made some valuable contributions to our culture.

Since I've not really experienced "all things common," I didn't know how well I'd adapt, but I did appreciate the Celo Community, Inc. model of community. I would not have made it so well during Arle's illness and after his death without the support friends in Celo Community gave me.

Arle wrote, "The farm in Mississippi is having its troubles, but we'll start again someday. . . . I will spend a good part of the winter with the folks."[42] And then a month later, "I don't know if I will be able to travel about as I had thought. We are more restricted under *conditional release*. . . . When I wrote to Hazel about increasing my family — nothing definite, her comment was, 'There needs to be a compromise in marriage — a give and take.' Of course that is true if one is thinking of *minor* matters and not a part of one's faith and principles. One cannot wholeheartedly love a person who causes one to go against one's principles . . . in order to live 'happily' with that person. . . . I have been away from women so long I do not know what they think. What *do* they think?"[43]

"Sounds like you are having a real back to the farm vacation. . . . Wouldn't it be easier to *train* the crows — they could teach their little ones not to eat thy corn — so in a few generations of crows they would all be living off of weed seeds and buds, and thee would never again have to use 'crow repellant.' . . . For Father's Day get [your dad] *Plowman's Folly* by Edward Faulkner.

"We have churches because we live such divided lives. We work here, play and worship somewhere else. If life were whole, there would be no need for church. There would be no difference between work and worship. . . . There are certainly grand and wonderful people working through all the churches. Perhaps a few may be drawn toward the common life upon the land."[44] "There are no valleys of hatred, and above the highest peak of human love stands this almost unattainable plateau of Divine Love where all persons walk always on the same level. A girl may not be greatly complimented by someone saying, 'I love you, but no more than [I love] the blind woman who sells pencils.' . . . We love to be attached to others and have others attached to us. Food for our ego."[45]

I doubt that I can claim it as a spiritual quality, but sometimes I have felt that my non-attachment was a fault. I love my family and my friends (of whom I have many wonderful ones), but it is not the clinging kind of love. I try to give them space. Often friends have said after my children have visited and gone, "Aren't you just devastated?" No, I am not! I loved having them, but now I know they have to go. I've often wondered if moving so many times when I was a child shaped my attitude — a kind of defense against being unhappy at losing friends over and over. I discovered I always found new ones in the next place. I think someone who was born and had all their schooling and most of their relatives in one place tends to be more dependent. Martha Almon, my co-worker at Crossville, Tennessee, *never* did understand my non-attachment.

"Phil and Eleanor were to come back to see me but were picked up by the local Texarkana police for having spent the night with a very cultured Negro family. After almost a week in several jails they were released on condition that they leave the county. Think of how many boys — Negro and white — who are fighting and dying for democracy."[46]

"I suppose I told thee that I was working 8 P.M. until 12 A.M. in the hospital. I like that shift because there isn't so much to do. . . . We work on the farm from 5–8 P.M. . . . So far I have been out twice and drove the tractor both times."[47]

"In a 'state of semi-consciousness,' the gates of [the] inner self were lowered so all within flowed freely to the surface, and there before me danced the naked thoughts of my real self — some noble, some ignoble, some pure and holy and some otherwise. I was neither proud nor ashamed for they were my real self. . . . Then I am awake, and they are gone. . . . To be proud of the good and beautiful is to destroy them. To be ashamed of the ugly is to cause it to be more careful and cause it to slip out and dance only when the night is darker and no one is watching — not even me."[48]

"Has the new preacher arrived? I think thee should get married. Phil (for about a month I thought I would marry him) said thee would make someone a good wife. I've always thought so, too. Hope the new preacher has brown eyes. Maybe he'll have a chance if he does."[49]

Arle was talking about Vladimir Hartman who was working in the Cumberland Mountains and staying at our house. I don't remember about his eyes; but I feel sure he would have asked me to marry him if I had not decided to marry Arle.

Arle's last letter from prison was written the day before he was released. On July 10, 1944 he was paroled, but his two-year term would not be up until December.

From Arle's home in San Marcos. "Dad and I have been working in the orchard and garden, and it is a great joy for both of us, I believe."

"How is thee getting along with the new preacher? Not too well, I hope. The folks said thee was a good worker and they like thee. We'd like thee to come again soon.

"I've looked the situation over and decided I couldn't do much better. I'm sending a picture of a house designed for functional living. The only trouble — it's designed for at least two. I just wondered if thee knew anyone who would like to share such a home. . . . Elva looked at the picture and said, 'What do you want to do, discourage her? Now a woman would *have* to love a man to live in a place like that!'

"I'm fixing up a room in the little smoke/junk house in the back yard. . . . They really do love thee. I suppose I might as well tell thee that I do, too."[50]

"Come on down so we could have a good visit. . . . Just tell 'em you received a call from the Lord to do a little missionary work in Texas. . . . They'll probably pay all your expenses and give you a bonus. . . . Hon, I hope you won't be disappointed cause I guess I am funny in many ways and beliefs. . . . I think we like each other."[51]

I did go for a visit the first of August. We *did* need that time to know our own hearts. The first few days he said sadly, "Thee doesn't love me." One morning I awakened and rushed to the garden where he was watering his *precious* okra. I knew I loved him, and he never doubted it again. I returned to Crossville and finished my four year commitment to the women of the Methodist Church. Before I left Texas, we had agreed that I would return and marry him in October.

August, 1944: "I want you to know that Dad and I [will be] *very* happy to have you with us and hope you will be happy, too. Lots of love, Mom and Pop"[52]

"Hazel quit work at the base. "The gang where she worked gave her a size 6 slip. They left the tag on so she could exchange it if she had to. . . . She did. I don't know why . . . just *think* of a slip costing $6. No wonder women let 'em show.

"The old cat brought her kittens out . . . and carefully placed them in the smokehouse (before we [take] over). We'll be crowded with kittens and chickens in an eight-by-eight-foot room, especially when we get the baby crib in."[53]

"The Service Committee needs someone . . . through the winter or longer. I feel that I'd like to be here, so I guess that is out . . .

"I would like to stay here and develop a small educational community. . . . The folks thought it would be fine and suggested a spot for a rock house. . . . I mention something I have written to thee, and they figure that I ain't much of a love-letter writer . . . but thee knows I do care, and important matters such as one's love for another look flat and cold on paper."[54]

"Thee'll get to see thy home when we fix it up a bit, but I'll let thee *walk* in if thee doesn't mind. The idea of carrying the blushing bride across the door sill is part of the old conception of the helplessness of the woman and the strong arm of the man . . .

"I do miss thy singing, hon, and look forward to being sung to sleep every night."[55]

"Dearly Beloved and all that — . . .I finished my monthly report and asked the probation officer for permission to visit the farm and then go up and adopt thee officially. . . . Would thee like to help pick a ring or what's the proper procedure?

". . .The other day Dad sent me in the house to get a red ring to mark a hen's leg. . . . I was standing on the back porch looking at the red ring and smiling to myself. Mama saw me and said, 'I know *exactly* what you are thinking,' and she was right. . . . I was going to send it and say, 'Mama gives red rings to the hens she wants to keep. I'm sending one to the girl I love and want for keeps.' I decided not to — it might not strike thee as funny. I'll have to find a blue one for thee. I like thee in blue. I like thee all the time — blue or nothing, but the blue dress thee wore here I liked especially."[56]

I had sent Arle a picture of the place I worked in Crossville, Tennessee. He thought the Methodists did things too lavishly. The place had been a school with classrooms, dormitory rooms, kitchen and dining room, laundry, etc. I think Friends go there for a yearly meeting now. Arle had hoped he could get permission from the parole board to come so we could be married there with my friends. He thought it would be nice to be married by the small lake on the place — with a full moon on October 1. He did *not* get permission. In his letter dated September 20, he said some things he wanted included in the ceremony.

"As we join our lives together, we do so believing that in such a union each may aid the other in the growth of the spirit. By joining our lives in an intimate relationship we do not in any way withdraw from the friendship . . . of people who mean so much to us."[57] (An example of this point-of-view can be seen in this incident: Arle's brother-in-law, Roy Rose, was outraged when, soon after we were married, we went to San Antonio and Arle went out to lunch with a former prisoner's girlfriend while I ate with Arle's sister Hazel. I thought it was okay.)

There was much more, and we did work on it together.

"I do not want a preacher to pronounce us man and wife 'by the authority vested in me.' The minister may sign the certificate in the name of the state since it seems interested in having a record of our marriage."[58]

"We all want thee to come on if it is at all possible. . . . I do not feel moved to violate my conditional release. . . . I know that the girl usually likes for the man to come after her. . . . Darling, please come on! There is much work we can do together. Instead of waiting until I can go there, come on, and let us be married here."[59]

"Received a letter from the National Board of Religious Objectors. The Department of Justice is releasing me to Selective Service which means . . . that shortly I shall receive notice to report for CPS or the army. I'm sure that this time it will not be less than three years. . . . Thy letter came. The Selective Service will probably take me before thee. If thee prefers waiting single, it's thy choice. I prefer marriage and family. I'm 35, and thee will be 30 soon. It's up to thee."[60]

"I cannot say much about the future, except this: if we are not willing to be married in the shadow of the prison walls, we will never be married. . . . I'm sure thee knows I love thee and want you to come as soon as possible. If thee really feels thee would rather wait until we hear something more definite, then do as thee really wishes. . . . We would like for some of thy folks to come."[61]

On October 12, 1994, he wrote:

I'm finding it harder and harder to write to thee 'cause I know words can't express how very glad I am that thee is coming — and soon. . . . Tell all the folks there hello and I am sorry I can't come up there now. I love ye, I love ye.

    Always & always,
    Arle

P.S. Come soon
P.S. Hurry up

P.S. I love ye.[62]

I don't know *how*, but Walter Longstreth kept Arle from having to deal with Selective Service any further.

I had made a blue suit dress for the wedding — a very simple dress. Since Arle was not coming to Crossville, I decided to wear the dress to church the last Sunday I was there. Martha, my co-worker, was horrified and said I just *couldn't* do that — but I did! The people had a generous shower for me.

A few nights before I left, someone played the piano and sang a song — I think translated from the French. I said, "Oh *that* song is for Arle!" I copied it, and it was one he liked to hear me sing:

The Florian Song

v.1: Oh, is there in your village dwelling
A gentle shepherd, tall and fair?
Oh, treat him kindly is my prayer.
I love him far above all telling.

Chorus: My love is he, give him to me.
His love is mine, my heart has he.

v.2: His voice is sweet, so sweet and gentle.
The woods in echo vainly vie.
The mountain peaks to him reply.
His voice in softened strains they render.

Chorus

v.3: My love is kind to all about him,
Alike to him the rich and poor.
Oh, tell me has he passed your door?
No longer can I live without him.

Chorus

We were married in the front room of the Brooks home place by Rev. Hendrickson who allowed us to do the service as we wished. It was on October 22, 1944.

We let Mary and Dad go on our honeymoon to San Antonio and we had the place alone. We stayed with the folks that winter. The next summer Arle disked in the Johnson grass as often as any green appeared, and in the fall planted a *huge* garden. He and Dad worked some for neighbors. I worked at a photo studio in San

Marcos until close to the time for our daughter to be born on Arle's birthday, August 28, 1945. At least once during that first year Arle was ill.

Probably in February, 1946 — about the time to harvest that fall garden — Arle went back to work for AFSC; so Dad and I harvested onions, carrots, beets, and spinach and sold them in town. I had *never* seen such vegetables! A mature spinach plant covered a bushel basket (the flat kind).

In May Paula and I flew to my home in West Virginia and from there joined Arle at the Brudercoop in Philadelphia. Most of the story from this point is told elsewhere; but there are a couple of additions I need to make to complete the story.

As I have told, Arle's illness increased in frequency and severity for seven years. In 1951 he had a chance to ride to Texas to see his folks, who were not well. Even though he had had a clear spell, he was ill before he reached Texas, about the first of September. I kept writing to encourage him to come home on the bus. Finally Hazel wired that I would have to come. I was not prepared for the way I found him — almost totally paralyzed, able to move only one hand. They said he'd begun to improve as soon as he heard I was on the way, but I didn't see how he could have been worse and still be alive.

Strange as it may seem, when I went to bed with him that night, he let me know he had an erection. It lasted just long enough for him to feel our oneness again, and gain strength from my presence with him. In fifteen days I took him back to North Carolina by bus even though he could not stand alone. The bus driver from San Marcos to Dallas came to me and said what a pleasure it had been to have Arle as a passenger — as did the men I had to ask to take him to the toilet.

He seemed to get along pretty well until mid-November, when he became very ill again. It was at that time that I felt *black despair*. I lay down to rest one day, and suddenly I was paralyzed with fear. I could *not* move. What would I do? A sick man, no income, no hospitalization, and three little children to care for. That lasted about five minutes, when the assurance came that God was with me, and I had only to ask and help would come from family and friends.

A way was made for Arle to enter the hospital in Philadelphia, and the nurses in the ward loved him so much they fussed because the doctors never sent him back to them in the ward. Instead, Arle was kept in recovery thirteen days, and those nurses followed him to the taxi the day he was released. Even in illness, he blessed those around him. Back in our mountain home, the day Dr. Ohle pronounced him dead, July 6, 1953, he said, "He put a lot of love in this community."

Why did a man that loving have to die so young? I have pondered that question. He was in perfect health except for that tumor on his brain. He lived in a clean environment and ate healthful food — so why? I feel it was a kind of heartbreak or frustration to find his dreams could not seem to come to fruition in this imperfect world. I tried to help him achieve his goal — even to practicing celibacy the last year and a half of his life. He had said when we were married it was only for forty years, then he would go into a monastery.

I suppose in one way it helped me after he was gone because our union was more spiritual than physical. He ended a piece he had written, *Tomorrow is Now*, this way, ". . . to be completely aware of our oneness and to know that we are an inseparable whole; therefore the miles of ocean or the hand of death cannot separate us from loved ones who are united with God. So dream not of happiness or peace tomorrow. For these are yours already if for you tomorrow is now."[63]

Arle also wrote the pamphlet for the Service Committee, *We the Offenders*,[64] the thesis being that the society we live in, which we support in some way, involves us and makes us also offenders, as well as those who are behind bars.

In the late fifties, thinking that I would write about Arle's life, I put an ad in the *Friends Journal*, asking for remembrances of him. Excerpts from letters received, together with letters received from friends after his death, are included below:

Emily Longstreth: "Walter said that he himself had not thought it was wrong to register until he saw Arle's sacrifice in upholding his ideals. You know Walter did not register.

"I can think of no one who lived [more fully] as though the Kingdom of God were here now . . .

"I am enclosing a gift for you, hoping it will ease the strain a bit."[65] (Which she did *many* times before she died.)

Naomi Binford to Arle's family after he first went to prison: "Be thankful that you helped lay the basis for the deep spiritual strength that made possible [this man] . . . for whom the Brotherhood of man and true democracy came first . . . and making him available to our country at a time when hate and fear toward other nations [prevail] rather than growth toward the understanding of the brotherhood of all men."[66]

John C. Parsley, who was with Arle at the Patapsco, Maryland, CPS camp: "Arle's gentle, kindly manner and his strong religious convictions impressed all of us in the camp."[67]

Harley Patterson, pastor of the United Church in Oak Ridge, Tennessee, wrote: "He was unquestionably the most unselfish person I ever met. He would literally give you not only the shirt off his back, but the shoes off his feet and the last cent he had."[68] Harley was Arle's roommate at Texas Christian University.

Marion William Byerly, of the Kuhopos Friends Center, in McCloud, Oklahoma: "His visit to us is indelibly stamped on our minds. Hundreds of people visited us in behalf of peace . . . but I can truly say that none made a more clear-cut and positive witness than Arle Brooks. It was as if he realized and embodied in his life the conviction, 'I shall not pass this way again. Therefore, any good that I can do, let me not defer or neglect it.'"[69]

J. Bernard Walton, from the AFSC wrote: "When Arle came to the Service Committee he impressed me as one of our ablest men — in clarity of purpose, vision and friendliness . . . the judge when he sentenced him said, as you know, 'I feel like Pontius Pilate . . .'

"Arle's search since he left social work . . . was to find a way of life that would lead us all out of slavery and dependence toward freedom and brotherhood with joy in simplicity."[70]

Agnes Hole, a member of First Friends' Church in Indianapolis, wrote: "He made a tremendous impression on the young people in the Mid-west. . . . His direct approach to his testimony, his personal charm and great integrity made such an impression on me that when I learned of his going to prison for his convictions, I felt very happy. . . . When I heard of his death I felt very badly indeed, knowing that he had a great deal to contribute."[71]

Avery D. Weage, who was with Arle at the Chicago Theological School, became minister at the First Congregational Church, David City, Nebraska. He wrote: "Arle . . . and I were discussing the urgent problem of securing enough to eat . . . at a price we could afford. . . . An idea occurred to me, 'Do you suppose the students would be interested in organizing a co-op dining club?' Arle agreed to bring it to the attention of the other students. . . . President Albert W. Palmer agreed to the idea. The seminary turned over the entire first floor of a building it had recently acquired [for the purpose]. The co-op dining club was a success from the start."[72]

James A. Crain, executive director of the Joint Board of Christian Churches, wrote: "Arle was the first of about 100 Disciples of Christ men who took the CO position, and he was the one who perhaps more than any other among them paid a high price for his convictions."[73]

Clay Marks wrote: "He lifted the hearts of volunteer work campers when he visited. We regarded him as a quiet, lovable man with great courage and the kind of insight that penetrates to the heart of the problem."[74]

***

When I began this chapter about Arle I expressed the hope that it would be a blessing to all who read it. As I spent four days (and many hours of the nights) reading his letters, I was certainly blessed! I shared with him his conviction that "if war solved our problems, wouldn't we have a world of peace and brotherhood by now?" He was spared Vietnam and Desert Storm. I can see that World War II, at least, stopped Hitler's aggression and the holocaust; but I have trouble justifying the above two wars.

My sentiments about the Gulf War were admirable expressed in a letter to the editor of the *N.C. Christian Advocate* by Harlan L. Creech, Jr.: "The Persian Gulf War was a sanitized television extravaganza. . . . The smart bombs were fantastic. The Pentagon and generals are jubilant; the hawks are all smiles and the president's rating is above 90 percent. . . . The war has brought no solutions. . . . Most Americans believe every life is of infinite worth . . . think of the casualties . . . ours were light; theirs were heavy. It has been estimated as many as two hundred thousand men, women and children were killed and wounded. . . . Surely a people able to make smart bombs, patriot missiles and put a man on the moon can also find a better way to solve human problems."[75]

I often wondered if the returning military personnel might not have been a little embarrassed at all the hoopla our nation exhibited — trying to salve our collective conscience for the way Vietnam veterans had been treated — a *ticker-tape parade*, no less! (All that paper — all those trees — all that trash to clean up.) When the "glory days" are past, the veterans tend to be forgotten; so I now contribute to several veterans organizations to say "I know you did what you were called to do, and I remember." I think Arle would feel the same.

But it is also evident to me that there are areas of Arle's "thought life" where we are *not* as one. As long as he lived I tried to support him in his efforts to see his dream come true. He had the strong conviction that "We must commit ourselves unto the power that we call God and into the hands of our fellowmen ... a complete abandonment of possessions and of self ... complete sharing and complete absorption in the spirit of love. ... Possible through *hours* of meditation and contemplation beginning by faithfully keeping short watches morning, noon and night."[76]

I do not live up to those ideals. I do not live in functional poverty. I have not abandoned possessions. (Once when I thought my mobile home might burn down I prayed, "Lord, I *can* live without these *things* — but I'd *rather not!*") Scorched leaves from the trailer burning below mine touched my home, but my trailer was left intact. I *gave* my inheritance from my mother ($3,000) to the owner of the trailer that did burn in gratitude for mine having been saved. He insisted on repaying me — which I feel sure he did, but I kept no accounts. My *needs* are pretty basic and my *wants* are very few. I do eat meat, but mostly fruits and vegetables, which I spend the least time possible preparing. So I *feel* Arle's influence in these areas, but *hours* of meditation? I really fail there!

I have found in (short-lived) spiritual diaries (that I still have) that I kept from college days on, I was always berating myself for my lack of *spiritual discipline*. It has taken a long time, but I am finally convinced that I am not a *contemplative* person! I am also not a *charismatic* in the tongue-speaking sense. I've known persons so classified since the early fifties, have attended meetings and had friends try to induce me to speak in tongues. I went with a group of twelve to South America in 1971 to encourage English-speaking missionaries there. I appreciated the teaching of Francis McNutt and was enthralled to hear several hundred people "singing in the spirit" (speaking in tongues). But after almost a month with the group I came home giving thanks for my own gifts of love, patience and understanding.

I try to be open and appreciative of all the many paths people find to love and serve God. For *me* — "Jesus is the sweetest name I know. And he's just the same as his lovely name. And that's the reason why I love him so."[77]

I *know* God loves me, forgives me when I fail, and has supported me in my efforts to share his love with all whom I have met "along the way." I am not afraid to die or face the final accounting for the life I have lived. Thanks be to God!

NOTES

1. Arle Brooks, *We the Offenders*, (publication information not available.)
2. American Friends Service Committee, *United States of America vs. Arle Brooks*, (publication information not available.)

3. Letter of Arle Brooks to Arthelia H. Brooks (henceforth referred to as LA), March 26, 1940.
4. LA, April 6, 1940.
5. Ibid.
6. LA, April 12, 1940.
7. LA, August, 1940.
8. Ibid.
9. LA, September 14, 1940.
10. LA, September, 1940.
11. LA, September 14, 1940.
12. LA, October 17, 1940.
13. LA, December 20, 1940.
14. American Friends Service Committee, *United States of America vs. Arle Brooks*, (publication information not available.)
15. Letter of Charles R. Swift, M.D., to Arthelia H. Brooks, June 23, 1959.
16. LA, June 5, 1941.
17. LA, June 18, 1941.
18. LA, July 23, 1941.
19. LA, August 20, 1941.
20. LA, September 23, 1941.
21. LA, November 23, 1941.
22. LA, December 6, 1941.
23. LA, January 14, 1942.
24. LA, February 22, 1942.
25. LA, March 13, 1942.
26. LA, June 25, 1942.
27. LA, July 27, 1942.
28. LA, September 30, 1942.
29. LA, November 8, 1942.
30. LA, December 9, 1942.
31. LA, December 21, 1942.
32. LA, January 9, 1944.
33. LA, January 31, 1944.
34. LA, February 7, 1944.
35. LA, February 26, 1944.
36. Ibid.
37. LA, March 19, 1944.
38. LA, (date not available).
39. LA, March 30, 1944.
40. LA, April 17, 1944.
41. Acts 4: 32–35 (NRSV).

42. LA, April 17, 1944.
43. LA, May 14, 1944.
44. LA, May 21, 1944.
45. LA, May 31, 1944.
46. LA, May 31, 1944.
47. LA, June 15, 1944.
48. LA, June 23, 1944.
49. LA, July 1, 1944.
50. LA, July 14, 1944.
51. LA, July, 1944.
52. Letter of Mary Brooks to Arthelia H. Brooks, August, 1944.
53. LA, August 19, 1944.
54. LA, August 21, 1944.
55. LA, August 27, 1944.
56. LA, August 31, 1944.
57. LA, September 20, 1944.
58. Ibid.
59. LA, October 3, 1944.
60. LA, October 6, 1944.
61. LA, October 8, 1944.
62. LA, October 12, 1944.
63. Arle Brooks, *Tomorrow is Now.* (Unpublished manuscript in the possession of Arthelia H. Brooks.)
64. Arle Brooks, *We the Offenders*, (publication information not available.)
65. Letter of Emily Longstreth to Arthelia H. Brooks, February 19, 1959.
66. Letter of Naomi Binford to Arthelia H. Brooks, January 20, 1941.
67. Letter of John C. Parsley to Arthelia H. Brooks, June 6, 1959.
68. Letter of Harley Patterson to Arthelia H. Brooks,, November 30, 1959.
69. Letter of Marion William Byerly to Arthelia H. Brooks, April 25, 1959.
70. Letter of J. Bernard Walton to Arthelia H. Brooks, October 12, 1959.
71. Letter of Agnes Hole to Arthelia H. Brooks, April 20, 1959.
72. Letter of Avery D. Weage to Arthelia H. Brooks, April 19, 1959.
73. Letter of James A. Crain to Arthelia H. Brooks, April 8, 1959.
74. Letter of Clay Marks to Arthelia H. Brooks, April 29, 1959.
75. Letter of Harlan L. Creech to the Editor of the *North Carolina Christian Advocate*, April 2, 1991.
76. LA, June 18, 1941.
77. Lela Long, *Worship His Majesty* (Alexandria, Indiana: Gaither Music Co., 1987).

Section IV
TRIPS

Favorite Scenes

← View from my Rocking Chair
← Styles Hill Burnsville, N.C.
←Photo Rachel Craddock

Crator Lake Oregon ↓

Golden Pavillion →
Kyoto, Japan

Niagra Falls, N.Y. ↓

Queen's Bath →
Big Island, Hawaii
Reflection

Favorite Scenes I

↑ Ogle meadows; Pappy kerl
Yancey Co., N.C.
About 1959

↑ Multnoma falls
Portland, Or.

↑ Roaring Creek falls
Yancey Co. N.C

↑ Machu Picchu
Peru, South Am.

← Cumberland Falls
Ky.

TEXAS IN AUGUST

When Arle was arrested for the second time — this time for not carrying his draft card — it was late fall, 1942, and he was living at the cooperative farm in Mississippi. He gave a friend his address book and asked that those in it be notified, and be asked to write his family in Texas. He felt they might feel isolated because their son was unwilling to fight for his country.

Since it was before Christmas and his mother's name was Mary, I wrote saying, "There was another Mary who had a son who did not listen to the same drummer as the crowd around him." His sister Elva chose to answer my letter, and so our correspondence began. In April I received from her the most memorable package of my life — special delivery. It contained Texas blue bonnets with the stems in a raw potato. Of course I had never seen those unique blossoms before.

It became apparent that 1943 would be my last year with Myrta Davis in the coal mining area of southern West Virginia. The coal dust bothered my sinuses and I had trouble with anemia. Arle asked his family to invite me to Texas for a visit. Perhaps the change of climate would help.

Since Myrta's family lived in Tyler, Texas, I decided to use my August, 1943, vacation to visit both families.

Texas in August is really no place for a mountain gal like me. I remember being very uncomfortable with the heat at Myrta's home.

When I was ready to go on to San Marcos, Myrta fixed me a sandwich to take on the bus. At lunchtime, though, a nice gentleman seat-mate asked me to eat with him, so I saved Myrta's sandwich for later.

At 2:00 P.M. our bus broke down in the middle of nowhere. We did have the shade of an old building to sit in, but the air was so hot it hurt to breathe it, and everything around us was burned brown.

A relief bus didn't come until six o'clock, and I didn't have any better sense than to eat Myrta's sandwich for supper! It was pure poison — ham with lettuce and mayonnaise, simmered for hours in the Texas heat! By the time we reached the small town of Hearne at 7:30 I was feeling ill, and a cup of tea did not help. By 8:00 I was vomiting, and by 8:30 I was hemorrhaging both ways. To try to stop the vomiting, a nurse who'd been on the bus with me got me a bottle of paregoric. (She was waiting for the next bus to her own destination.) I was too sick to get my luggage before our bus left for its next stop, and too sick to care. I asked the nurse to see if there was a hotel nearby. Yes, there was one, but it was full of soldiers, soldiers' wives, and soldiers' sweethearts, due to the army base just outside of town. Myrta and I had learned about the perils of wartime travel — we, as civilians, had been bumped a couple of times on our way to her home.

By 8:45 the hemorrhaging had increased, and I was going blind. I told the nurse to call one more time. I had to have a place to lie down. (For some reason I never considered a hospital.) She called the hotel again, and they said that she could bring me. I don't know how I got there, but the next thing I knew I was seeing, through my blurred vision, a white-haired woman standing at the foot of my bed saying she was the proprietor, I felt I was in good hands. They had the drugstore deliver another bottle of paregoric and wanted the name and address of my family. I said I would give it if they wouldn't call until morning. "I'll be okay by then," I said. The bus station in San Marcos had been called and the Brooks family paged. The doctor was called, and he said the nurse had done the right thing. He also said for me to eat chipped ice the rest of the night. The nurse left to catch her 9:30 bus.

All that Monday night the night clerk brought me the prescribed chipped ice. The white-haired proprietor assured me that he was a *nice* old man, and he was. Mercifully, the bleeding stopped about midnight.

Tuesday morning I *was* okay. The hotel didn't serve meals, but my order for a large glass of fresh orange juice was brought me by a soldier. My door was never closed, and only a sheet over the foot of my bed offered privacy. The same white-haired lady came to check on me that morning, asking who I was, etc. I told her that I worked for the women of the Methodist Church. She said, "I thought you were someone special. I saw you were *not* wearing an ankle bracelet."

I paid the doctor three dollars later that morning, and thought,

"It's a good thing I brought that emergency money I had tucked away. This hotel bill will have to be paid."

Arle's sister, Elva, arrived on Wednesday. Still the door to our room was never closed. My meals were brought to me, but Wednesday evening the proprietor took Elva out to dinner and a movie.

By Thursday morning I was well enough to go on to San Marcos with Elva. When I went to the desk to check out, the proprietor said, "Oh, my dear, you don't owe me anything. I am a Methodist, but in this job I seldom get to go to church; so it was a great joy to do this for you."

By Saturday I was able to mop the kitchen at the Brooks home. When I wrote to my mother about the trip, she answered, "I do suppose if you were dropped in the middle of the Sahara Desert there would be someone there to care for you."

Since Arle was in Texarkana prison in Texas, I visited him on my way home. The next summer, after he was out of prison and at his home, he wrote and proposed in this way: "I'm sending a picture of a house designed for functional living. The only trouble — it's made for at least two people. I just wondered if thee knew anyone who would like to share such a home with a dumb bunny? . . . She should be tall and blond and weigh about 145 pounds, kinda foolish at times, but always a searcher for truth. . . . They [the folks] really do love thee. I suppose I might as well tell thee that I do, too."

I went to Texas again the following August (1944) to find out if *I loved him. Yes!* And we were married in his home on October 22, 1944.

POINTS WEST AND THE UNEXPECTED

When Paula was ready to graduate from high school in the spring of 1963, I knew that would signal the beginning of the "flight of the birds from the nest" and thought we should do something special before it happened.

The Brooks family had been to see us more than once after Arle died in 1953, and the girls had been to see them, but I had not been, and they were beginning to wonder why. Since there was a Town and Country meeting near Minneapolis I was supposed to attend in connection with my work, I conceived the idea of borrowing our minister's travel trailer, and parking the girls somewhere close by while I attended the meeting. (They would have food and a place to sleep.) Then we could visit the Griffiths in Iowa, my sister Ruth in Oklahoma, the Brooks family in Texas, then proceed on to Mexico. I told these plans to our minister, Tom Rutledge, and he agreed to let us use his trailer. I had a young woman to dinner one evening, and when she heard about the plans and the meeting in Minneapolis, she said, "Oh, I know a family that lives on a lake in St. Paul. I just feel sure they would be glad for you to park the trailer there." She called and found it so. That was very encouraging, but I found myself with another problem still on my mind. I had a persistent feeling that if we undertook such a journey, we would have a wreck. I wrestled with this thought for several weeks, and finally I had the assurance that even if we had a wreck it would come out okay. So I went ahead with my plans.

I checked with Rev. Rutledge to be sure his trailer was insured, and I took out extra insurance on our Chevrolet. We put a trailer hitch on my car, and early in the morning we let Homer Price put a wide-angle side mirror on the car. He later told me, "I never hated to see anyone start on a trip so bad in my life."

I had never hauled a trailer, so as we drove I tried never to get into a situation where I had to back up — involving that tricky business of turning the steering wheel the opposite way from the direction you wanted the trailer to go. Once we stopped to eat, and a backing situation faced me, but a truck driver appeared and did the backing for me.

We got to Minneapolis about suppertime, and we stopped in a park to eat. I had no idea how to get to the home of the people on the lake. While we were eating, an older man walking his dog sort of hung around. I went to ask if I could help him. He said he just wanted to know how I liked traveling with a trailer. He was retired and was thinking of getting one so he and his wife could travel. I explained my problems with the trailer, and my main problem of how to find my destination, explaining where I wanted to go. He said, "You shouldn't try to go through the city. I don't have anything urgent to do; I'll just lead you by short cuts to a filling station, and you can call your friend to meet you and guide you the rest of the way."

That problem was solved, and I said, "Thank you, Lord."

The family we visited was lovely, and so was their place. The girls slept in the trailer but ate with the family, went swimming, and even tried water skiing. The lady took me to my meeting on Monday and returned for me on Friday.

Our next stop was to be with the Griffiths in Iowa. The driving in prairie country was most difficult. The overhang on the trailer caught the wind, and we were getting about ten miles to a gallon of gas. We had the oil changed at the Griffiths, and made sure the chain connecting the car and trailer was secure. Then we set out through Missouri toward our next stop with my sister Ruth, in Miami, Oklahoma.

Some time after midafternoon, well into Missouri, Marla asked if I would like to have her drive. She had gotten her driver's license in March and had driven a school bus the rest of the year. I got into the backseat, and before long I had the thought, "Marla will be driving when we have the wreck."

I didn't have long to wait. As Marla came to a bridge with three-foot walls on each side, the lane looked too narrow for the wide trailer we were pulling, and seeing no car approaching her in the opposite lane and no car behind that was visible in the side-mirror, Marla crossed the middle line. The driver of a car, which had been *close* behind her, sat on his horn, and Marla jerked the car back into her lane. The driver who sounded his horn got by, but the trailer jumped off the hitch leaving only the chain to connect it to the car and causing the car to jackknife. Before the chain broke, it pulled the car off of the road so that we went straight down a steep bank into dry marsh grass. The trailer was lying on its side in our lane of the highway. A trucker behind us saw what happened and stopped to help. The girls and I crawled up the steep bank, and I found my heart singing, "Oh, the Lord is good to me, and so I thank the Lord. For giving me the things I need, The sun and the rain and the apple seed. The Lord is good to me."[1]

The trucker called on his CB for a wrecker. He said there was something about that spot, that he'd pulled many trailers out of the same marsh. Then he inspected the hitch and said, "Whoever was driving this did a good job keeping the trailer on the highway." The socket, which had been worn out by the many trips the Rutledges had made over the washboard-like Alaska Highway, did not hold the ball securely. We had been traveling with a false trust in its strength, and it had taken only one sudden jerk to dislodge it.

While waiting for the wrecker, I noticed an old road coming into the highway just a little way ahead. I walked down to the car and decided I could drive it out, using that old road. Which I did. The only damage to the car was caused when the overhang on the trailer hit the back door when the car swung around. The glass was not broken but the door wouldn't open. (Cars were still made of heavy metal in those days.)

When we got back to the little town I called the Methodist church and explained our dilemma and asked if we could sleep in the church basement. The minister of the church apologized for being unable to take us into his home because they had company. I said we were in no condition to be guests anyway. He put a phone in the basement and we called Ruth, and then I called the Rutledges to tell them the condition of their trailer. We were able to get food from the trailer, which was only a few blocks away. We spent the night at the church, and the next morning we undertook the job of rescuing our clothes from the mess of broken jars of peaches and grape juice. We were fortunate that the trailer had been parked in a huge building that shielded us from the August heat, and that we had water handy for cleaning up the mess. The trailer windows had been broken on the side that had hit the pavement. Since the trailer couldn't be used, we left it in the hands of the Rutledge's insurance agents, took our clothing, and headed for Oklahoma.

I had a sense of real freedom now that the wreck was behind me, and we were actually okay. I realized as we drove that we no longer had a practical use for the trailer, anyway. It would have been a drag on us the rest of the way.

We enjoyed our visit with Ruth and continued on our way to Texas and Mexico. We came back by Ruth's and went to see if our household things were still in the trailer. It had been parked in a lot with abandoned cars. All our things were intact. We rented a small U-Haul to carry our things and we made our merry way home. Insurance money paid most of the cost of a new trailer for the Rutledges.

NOTES

1. From a traditional "Johnny Appleseed" grace. (publication information not available.)

Far East Trip
Pine trees
Michiko
Tonegawa
and Brooks
girls
← P. 245

Lois (Doan) and Norris
Gornto, Lela Doan.
P. 244

Christine (Wilson) Campbell
and family
← P. 244

Cary and Grandma
McConnell P. 244
↓

Betty and
← Tillie with
Leis
P. 246

Betty, Jimmy
Kikuchi, 245, and
Michiko at Red
Bridge ↓

Betty
Michiko
—
Minoru
Tillie

Leaving Hokkaido
↓ P. 251

THE FAR EAST – 1966

In 1962 the Women's Division sent a young Japanese woman to spend ten days with me in Yancey County. They wanted her to have some idea about rural social work because she taught in an agricultural college in Sapporo on Hokkaido Island in Japan. Her name was Michiko Tonegawa. Probably while she was here, I took her to see Betty Motsinger, because about three years later a young graduate of that school came to the United States and visited Betty. I did not meet him; his name was Jimmy Kikuchi.

Betty Motsinger came to Yancey County in September, 1959, after a life-changing spiritual experience. She bought the mountain at the head of George's Fork, near Burnsville, and moved into the main house that she had built there, on Thanksgiving Day, 1960. She dedicated the house to the Lord, and people began to come, seeking a deeper relationship with God and an understanding of more perfect ways to serve Him. In 1968 the place was incorporated under the name of High Pastures, and through these years, many other facilities have been added until now it is a first-class retreat center. High Pastures can accommodate 128 overnight guests at one time. I met Betty in the early sixties, and I'm now one of the undergirders of High Pastures. My Hilleary family reunion was held there in July, 1987.

In January, 1966, Betty came by my office on Academy Street in Burnsville. In the course of our conversation she took a card from her purse from Jimmy Kikuchi. "He says they are expecting a baby in March, and why don't I come to visit them? I think I will go."

"Well, I'll just go with you," I said. The reason this statement was not utterly absurd was because in March of the previous year I had been remembered in the will of my friend, Emily Longstreth. I assured Betty about intending to go if scheduling could be worked out with the Women's Division. We tentatively planned to leave March 19 and be gone two months. Because my itinerary included visits to several missionaries whom I had known at Scarritt, the Women's Division allowed me one month as a *learning* experience, and I used my vacation for the second month. Dena would stay with Lois Doan and her parents, Jeff and Lela on Possum Trot Road (Burnsville).

The beginning of my schedule included a stop in Texas to see the Brooks family and a visit with the Toness and McConnell families in Oakland, California. Betty joined me in San Francisco, and we flew to Hawaii where my former co-worker, Martha Almon, and Christine Wilson, a Bald Creek young person, were our hostesses.

A listing of our complete itinerary follows, but I will elaborate only on places where the experiences were memorable.

We went from Hawaii to Tokyo and other cities of Japan, the island of Okinawa, Taiwan, the Philippines, (landed briefly in Saigon), Singapore, Kuala Lumpur, Malaysia, Bangkok, Thailand, Hong Kong, Japan, Hokkaido Island, (the northernmost island of Japan), Anchorage and Juneau in Alaska, an overnight in Seattle, and home.

(Home! When I later showed the many slides I had taken to Aunt Lula Wilson on Jack's Creek, she commented, "Now, *that's* the prettiest place you've showed me." It was my green lawn at the log house at Celo. Home looked mighty good to me!)

In Tokyo we stayed in a hotel that Frank Lloyd Wright had designed.

Being March it was still cold in Tokyo; but nevertheless it was almost *imperative* that we see the cherry trees in bloom. It is a rite of spring, and families were having picnics, but a picture of me taken in the park shows clearly how cold *I was*. I think getting chilled caused my illness during the Conference of Missionaries at the Sagamia Hotel at Atami on the coast. Medical attention was available, and it postponed my introduction to real Japanese food, like raw fish. On this trip we were told that Mt. Fuji was up *there*, but it was covered with clouds most of the year, which was a great disappointment to me.

When the missionary conference was over at the Sagamia Hotel in Atami, we went by train to Kyoto, the old capital of Japan, where Akira Takagi, an old classmate of mine from Scarritt, was our host. There we saw what we were told was the largest statue in the world of Buddha. I took one of my all-time favorite pictures — the Golden Pavilion reflected in the lake. We visited Nijo Castle with the singing floor. The Shogun had built it with his living quarters in the center and all around a hall with a floor that squeaked so no one could slip up on him. When the whole tour group walked on it, it sounded like a thousand singing birds. I fell behind to hear the sound *one person* made — loud and unpleasant!

My visit to the Peace Museum in Hiroshima was a traumatic experience. I could not keep from weeping. The young girl guide said she had accompanied many Americans through the museum, but I was the first who cried. To me the three greatest blots on our national character are (1) the systematic destruction of the Native Americans, (2) the interning of loyal Japanese American citizens, and (3) being the first to use the atomic bomb to destroy a civilian population.

In 1966, it had been a little over twenty years since the bomb was dropped on August 6, 1945. The only visible scar remaining was the bombed-out dome of one building in the center of the city, and they were debating about removing it.

My visit to the Children's Monument, hung with the thousand crane origami streamers, is unforgettable. The paper cranes are constantly renewed by schoolchildren from all over Japan in memory of Sadako, a young girl of Hiroshima who thought that if she could make a thousand cranes she would not die from the effects of the atom bomb. She got to 644 before she succumbed. Each streamer made since then has one *gold* crane in memory of Sadako. A one-thousand-crane streamer hangs in my living room, made by Michiko's daughter for her father. He gave it to me when I visited their Episcopal parsonage home in 1987. Pat Styles gave me a printed version of the story, *Sadako*,[1] for Christmas, 1990.

In Hiroshima I also visited Women's College and left a note on Mary McMillan's desk. She was in my graduating class at Scarritt and was on furlough in the United States.

Our stops in the city of Osaka, and on the island of Okinawa were not very memorable.

Easter found us in Taipei, Taiwan, where we spent almost a week. We went to a sunrise service, breakfast, and morning worship at a Methodist church and Sunday evening attended a service at a leper colony. The highlight for me was meeting Kathleen Langston Smith. She had come from England to assist Gladys Aylward with the orphans she had brought out of China and into Taiwan during the Japanese invasion of China back in the thirties. I have tried to find the book, *The Inn of the Sixth Happiness*,[2] to refresh my memory, but the library does not have it. I had read the book to my fifth grade class in Spruce Pine in the late 1950s, and we also went as a group to see the movie. The memorable song was the march, "This old man, he played one, etc.," used to encourage the children on their trip through warring factions from the mountains to the sea. I was disappointed that Miss Aylward was in the United States while we were there, but we found Miss Smith to be a most remarkable woman. Betty Motsinger has been in touch with her all these years and says Miss Smith has received much recognition for her work.

As we flew from Taiwan to the Philippines, the captain called attention to the resort city of Baguio on the top of the mountain on the island of Luzon. We stayed in a Methodist community center in Manila with Miss Flora Clipper who was the director. I remember that she had to get up at 2:00 A.M. for her daily routine of getting water to fill the upstairs tub that was then used for many purposes.

When she was discussing what tours we might like to take, Betty said we were not very interested in "tourist things" but would like to meet the people. Miss Clipper said, "Well now, if I just had some way of getting in touch with Miss Walker who works with the Negritos (aborigines) at Tarlac, up in the mountains, she could help you. But one never knows when or where you can find her." Before an hour passed, Miss Walker came by. We took a few of our clothes and went with her to the deaconess graduation and then on to her mountain mission. At Tarlac, we were told five thousand people lived there, and there must have been a dog for every five persons — that barked all the time.

Miss Walker had a kind of compound, where she kept girls from farther out in the mountains. They would stay in the compound, help with cooking, etc., and go to school. Water was scarce — and it was hot!

On Sunday morning I said I was going to take a "talcum powder bath." Betty was not so sure it was a good idea but went along, and it helped. The district superintendent, the minister, and the local doctor were there for breakfast. We went to church early, then went with the doctor to a village farther up in the mountains where he treated those needing healing. One malady was a terrible skin disease that the doctor said was quickly cured *if* one could afford the medicine. I think Betty later provided the means to get the medicine for some of the people there.

At this village there was also a small, roofed church with about a three-foot wall and a gate. Miss Walker said, "Oh, children, you have left the gate open, and the goats are in the church."

After dinner Betty and I were wondering *how* we were going to cope with the excessive heat the rest of the day. Miss Walker had gone to sleep on the bench by the table. Soon she roused up and said, "I think we will go to Baguio City." Remembering that the pilot had said it was a *resort* city, we protested that we had not brought proper clothes. She said that it didn't matter, the Board of Missions had a house there. All the missionaries had to do was take bed linens and blankets, food, and fuel for the stove. Her driver took us in the Land Rover, and we spent a night and morning in that "heavenly cool place."

We flew out of Manila through a solid cloud cover. From my window seat I could see on top of the clouds a plate-size rainbow with the shadow of our plane in the center. It went along with us until we gained altitude; than a conventional rainbow appeared outside my window. I *needed* that assurance when later we flew into some thunderheads we couldn't get above, and experienced such precipitous drops that Betty (who had flown a plane) said, "I don't understand how the wings stay on." I did not feel afraid.

Someone on the plane told us that we would make a brief landing in Saigon. Since this was during the Vietnam War, they did not tell the passengers. I had just taken a picture when the stewardess said, "We will be landing in Saigon in a few minutes. No pictures are allowed." I *set foot* in that airport.

In Singapore only two experiences were memorable. One was the making of rubber, from the tapping of the trees to the operation of the little processing plant where they hung the latex out to dry. The other was seeing "the flags of Singapore." On all the high-rise apartment buildings (and there were many), both in the city and on the outskirts, were poles from each apartment window on which the residents hung their wash to dry, thus the phrase, "the flags of Singapore."

The airport at Kuala Lumpur was new and the most beautiful I saw on the trip. In fact almost everything looked new. As I understood then, it was the capital of the newly formed country of Malaysia, which included thousands of islands in the South China Sea and the Indian Ocean. Singapore was a separate country because it had withdrawn from the Federation.

Then on to Thailand.

I had read the book, *Anna and the King of Siam*,[3] and Arle and I had seen the movie in Philadelphia in about 1946; so it was a great thrill to see the real palace in Bangkok and the floating market, ride in a taxi boat on the Klongs, and have my picture taken on a water buffalo.

From Thailand we headed east again and spent a few days in Hong Kong. One of the traditional things to do there is to have a garment made; so Betty and I went to be measured. I decided on a tweed skirt and jacket with a Thai silk sleeveless blouse. Betty wanted a jacket dress. She emphasized that it must have plenty of room through the shoulders because she drove a jeep (and she demonstrated). I said no to pockets in my jacket. On the way back to our hotel I said, "I *wish* I had said to put pockets in the jacket." When we went to get the outfits, my jacket *had pockets* in it, and Betty later had to send back for material to try to make the shoulders in her dress larger. That experience was illustrative of the story of our lives. Betty had (except for money) *struggled* for everything she wanted in life — even her religious faith — while I always felt that before I called, God answered my need. This was further exemplified by the trip we made up Hong Kong Island. As we walked along the road we saw shells mashed by cars. We thought it rather remarkable that the shells were so far from the sea.

Betty determined that she was going to find a whole one, so I looked, too, on the left side of the road. When Betty crossed to that side, I went to the right and found the colorful, beautiful inside spiral of a broken shell that pleased me, so I stopped looking.

When we reached the top of the island, Betty continued to search for an undamaged shell. She finally went a short distance down the other side of the mountain.

In the meantime, I sat on a rock and wrote postcards. Then I began to think, "This is why Betty's spiritual life has so much more power and depth than mine. As with the shell, I am satisfied with less than perfection, while Betty persists until the best is found."

She *did* find a nice large, whole shell, but in speaking with another visitor she found that it was *not* a sea shell but a snail shell.

The next morning in our devotional time, I told Betty that I felt the seashell episode was indicative of my lack of persistence in my spiritual life. Then she reminded me that the analogy did not carry through to such a conclusion, "Because on the way back you found a small, perfect shell that I would rather have had." I decided that our experiences were unique, and I should stop making comparisons. But to this day, at least for me, "The lines are fallen unto me in pleasant places." (Psalms 16:6) I trust Betty has reached a place beyond struggle.

In Hong Kong in 1966, the residents were already talking about 1995, when the British Crown Colony would revert to mainland China.

When we returned to Tokyo, Michiko was waiting for us. We had lunch with her parents, who were long-time Christians. Her mother had been a nurse before her marriage, which was pretty unusual for that time and culture. Her father was a chiropractor. He gave Betty an adjustment that left her sore for a week. He said I was *loose*, so I escaped.

Michiko accompanied us on the pleasant train ride through the Japanese countryside to meet Jimmy Kikuchi. We saw some of his agricultural experiments. We met his wife and rosy-cheeked baby. We also managed to eat the special "noodle supper" with our chop sticks — even though a maid sat at our elbows with a fork.

Jimmy took us to his church in Sendai where we spent the night in a Sunday school room. Their rooms, bare of furniture, can be adapted for many purposes. During worship, the same room was the nursery.

Sendai was the port city from which we took the ferry overnight to Hokkaido Island. We had berths. It was a very rough passage, and I was seasick. By lying on my stomach and breathing through my mouth I managed to keep my food down, but I have avoided ocean travel since that experience.

We had another train ride to Sapporo, where Michiko taught in the Agricultural College and lived in a Quonset hut left by the U.S. army after World War II. We met her "hut mate," Noriko Satsuma, who had become engaged to Minoru Yamada the day before we arrived.

Minoru was a native of Hokkaido, a member of a close-knit Christian community of dairy farmers. They had been introduced to the idea of producing milk by a Presbyterian missionary in the last quarter of the eighteenth century.

In 1925 the Hokkaido Dairy Cooperative was formed "to enhance the nation's health and physical constitution" and it became the Snow Brand Milk Products Co., Ltd. They had sent Minoru to Wisconsin to study dairying the previous three years.

He had learned to like many American foods and wanted his fiancée to learn the domestic arts. They asked Betty if Nora could live with her and learn, but she declined that teaching role, so they asked me. I said I would keep her if they paid her air fare to the United States and back. Before we left, we made the necessary arrangements for her trip, the dates to be decided later.

On the flight from Sapporo to Tokyo, I told the flight attendant of my disappointment about Mt. Fuji and asked that if it became visible would she let me know. It apparently was known to *all* the other passengers because when Fuji became visible above the clouds everyone on that side of the plane offered their seat so I could see. It was the icing on the cake of my visit.

Now we were ready to head for home. We boarded the plane in Tokyo at 5:30 P.M., Friday, May 13, flew across the Pacific Ocean, and landed in Anchorage at 4:20 A.M., and it was *another* Friday, May 13. That experience dispelled any lingering superstitions I may have had about Friday the thirteenth.

It was good to have a visit with my sister Olive, her husband and three children in Juneau, as well as with my daughter Paula, in whose apartment we stayed. I chastised her for not having food for our breakfast. (Any visit with Paula since that time there has been an abundance of food.)

Paula went with us to Seattle for a visit with her Aunt Elva and Uncle Harold. We arrived home on the sixteenth of May.

NOTES

1. Eleanor Coerr, *Sadako*, (New York: G.P. Putnam's Sons, 1977).
2. *The Inn of the Sixth Happiness*. Out of print. (publication information not available.)
3. Margaret Landore, *Anna and the King of Siam*. (New York: Harper Collins, 1944; reprinted by Buccaneer Books, Cutchogue, N.Y., 1990).

Japanese families I And Far East Trip

Yamada family and Tillie with minister

Mt. Fuji (background) Minoru, Tillie and Nora

Tillie (writing), Michiko Sato - at her home in Tokyo

Special guest dinner - standing Minoru's niece and nephew - L to R - Nora, Minoru, Tillie, Mikage and Nozomi.

Yamada family and Tillie (Christmas card)

Japanese Families II and Far East Trip

Michiko Onuki, her three children, and Tillie - in Hokkaido 5-9-87

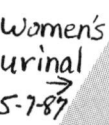

Women's urinal 5-7-87

p 260

Dane and Emi Norman with Tillie in her apt. 2-9-92

Yamadas, Marla, Derek, Jamie with Tillie in her apt. 5-3-90

Emi's college graduation - her parents, Marla and host family Fred and Jean Macon 5-13-90

MY JAPANESE FAMILIES

As mentioned in the previous story, Betty Motsinger and I visited Hokkaido Island in Japan in May, 1966. Before we left there, we made arrangements for Noriko (Nora) Satsuma to come live with me for a year. Nora was the Quonset "hut mate" of Michiko Tonegawa, who had observed rural social work in Yancey County in 1962. Nora intended to learn Western cooking and housekeeping skills, "domestic arts," at the insistence of her fiance, Minoru Yamada. In July, 1966, I had word that she would arrive at Asheville the first Wednesday in August.

U.S. Immigration was quite disturbed when she landed in Hawaii with only a weekend-sized suitcase and a JAL shoulder bag, saying she was going to spend a year with Mrs. Brooks in North Carolina. Since the forty-two dollars she had was not enough to send her back, they let her come on. On the way, she was scheduled to visit Minoru's cousin in California, who called me to tell me of the Immigration problem, and to warn me that Immigration expected her to check in with them as *soon* as she got to North Carolina!

The girls and I were as amazed, as was the U.S. customs agent, when we saw her luggage. Later when it got cold and she had no winter clothing, I asked her *why*. She explained innocently that Minoru had told her that houses, cars, and public buildings in the United States were all heated. And *he* had been in Wisconsin three years!!

The nearest immigration office was Norfolk, Virginia. Fortunately, my next-door neighbor, Gertrude Barrus, had a very aristocratic friend who lived near Norfolk whom she would *love* to see especially since the friend was blind. She lived in a beautiful antebellum home where we could spend the night. Her brother took us to the immigration office the next morning.

I was able to convince them that indeed Nora would be treated as a member of my family — convince them, at least then, — but in January an officer came to my office in Burnsville to check on her well-being.

I said, "I thought the officials in Norfolk were satisfied that she would be treated right; but if you want to ask her if she is being well cared for, she's at the library across the street."

As if on cue, Nora burst into the room, "Oh, Mother — ," and then she saw the man. He looked at me and said, "Okay, okay. We'll not bother you again."

Nora learned the domestic arts, cooked the evening meal, and made three tries before producing an edible lemon pie. She did most of my housework and learned to sew — she had winter clothes to make. She went with us to Celo Church, sang the Lord's Prayer at Marla's wedding and went with me to all Women's Society of Christian Service (WSCS) meetings — even when I spoke at district meetings. She stayed with Mattie Lula Britton, my former Scarritt roommate, while I attended a short course in Nashville. She also went with me to the WSCS annual meeting at Lake Junaluska, North Carolina, where I presented the need for help with her plane fare home. I thought they paid part of the fare, but Nora told me later they paid it all.

It was most remarkable. She was never homesick and only twice was she the least bit unhappy (I think during her period). Once she wanted Dena to turn down the volume on the radio. Dena said, "I live here, too!" The other time a photo finishing place returned an eight-by-ten-inch enlargement of her with the face scratched. She thought it was done deliberately because she was Japanese — even accused me of doing it. I had taken special care in taking the snapshot — had draped her in a rich-colored fabric. It was to be a Christmas gift for Minoru. I explained to her how a negative could be dropped and stepped on in a darkroom and then said, "If you *think* I would go to all this trouble and then scratch the negative, just go ahead and believe it." She sulked one day, and then on the next the house was all cleaned and my favorite supper was prepared when I came home. Nothing more was said. She was *so* happy with us that Dena (a little jealous) once said, "When she goes back home and is just another Japanese, she'll be *hurting*." Her prediction came true. She was so homesick that she wrote, "The only time I am happy is when I go to church and close my eyes and think I am with you in Celo Church." It made it harder for her to readjust because her parents were Buddhist.

She had returned to Japan the last of July and did not marry Minoru until early November. She sent a wedding picture, and I was distressed to see that she *did not* look happy! That was not explained until twenty-one years later when I was trying to reconcile the two dates I had for Emi's birthday. It turned out that Nora had been four months pregnant in the wedding picture, and they were afraid I would be disappointed in them if they told me. (I felt their engagement ceremony was a real commitment, and after their year of separation, I would have understood.) Emi was born April 20, 1968; Nozomi, June 7, 1970.

For many years after Nora returned to Japan, I wrote to her weekly as I did my girls, my mother, and Arle's mother. For my birthday in 1989 Nora sent a bound book, *Letters from Mother — 1967–1988*. It is a pretty complete diary of what had happened in my family during those years. The gift was especially touching because I had not received *answers* to all those letters, but unfailingly on special occasions I did receive her "Dearest Mother" greetings or gifts.

In her Christmas card in 1986 Nora said, "Please come to Japan next year after March. We hope to invite you, Michiko, too. [Michiko was Nora's friend from the Quonset hut.] Please don't be anxious flying cost. We hope to pay half of your trip-fare."

As soon as I read those words, I knew it was something I very much wanted to do, and through all the planning I anticipated this trip with more real excitement than I ever had anytime before.

On Tuesday, April 28, 1987, I got up at 4:45 A.M. to make the trip. Marla took me to Asheville, and the plane left at 7:00 A.M. Paula and her close friend Warren spent the three-hour wait with me in Portland. I had flown across the United States including the Grand Tetons, and now, at 3:00 P.M. Pacific time, still on Tuesday, I was leaving to cross the Pacific non-stop.

I arrived at Norita airport at 3:15 A.M., Wed., by my Eastern Standard Time watch, but it was 4:15 P.M., Wed., in Japan. I had flown into the sun the whole way. Every time I raised the blind, the sun was in the same place. I was 26 hours en route from my home to Nora's - 15¼ hours in the air and 9¼ of those over the Pacific. The whole Yamada extended family met me, and it took about the same amount of time to get from Norita airport to the Yamadas' as it did to fly across the United States. Much to the surprise of the family, I did not have jet-lag.

On Thursday we spent most of the day at the botanical gardens — azaleas and dogwood were in bloom. I noted that the season was very similar to ours in the mountains. More than the flowers, I loved watching the hundreds of kindergartners — all dressed exactly alike — on special school trips.

Friday I rode the train with Nora to her class in ancient Chinese poetry. They chanted it. Their teacher was lovely, and the class members gave me small gifts.

Saturday night Nora prepared a *big* dinner. The invited guests were Michiko's daughter, Minoru's brother's son, and his sister's daughter. I showed slides of my previous trip to Japan and of my home and family.

On Sunday we all went to the Presbyterian church in the new part of Tokyo. The building was only about five years old. The church had very active members and was full of people who sang extremely well — an unusual treat to be with a Christian congregation in Japan where less than 2% are Christian.

Without actually planning, I had arrived for the *best possible* week in Tokyo — Golden Week it was called. It started with the Emperor's birthday, the last Tuesday in April, through May Day and Children's (once Boys') Day the next Monday. Since Minoru was on vacation, we spent most of his last vacation day looking at furniture. They wanted me to suggest ways to redecorate their apartment.

On May 5th we attended the wedding of Minoru's first cousin, Shigeru Yamada, a Presbyterian minister on Hokkaido Island. The bride was Julie Toll who had lived in the United States for thirty years. Her maid of honor was her daughter, who could not speak Japanese. The wedding was arranged by Cho Kuroyanagi, a famous TV personality and a liberated woman! She wore *boots* to the wedding.

On May 6 Nora and I visited model homes in Tokyo that had some innovative features — like a kind of trap door in the kitchen floor opening to steps to a storage space below for vegetables, etc. A home like this was priced at about 33 million yen — $235,714 with the yen at $1.40.

On May 7 I took a plane to Hokkaido to visit Michiko and her family. Masao (her husband) came back to Tokyo with me on the eleventh. He was going to attend the celebration in Osaka of a hundred years of the Episcopal Church in Japan. He served two small Episcopal churches in Abashiri and Kitami.

The memorable events of the four days with Michiko were: (1) Bible study, singing, and eating at a fisherman's home; (2) participating in the tea ceremony with Michiko's adult English class in an antique Japanese home; (3) a ride to the observatory above Abashiri and a visit to the prison gift shop (we had previously visited the original, inhumane prison); (4) a spaghetti lunch with the surgeon's wife and daughters; (5) attending Masao's church in Kitami and then calling on Minoru's sister and family in their parsonage home.

Although I was at Michiko's on Mother's Day, no mention was made of it in the home or at church; but I knew it would be celebrated when I returned to Nora's. We had a very special dinner with flowers and Mother-Daughter sweaters from Minoru ($165 each). I really took him to task for spending that much money, especially since he had bought my plane ticket to Hokkaido, which cost $468. He said, "You did *everything* for Nora for a *whole year*! We *must* do these things for you."

On Tuesday, the twelfth, Nora and I went to Tokyo Disneyland — on land filled in with Tokyo garbage. I *had* to have my picture made with Nora in "Western Land" in a *much* too small dress. I had felt an earthquake at 6:55 that morning. The paper said that from midnight the tenth until 9:00 A.M. the eleventh there had been 728 quakes under the sea, and the next day there was at least one on land.

Nora's aunt and uncle bought us tickets to see a play. I could not understand the language, but the costumes and pantomime told the story pretty well.

Now my visit was nearing the end, and again I had not seen Mt. Fujiyama. On the *very few* smogless, cloudless days in midwinter the mountain *can* be seen from the Yamadas' balcony! They once sent me a picture taken at such a time.

Minoru was determined that I not miss this most typical of Japanese tourist attractions. He watched weather reports and kept in touch with a weatherman friend to find a day when Fuji would be visible. If necessary he would take a day off from work. But it turned out that the best day to see this mountain, over twelve thousand feet high, would be Saturday, the sixteenth — if we went early. So he was easily free to go.

The three of us left about 8:00 A.M. My hosts bought food for both breakfast and lunch at 7-Eleven store(!), and we had our first glimpse of the snow-covered peak from the highway. At a rest stop we saw great crowds — many buses headed for Fuji Park; but Minoru had been advised *not* to go there, but instead to go to the small village of Oshino at the foot of the mountain. I was delighted because I had bought a commercial slide of that village and of Fuji on my first trip to Japan.

The three of us spent several hours there with only a very few other visitors. The clouds were creeping up on Fuji by the time we ate our lunch by Lake Yamanaka, and by three o'clock it was completely hidden.

At three places on the trip, my hosts had gone to the rest room and asked, "Mother, don't you want to go?" I knew the women's facility was like a men's urinal (only in the floor like the one at the Sunday school at Michiko's church, where I had slept in a classroom). Since I cannot squat, I said no. By the time we were ready to start home, Nora was worried about me (or their car). There was a resort hotel by the lake — so she went in to see if they had "mother's kind of toilet." They did, but I *could* have made it home.

On Sunday the three of us went to church, and I paid for us to eat out. Monday was a good day. In the early part of the morning I went with Nora to her physical therapy session for her hand (a birth defect), and then to Michiko Sato's for lunch and the brush painting lesson that Nora and two other women were taking. The lunch was especially for me — all Japanese, even to sake. I even tried my hand at brush painting. They were very kind. They clapped and said I did well. The Japanese characters, translated, said "Peace from God." I have it framed as a companion to the picture Nora had done for me in that class.

Late in the afternoon a young man delivered a breadmaking machine Michiko's husband had bought her. The mix, water, and yeast were put into the machine, and the man said that four hours later a nice, brown loaf would emerge. I had Nora tell him, "On TV in the United States they would have had the final product to show us." Tuesday evening, before I was to leave on Wednesday morning, Michiko brought four slices of the bread. It was delicious.

I showed Nora all the gifts I brought back from Michiko's. She said, "Oh, we have *many* gifts for you in the closet," and she got them out. I knew at once that I would have to mail them by surface mail. I packed two boxes, and it took eighty-six dollars to send them.

Also that day Nora said she would have to go to the bank because she had saved money from her teaching of English to give to me. I *begged* her not to do that, but she went when I didn't know.

Her aunt and uncle came for my special farewell supper. Mrs. Sato's bread was part of it. And we decided on a few more things "one *must* do." Minoru said they *must* take a family photo. I suggested that he have his equipment all set up, and when we were dressed ready to go on our way Wednesday morning he could take the picture. Not only did he do that, but he was up until 1:30 A.M. making a copy of the videotape of my visit for me to bring home.

We got up early and did the picture — *very* good! They used it as their "family Christmas card." At the hotel where we got the limo to the airport, Minoru gave me a *good* hug "before God and everybody," which was most unusual because Japanese men *do not* show affection in public (Masao did not say good-bye to Michiko when we left Hokkaido).

Nora went with me to the airport — about a five-hour drive. I took her to lunch at Shoney's Big Boy at the airport and gave her the rest of my yen not knowing I needed 2,000 yen to get through the gate, so Nora had to pay it. She had given me a pretty envelope that I was to open later, after we had said good-bye.

The plane was to leave at 1:45 P.M., but the plane's storage door would not close. After two trips to the plane and back we finally took off at 7:25 P.M. I had called Paula to say I would be late, which was actually more convenient for her. The last thing I ate in Japan was Orville Redenbacher popcorn. I slept most of the way back. It was a wide-body plane, seating about four hundred. There were only forty on the flight.

Now to account for finances. Nora had sent me $800 with which I paid about three-quarters of the round-trip airfare. The first day I was there, Minoru left me ten thousand yen (about $71). I gave him a hundred dollar bill to get changed for me. He did, at the $1.35 exchange rate, which was the *lowest* it had ever been. I mentioned the $468 trip to Hokkaido, then all the bus and train fare everywhere we went, and all the entrance fees. There was the $165 sweater, the two-thousand-yen gate entrance fee — and now the envelope!!

First, there were *my* very own bills — one hundred, two twenties, and a five — that I had given to Minoru to have exchanged. He had brought me the yen, but here were my bills! Then the money from Nora's teaching — thirty thousand yen that exchanged into U.S. currency as $213. I just *thought* I had spent my money. All I spent was what I charged to Visa — gifts for the girls. I got back with over a hundred dollars more than I took to Japan, so I paid for the Memorial Day weekend trip for Paula, her friend Warren, his mother Betty, and me.

Early in 1988 Emi wrote asking me to send material about junior colleges in some place not *too cold* or *too hot*. From those I sent information about, she chose Brevard College, a Methodist-affiliated school near Asheville. I helped make some arrangements, and she came that fall. Her host family was Fred and Jean Macon. He was pastor of First UM Church in Brevard. Emi sang in the choir.

She spent most of the Christmas holidays with me the first year and other less extended times during her two years here. Her whole family came for her graduation in May, 1990. She graduated *magna cum laude*, which I thought quite remarkable.

Between the two of us, Betty Motsinger and I were able to show the family the main tourist attractions. One special place that Nora wanted to visit was the log house. We had a picnic there, and while we were eating, John and Reva Griffith came by. They had spent the first three months of their marriage in the log house forty-three years before. They had planned to come by to see me, but would have missed me.

Emi worked in Tokyo for a year. In 1991 she came back to the States and was in college in Lake Charles, Louisiana, then married Dane Norman (whom she had met at Brevard) and transferred to UNC-Asheville. They have lived in a mobile home near Asheville and visited me a couple of times.

Nozomi was accepted at Brevard for the 1992–93 term — especially for flute instruction. She spent about a month with me, learning English and practicing the flute — for the cows. Emi and Dave came for her when school started in August.

On the Friday before Mothers' Day, 1993, Deanie's Florist here in Burnsville called to see if I was home; they had an arrangement to deliver. I guessed that it would be from Nora, and I was right. However, when a florist from Asheville called early Saturday morning to ask for directions to deliver another floral gift, I was at loss to figure who the donor could be.

"Why all the way from Asheville?" I asked. "Can't it be sent from Burnsville?"

"No, we're the only florist in the area that has the item the customer wanted, and she is insistent that nothing else will do as a substitute." I had to give directions the second time before the poor man got here about nine o'clock. I gave him a warm bran muffin and a box of fruit juice because I knew he'd had no breakfast.

Now to solve the mystery. This arrangement was also from Nora, and the driver had instructions to take the Friday one back. How strange! They were from different florists. The second one *was* in a different *class*! It was a delicately painted, real teapot holding the cut flowers. I've still not had any formal explanation; but this is the way I figured it out.

Nora had wired the arrangement that the Burnsville florist delivered on Friday, then she saw an ad on TV showing the lovely FTD teapot, and she thought, "That is what I want to send to mother." So she called Emi in Asheville and asked her to find it and have it sent. Emi, a dutiful daughter, called florists until she found it. I still don't know about taking the Friday one back. Maybe she got a discount.

Both girls visited their parents, Nora and Minoru, in their new home on Hokkaido Island during the summer of 1993.

Emi and Nozomi had lunch and spent two hours with me in October of 1993. I had Christmas greetings from both girls, pictures of me with them from Nozomi. They came for my birthday, Friday the eleventh, and had baked me a pretty fruit pie, but I was out to dinner, and missed them. The pie *was* delicious!

NEW ENGLAND

After I retired from the National Division (UMC) the last of August, 1980, I stayed on at the Lakeland Parish and began compiling a list of prospective residents for the Lakeland Wesley Village that was being constructed near Kentucky Lake, Kentucky.

I had been informed that I would serve as resident manager when the facility was complete. Robert Werle, the executive director, thought I would benefit from attendance at the American Association of Homes for the Aging conference being held in Boston that fall, from Friday to the following Wednesday noon. Since I had never been to the New England states, I extended my reservation to return on Saturday.

I drove to Nashville where Bob lived and followed him to the airport. He would leave his car in airport parking, but since I was staying longer, he suggested I park in a field on a nearby hill to save parking fees. We had to rush to make our flight, so I did not fix in my mind the parking spot.

On Monday morning of the conference I decided to see if being a deaconess in a "connectional church" could be helpful to me. I found the number of a Methodist church in the directory and called. To the woman who answered I said, "I am a Methodist deaconess attending a conference in your city. It is my first trip to New England. My meeting ends Wednesday noon, and my plane does not leave until Saturday morning. I was wondering if there is a woman who would take a tour with me if I paid the way."

The woman said, "I wish I could take you up on that offer, but I cannot; however, I'll see what I can do. What time will you be back in your room?"

"About four o'clock." The call came at that time.

"Please hold for the bishop's office," the girl said. It was *not* the bishop, but it *was* the editor of the conference newspaper, C.T. Whitehouse.

He said he and his wife, Libby, would be delighted to spend Friday showing me their historic area. He asked about my hotel accommodations. I told him I was staying at the downtown Boston Sheraton, paying forty-five dollars a night for a room so small I had to climb over the foot of the bed to get into the closet. He said he could get me a better deal. He was on the board of an Episcopal guest home for missionaries, and he would check to find out if they had a room available. He would come for me after he got off work on Wednesday.

He was as good as his word and took me to the home in Auburndale, a lovely suburb of Boston. I had a "suite of rooms" on the ground floor for five dollars a night, with breakfast for a dollar and the evening meal for three dollars.

I took a walking tour of the neighborhood and found a tree to add to my collection of "memorable trees." It was a *huge* copper beech (new to me) on the grounds of a Catholic church. The outer edges of the lowest limbs were about three feet off the ground. I took a photo looking down through the leaves to the grass below. It made an unusual picture. It is enlarged and hangs in the photo gallery throughout my apartment.

On Thursday I got up enough nerve to go back to Boston on the train by myself to see at least a few of the main tourist attractions — the Old North Church, the Boston Commons, and to see and read an account of the outstanding facts about the fabulous organ at the Christian Science Church. I had heard the organ on Sunday; since the church was near my hotel, I had attended worship there.

C.T. and Libby arrived at the missionary home at 9:00 A.M. on Friday as he had promised, and our tour began. They drove through the Brandeis University campus, and then we did the historic highlights — Lexington and Concord and several homes of renowned American authors. We ate lunch at Rockport and I took a picture of what is said to be the most photographed scene in the United States — the harbor with its many sailing vessels.

It was so pleasant to be with those two — like old friends. We had plenty of "Methodist subjects" to talk about. We ended the day sitting on the front row at an auditorium where on the stage a young man acted out the complete book of the gospel of Mark.

(In November of 1993, when I looked in my address book to be sure of their names before starting to write this story, I found a telephone number as well, so I called to say hello. C.T. seemed fine but Libby has had some health problems. They may make a trip to Florida in the near future. I invited them to stop with me for a night.)

I arrived back in Nashville after dark on Saturday. I hired a taxi to get to the place where I expected to find my car, which in the dark I was unable to do. A fellow Church and Community worker, Laura Wells, lived in the city, so I called her for a night's lodging. We found my car the next morning, but again the "Methodist connectional system" had come to my rescue.

A BUS TRIP HOME

Venice, Florida, January 30, 1991 — 3:30 P.M.
to Asheville, NC, January 31, 1991 — 3:40 P.M.

I decided to write a "thought journal" of this trip because I thought it would give some clues as to how I, at age 76, could make such an overnight bus trip, and have dinner with Marla at the end, feeling much as I do at the close of an ordinary day.

We left my sister Lucille's apartment at 3:10 feeling that was ample time, but a car blocked our line of traffic at an intersection, and we sat there, watching the minutes ticking away. I had mental images of what would happen if I missed that bus. Lucille said she was sure the bus would be late. Fortunately, we found an alley we could duck through to the next street. I was glad I had bought my ticket when we'd checked out the location on Saturday. We arrived at 3:30. The bus *was* fifteen minutes late leaving.

My thoughts, as I rode from Venice to Sarasota, were an overall reliving of the visit. The first thing I was thankful for was the weather. During my visit it was cool — even down to upper thirties some places in Florida, and an all-day downpour furnished much needed moisture. Then the day before I left, it turned sunny enough for a few hours at the beach to look for sharks' teeth. Another thing I was thankful for was the time I had with Lucille; it was the longest we'd spent together since we kept house for our younger siblings, boarded the school teacher and "burned the house down" on Cheat River in 1933–34. [Details of this time are in my Mini-autobiography, earlier in this book.] I was glad to finally meet Margo, Lucille's sister-in-law, and have a Chinese dinner out with her; and I felt pleased with my shopping — even to getting into the smaller-sized pants I had bought before I left. I noted that the bus was alternating between I-75 and U.S. 41.

Then my mind went back to the very beginning of the trip — how I decided to go before the Disciple study was finished, and the members' tribute to me the last night I was there. How I'd been hoping someone from our church would be driving to Florida and looking for someone to ride with them. How in the January church paper there had been such an invitation — no name, but a note to call 682-4496. I went through the whole Burnsville directory looking for 682-44__, then finally gave up and called. Doriscey Young answered. I didn't know her yet, but we made plans to travel together, leaving Friday, January eleventh. As I rode the bus home, I thought about how we spent that first night in a very nice Econo Lodge in Byron, Georgia. How much of the Saturday driving was spent listening to the Senate debate on whether we would continue to favor sanctions against Iraq, or authorize the president to use military might if the U.N. deadline of January fifteenth(?) was not met to get out of Kuwait. Doriscey spent Saturday night with Lucille and me.

On the next leg of the journey home, from Sarasota to Tampa, the sunset was so lovely that it brought back the night before when Lucille's friend, Gayloree Hammond, had driven us to Sarasota to eat at Marina Jack's and to see the lovely yacht with the huge lighted heart and its message, "Be my real Valentine." The boat had docked while its occupants came in to dine.

I changed buses in Tampa. I had eaten a sandwich of banana bread (I had made) and cream cheese, apple and cookie, so here I got a milkshake.

Riding on the right side of the bus out of Tampa I enjoyed the full moon in the east as we alternated between I-75 and Hwy. 301 into Ocala and Gainesville, Florida. Then the clouds came and it began to rain hard. It must have been about this time that I got four or four-and-a-half hours sleep.

I knew when we stopped at the Georgia towns of Valdosta, Tifton, Cordele (I remembered Cordele as a place where I'd stopped overnight on one of my solo drives to Florida) and Macon. We were mostly on Hwy. 23 but sometimes on I-75, as we came into Atlanta.

I had to change buses again. The bus management's food supplier of choice seemed to be Burger King. This time I got egg, bacon and cheese on a croissant and milk. As I was eating, a tall, very shabbily dressed man came to my table and sat down. "Could I ask you a question?" he said. I never could understand his questions, but did get the gist that he wanted money for food. Even though I could smell alcohol on his breath, I gave him two dollars. He thanked me profusely and said "You are a very generous lady." I said, "That was *not* a generous gift, but I'm not in a position to give money away, since my billfold was stolen recently." He professed much concern that anyone would do such a thing to me!

I left Atlanta on a Trailways instead of a Greyhound bus. I saw we were on I-85 at times, but soon left it for U.S. 23, and my conversation companion got off at Gainesville to go to her home in Tennessee. There we took U.S. 129 to U.S. 19 into Blairsville, Georgia.

The itinerary *in my mind* took me through South Carolina and into Asheville from the east, but that was *not* the one we would take. U.S. 23 headed for North Carolina and places that brought back so many vivid memories.

When we were on U.S. 441 for a while, I thought of the bus tour I had brought Zesta Club senior citizens on from my work in Kentucky. We were headed for the Smokies on 441 when we came to a sign that said buses could go no farther on that road, so we had to take a less direct route. It was a good trip — even the touchy maneuvering of the bus through Lost Cove.

When I saw a sign to Sky Valley, I wondered why that rang a bell. Then I remembered that Dave Salstrom had been there before he came to be with us at Celo. It was a kind of intentional community that was very health conscious, and Dave had told me this story about it: The native people told the community members that they ate the poke, which grew abundantly around them, for greens. What they failed to say was that it had to be young and cooked, or it would be poisonous. The community members, in their zeal, of course, thought *raw* would be better. Fortunately for them, they had mixed the poke with other greens, so it only made them ill.

When we came to the town of Murphy, I thought about the North Carolina saying that describes the east-west extremities of the state with the words "From Murphy to Manteo" — like the Biblical "Dan to Beersheba" that describes the north-south limits of Palestine.

From Murphy I traveled ahead in my mind on U.S. 64, because it was so familiar — through Hayesville, by Hinton Rural Life Center and Shooting Creek, over a couple of big mountains into Franklin. I had been at Hinton Center for meetings of the Small Membership Church, but especially for the executive committee of the United Methodist Rural Fellowship. I had served as treasurer for eight years, but was unable to go to Louisville last year for the Jubilee (fifty-year) celebration. I was at a meeting at Hinton when word came on TV that Martin Luther King had been shot.

I saw the sign to Hayesville, but we stayed on 19 to Sylva and Waynesville. It was there that the *big* memories kicked in, because Lake Junaluska was nearby, which is our conference center for the Southeast jurisdiction.

During my eleven-plus years working here in the Western North Carolina conference, at least some part of each summer was spent at Lake Junaluska. One of my early experiences was as a counselor for Senior High camp. One night I had thought every one of my girls was accounted for and asleep, when I was awakened at 3:00 A.M. with uncontrolled sobbing next door. When I went to investigate, the girl said her roommate was supposed to meet a boy to go get married, and if he didn't come she was going to drown herself in the lake. I had to go to another building and alert the camp directors. They found her *not* drowned and *unmarried*; but I could not be persuaded to work with Senior Highs after that.

Between Waynesville and Lake Junaluska we passed a Methodist church with a wooded area behind it that *really* triggered a vivid memory.

Since there were in the WNC conference several Church & Community workers in the 1960s, the Conference utilized us to train women college students to work in the small churches during the summer. They received special instruction in conducting Bible school, day camping, and general youth work.

One year the setting for our day-camp experience was the church I mentioned above. We were divided into about four groups to establish our "Home in the Woods." One of my girls came bounding down the hill through the woods. She suddenly stopped with a scream. She had stepped on a metal spike of some kind, hidden in the leaves. On investigation I found it was part of a rack, like the kind we used to put jars in a hot water bath. It had gone through her tennis shoe and was almost through the top of her foot. I pulled the spike out, she was taken to the doctor and "her family" said a prayer for her. She did not experience extended effects.

When this group first met at Lake Junaluska we stayed in the apartments there. I was allowed to take my three girls. The last couple of years we stayed in one of the large houses on the hill facing the lake. Two episodes from those last couple of years before I moved to Kentucky stand out in my mind.

The first episode I remembered was one evening after dinner when Laura Wells said, "Tillie, I think you should tell these girls the story about you and Arle, the one that you told me when we took that short course at West Virginia University." There on the porch, I began the story of our odd meeting, our strange courtship and our eventual marriage. [It is mainly the story I've told in the Arle section, earlier in this book.] It took so long to tell that night, that we had to move inside before the final sad — yet triumphant — end came.

The second episode must have been the last summer we had the training — perhaps 1968. The other workers had asked me to do a morning devotional study with the group. It was the day we were to do the day-camp actual experience, and the topic for consideration was "Praying with Faith." We had chosen a site in a little valley on our side of the lake. The forecast was for rain — which it did *very* easily at Lake Junaluska. *My* faith dilemma was — could I encourage us to pray that it would not rain on our plans.

I got up quite early that morning and went down by the lake. Sitting on one of the large, low posts by the walk, I told God that I thought it might be best to stay clear of the rain question, because failure of our prayer might damage the faith of these young people for the rest of their lives. That was pretty much settled when I saw a shower coming across the lake. I sat still. It came to the edge of the lake in front of me and stopped. "Okay, God. I'll go out on a limb and we'll pray that *wherever* it might rain, that it *not* rain on us." Which we did.

Later that day, out in "our homes," we saw the rain coming. They ran to me. "Tillie, shall we gather up our things?"

"No, let's wait and see. Water won't hurt us, or anything we have."

Rain was all around us, but skipped our little valley with only a sprinkle or two.

I suppose it was seventeen years later when the Conference UMW had a luncheon at Lambuth Inn for those of us who had retired. A woman came to my table. "It's good to see you, Tillie Brooks. I've never forgotten the day when it *didn't* rain on 'our homes in the valley.'" She had been one of the trainees.

Before my "first retirement" in the fall of 1980, I got to attend Jurisdiction Conference at Lake Junaluska as a lay delegate from the Memphis conference. It was an enlightening experience. That is where the election of bishops takes place every four years. Jerry Carr (a ministerial veteran of other such conferences) was a bit apologetic for the "politicking" that went on, but on the flip side it was interesting to learn that a council of ministers and lay people decided where the *bishops* would serve!

I believe it was at this meeting that Peg Neal asked me if I had been to the new Terrace Inn. The answer was no. She said I should go there, to the main lobby, because there was an enlarged photograph of my red-roofed barn at Celo, taken by John Morgan.

Peg had lived in the front room of my log house and looked at that barn from a little different angle than John had when he lived in our crib cabin and took the photo. I did go to see it, and other pictures of his nature scenes in the halls of the Inn.

As I went by on the bus, I could see the Terrace, Lambuth Inn and the cross overlooking the lake. I thought of the blown-up photo of the cross I had, enlarged from my own snapshot.

It took a lot less time to *think* these things than to write about them; not unlike the way your whole life is said to flash before you in a death-threatening situation.

By taking this alternate route the bus arrived at the Asheville station at 2:05 instead of 3:40. I still had to wait for Marla to get off work at 4:30. The bus station was within walking distance of K-Mart and Gimbles.

I had determined to try to find a folding umbrella to send back to Lucille with the pillow she'd lent me to use on the bus, and decided this was as good a time as any to find it. I disliked being remembered as the donor of a malfunctioning umbrella, which she kept in her car, and which I had been unable to open when we needed it.

I walked the four to six blocks in bitter cold and very strong wind — and I later heard that the wind-chill factor was below zero. Marla came at 4:40, we ate at Ryan's, and I got home to Burnsville at 7:30, feeling fine. About ten o'clock, though, I began to feel effects of the cold, which stayed with me for several days. I still think the *bus trip* was fine! And my thoughts kept me very good company.

Marla Brooks Lang
I

Charles and Marla Lang, Paula and Dena Brooks

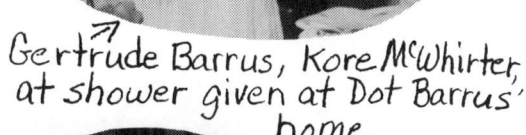
Gertrude Barrus, Kore McWhirter, at shower given at Dot Barrus' home

Dena, best friend Julie Rutledge, Nora, Paula, Me and Charles.

Dena, Mama, Me, and Paula - wedding in Alabama

Dena, Susan Lang, Paula, Charles, me (pregnant with Robbie) Vi Lang, Henry (Hank) Lang and Tessa Swink. Log house in Celo

Marla Brooks Lang II

↗ Willard and Mary Lee Hill with Robbie

Robbie about 4 yrs old →

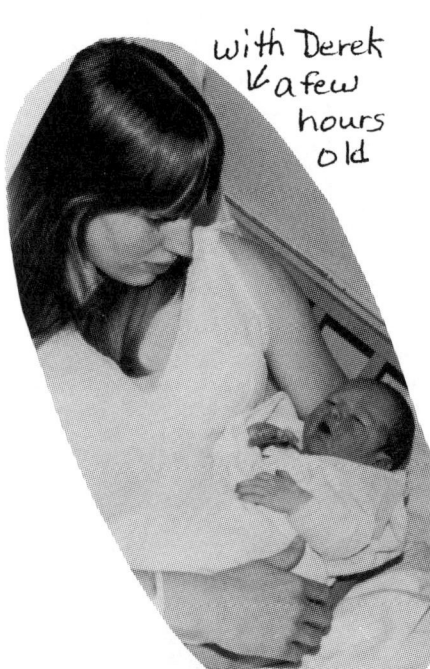

With Derek ↙ a few hours old

Robbie, Derek and me ↖ at Mom's in Ky.

Derek and → Robbie - ready to help mow

Marla Brooks Hoover
I

"Buster" James and Debbie Hoover, Mary Rutledge, at wedding breakfast
→ 5-9-71

↖ Tom Rutledge, Cathy Thomas, me, Robbie, and Jerry during wedding on lawn at the log house
5-9-71

↑ Derek, Jamie and Robbie

Robbie, Mama, Jamie and Derek
↓

↖ Jamie kicking (left foot) ball at Mama's in Ky. about 2 yrs old

Marla Brook Hoover
II

Derek, Dena, Me, Mama, Robbie, Paula and Jamie at my house in Burnsville, N.C.

my grandson Jeremy age two

Jamie, Robbie, Mama, Robbie's son Jeremy, step-son Josh, wife Wendi, Derek and me at Higgins UMC

Robbie and Wendi with Jeremy - spring '93

Great-granddad James Hoover, Jeremy, Uncle Derek and great-grandma Nelle

Marla Brooks Hoover III

Jamie, Robbie, Me, Derek ← and Mama at Derek's graduation from Mars Hill College 5-10-92

Charles Lang, Derek, ← and Vi Lang at Derek's graduation

in Norfolk with Josh, Robbie and Jeremy →

Derek, Charles, Susan ← Lang's husband Bob Harris. and Jamie

Section V
SPECIAL OCCASION WRITINGS

HEALING SERVICE

Higgins Memorial UMC Background Experience
by Arthelia (Tillie) Brooks, August 18, 1991

The book *Final Exit*[1] by Derek Humphrey made the top of the *New York Times* bestseller list last week. It is a "how-to" book on orchestrating your own death. It is selling best in Florida. When an expert was asked to explain why the sales were outdistancing the promotion, he said, "(1) failure of the family structure, (2) failure of our health care system, and (3) failure of our religious faith to meet the needs in this area. People want control — not only of their life but of their death. They are afraid of being kept alive artificially, of living beyond their mental capacities, and of being a burden and expense to their families."

With these, and other disturbing accounts in the media about the right to die, we do have a few encouraging signs for which to give thanks: (1) Mother Theresa and her world-wide ministry; (2) Elisabeth Kubler-Ross, who has spent many years writing and lecturing on death and dying; (3) St. Christopher Hospice in London for starting that helpful movement; (4) for Dr. Hagler and his awareness of our need to learn how to deal with the loss of a loved one and our death; (5) for an increasing number of hospitals using teams composed of doctor, nurse, minister, and psychiatrist; and, (6) for this church desiring to help us achieve holistic health through these healing services.

Except in a broad sense, I would not claim healing as one of my gifts. Scott Kisker identified my gift, but I'm not sure what he said. I think it had to do with communication. If so, I pray that as I share my experiences, the Holy Spirit will give you understanding and fresh insight into the areas of your life that need healing.

LET US PRAY SILENTLY FOR ONE ANOTHER

Health of the whole person has its foundation in Matt. 22:37–39. "You shall love the Lord your God with all your heart, and with all your soul, and with all your mind. This is the first and great commandment. And a second is like it. Your shall love your neighbor as yourself."[2]

It could have stopped with "You shall love your neighbor"; but Jesus, in his wisdom, knew that love of self was important. Indeed, if one cannot affirm, respect, forgive, and love oneself, it is next to impossible to love God or neighbor.

My experience of the truth of this came in January, 1971, when I was probably the only non-charismatic member of an ecumenical group of twelve that went to South America for nearly a month to encourage and minister to English-speaking missionaries, priests, and nuns. My former pastor at Celo, North Carolina, Joe Petree, was the organizer of the trip. I went not as a leader, but for the experience. I paid my own way. Four of us spent the first weekend in Quito, Ecuador, with two women Catholic missionaries, then joined the others in Lima, Peru.

At one of the initial meetings, the Catholic priest (who did most of the teaching) and a psychiatric nurse led us in a healing of the memories. They began in the womb where we may have been unwanted, through the trauma of birth, taking our first steps, leaving the security of home for first day at school. On through puberty, times of rejection, choosing a vocation, courtship, marriage, broken relationships — perhaps divorce; and any sins of commission or omission. *Anything* that had left an unhealed wound. I went with them through all these phases and could not find *anything* more than a few faint scars. But apparently it was not so with most of the audience because counselors, one-on-one, were kept busy long hours through the week.

This demonstrated to me the necessity of dealing with the self; but I also began to be aware that some problems within our group of twelve could use some healing. There were disagreements as to methods of ministry (the Illinois farm woman left the middle of the first week because she felt her ideas were rejected); there were questions about distribution of funds, favoritism and inequity in housing; and complaints that the Catholic priest drank too much wine. These were the ones I knew about.

The first retreat in Lima was at a Catholic girls school, and the next in Chimbote, was also at a Catholic school. This town was near the epicenter of the 1970 Peruvian earthquake. The Catholic school and the tiny Methodist church were about the only buildings left standing. The group also ministered in another place in Peru; but David and I went to Cuzco and Machu Picchu because the ladies in

Ecuador said it was a *must* if we never expected to return to South America.

The last retreat was in Cochabamba, Bolivia, at a Methodist school and we had a much smaller group. Perhaps I felt more at home; so this one was more meaningful to me. At the beautiful chapel in Lima, I had not felt free to take communion because I did not believe in transubstantiation. However, I was enthralled by several hundred people singing in the spirit.

At our final communion in Bolivia we were on the third floor of the main building. The sides were open to the tree tops. As the group sang *Fill My Cup, Lord*[3] the priest elevated the cup; we then sang *Bread of Heaven, feed me 'til I want no more*,[4] and the bread was lifted. I could participate in that. The Holy Spirit came in great power, God was praised, and any who still harbored resentment against another asked forgiveness and were reconciled. It was an unforgettable experience, a true healing of relationships.

Sometimes I have my own relationship problems. I have a friend here in town whom I've known since the sixties. She has serious health difficulties, lives with regrets of wrong past decisions and a present concern for her only daughter. Through the years of trying to be helpful, I have felt so inadequate to meet her real needs that periodically, in pure frustration, I have lost patience and said things I shouldn't have said. I did it again over the phone on a Wednesday night. My friend told me she did not need a lecture from me — that I had no compassion for the pain she had to endure daily, and she would pray that God would deal with me. I said, "God and I are getting along just fine in this matter." But I really regret these failures to be considerate and loving, and God knows it. I love His sense of humor in teaching me. At three the next morning (my praying/worrying hour), I read a daily devotional book in which I was a week behind. The paragraph for my instruction was, "It is important to remember that love is more than a feeling . . . the real test of any loving [for me] is not that I feel loving but that the other person feels loved by me. Love is what I do to create this sense of being cared for. It is independent of my personal feelings."

I usually don't say I'm sorry after these episodes, so I just went back on Friday and shopped for groceries for her. When I went to leave, she handed me a picture frame with a poem in it. God has given her the uncanny ability to pull from the multitudinous array of papers, books, and magazines in her apartment the exact thing to meet her or someone else's need. One verse of the poem said,

> "If you can give your help without begrudging,
> The patience, time and effort you impart.
> Or look at the other's weakness without judging
> And see not with your eyes but with your heart."

and ended,

> "You'll be a woman, and all those around you
> Will be richer for your womanhood."

My chief experience with illness of the body was with my own husband whom I met at Scarritt College in Nashville in March, 1940. He became ill while we were having dinner with a friend on our first real date. He recovered sufficiently to propose marriage later that night. I said no, because I had promised the Methodist women I would work four years to repay my scholarship. We were married in 1944, and every six months or so he would have one of those attacks.

By the time we moved to Celo in 1947, the attacks were becoming more frequent. In consulting with our physician, Dr. Ohle, about him I said, "I think it is a tumor on his brain, but we have no insurance or savings to pay for the electroencephalograms needed to find out."

I suppose that during my years studying at Scarritt, I accepted the healing miracles as something God was able to do through Christ. Although I had heard much about faith healing, intellectually I had real trouble relating it to my ministry. But God was most gracious in teaching me by using circumstances that surely only He could have devised.

A diary entry for July 15, 1950 reads, "Reba Hooks from Bennettsville, South Carolina, came by for half an hour." Reba's parents lived in Marion, North Carolina. Someway, the Lord had been preparing her for a coming ordeal, and she was seeking deeper meaning for her life. She had heard a Methodist minister speak at PTA and felt he would understand her needs better than her Baptist minister. He was the father of John Griffith who had been at our retreat center earlier (1947); so Brother Griffith suggested that since Reba was coming to see her parents near Marion, that she go see Arle and Tillie. Brother Griffith couldn't remember our last name; so Reba came up the mountain and found us. We met for only half an hour, but a real bond was forged. In November my daughter, Dena, and I went to Bennettsville and spent almost a week there. Reba was part of a prayer group of women in their early forties as was Lem Crosland (now Lem Anglin, living here in town). I felt real kinship with these women. In early spring of 1951 one of them wrote that Reba had had an operation for cancer.

Arle was becoming ill more frequently. I wrote in my diary for July 11, 1951, "Arle's sick. Marla is not sleeping well. This was the lowest day of my earthly existence." Then during August, Arle felt pretty well. Since he had a chance to ride with a friend, he decided to go see his parents in Texas who had not been well. He became ill on the way and then got progressively worse. In late September his sister wired that I would have to come to decide what to do for him. I left the three girls with neighbors and arrived October first.

He was almost paralyzed — couldn't even swallow. In two weeks, although he could not stand alone, I was able to bring him back on the bus with a two-night stop in Tennessee. He made the trip well, but was soon ill again.

In a borrowed car, a friend and I took him to the Friend's Psychiatric Hospital in Philadelphia — mostly because they would take Arle because he had worked for the Friends Service Committee. He was admitted November 14. I still felt my early diagnosis was right, so I *stressed* that they should check for tumor before any other treatment.

I got home Saturday and collected the girls. Sunday night the word came that Arle was in Philadelphia General Hospital. They thought it might be tumor on the brain. His former secretary, who knew of our lack of funds, had put on a doctor's coat, hired an ambulance, and admitted Arle before they had time to ask questions.

I took Dena and returned to Philadelphia by train on Tuesday. We stayed with friends for Thanksgiving, and then a Quaker friend rented a third floor apartment ten blocks from the hospital and came to stay with Dena often while I visited Arle.

Arle served as a guinea pig for three weeks (and became most beloved by the hospital staff). They could not be absolutely sure of the tumor — his body was so strong. They didn't know for certain until they did electroencephalograms before his eight-hour operation on December 6. At the end, the young intern from North Carolina said, "I'll not pull any punches. I don't see how he can possibly live." I assured him that he would because on *that Monday morning* as I prayed in the wood yard (where I'd gone to pick up chips to build a fire), I had received this instruction: "Tell the older girls you will have to leave them again; but Daddy will be okay, and we'll all be together at Grandma's for Christmas." On December 19 he walked the three flights of stairs to the apartment. On the twenty-second my younger brother, who worked at the Pentagon, came for us. My other brother had already brought the two girls from North Carolina. We were together at Grandma's for Christmas. We stayed until the last of February.

In April I had word from Lem that Reba was not expected to live. Could I please come? I went on April thirtieth. Trying to deal with my intellectual doubts about God's healing today, I had been reading Agnes Sanford's *The Healing Light*.[5] I finished it the night before I left and prayed, "Father, if there is something you need to show me, this would be a good time. If you could just ease her pain so they wouldn't have to give her strong medicine . . . so she will know me . . . that would be a good sign."

I arrived at 4:00 P.M. on Wednesday. The first thing I was told was that she had not had a shot since last night. I gave thanks! I went to her bed and took her hand and whispered, "This is Tillie." She opened her eyes and looked rather wild; then opened and shut them three times before she could believe. Then she said over and over, "Oh, Tillie. You are so beautiful! How did you get here?" I said, "By bus." And she said, "Oh, no, you didn't. You just rolled down the mountain."

Since Brother Griffith was at General Conference on the west coast, I asked the young Episcopalian priest who had become a friend to the family to give me communion for my personal cleansing that I might be a vessel fit for the channeling of God's healing love to this, His child, whom I loved so deeply. The prayer group also prayed earnestly.

On Tuesday Reba's doctor had said she could not live more than forty-eight hours. Her eyes were yellow as gold, her abdomen swollen tight as a drum. Her kidney and bowels had ceased voiding. Her systolic blood pressure read 65, and her pulse was soft.

I spent Thursday praying as I looked at her wedding picture, and periodically going to her room, touching her abdomen, and asking for Jesus's mercy. That evening at seven o'clock, I watched as her doctor examined her in complete amazement. She had taken food, she voided twice, her pulse was stronger, and her blood pressure was 110. The doctor said, "The longer I practice medicine the less I understand some things. Reba, you are better in every way."

When I got to the house the next morning, Reba's mother said Reba was saying, "Tillie's gone. I know she's gone." I assured her I was still with her, but I did have to go home to my girls and ill husband. Reba died the next Wednesday, May 7, 1952. Why did she have to die?

I went to see Reba's parents soon after. Her mother echoed

Martha's remark to Jesus, "If you had stayed, Reba would have lived." We both knew that was not true, but it took us a year to sort out what we had experienced. These are some of our conclusions: (1) my coming, not having witnessed Reba's decline, brought new hope to the family and prayer group; (2) Our prayers did avail much. We did witness her healing — as Jesus said about raising Lazarus, "That they may believe." (I have never again doubted that God *could* heal miraculously.) (3) So there must be a reason why Reba was not meant to live.

I have long felt that one of the causes of cancer is negative feelings — fear, anger, worry, frustration, hate, etc. Reba had two children, the eldest — a mentally retarded daughter — was coming into puberty, and Reba didn't know how she was going to cope. Even in her delirium, she worried about Nancy. To me *that was the reason* she could not be well; and her mother agreed, especially after the wonderful things that happened in the family after her death. George, her husband, married a lovely woman who was able to help Nancy in a detached yet loving way, and other good things happened that made her mother believe that Reba was directing them from her newfound freedom.

During the summer of 1952 Arle was able to raise a garden and try to cope with his inability to express his thoughts in speech or writing — something he had done so well before his brain operation. In June of 1953 when I began working with the churches in this county, he worried every time I drove away that I would be killed and he would be left with the care of the children. He began to be paralyzed, and we could see the skin over the hole in his skull puff out. We both knew what that meant, and were at a loss to know where to turn. On the evening of July fifth, Arle took the girls swimming in the South Toe River; then the vomiting came back again. He went into coma at 3:00 A.M. and died at ten minutes after noon, July 6, 1953. "Hemorrhage of the brain," Dr. Ohle said. "He has been spared indescribable pain."

One more thing I think my experience has taught me: when we ignore what we feel is God's will for our life, our body responds negatively. In 1961, in one of my churches in Yancey County, North Carolina, the father of three children, Fleet Proffitt, was dying of cancer. He had been sent home from the hospital without hope of recovery. Probably because of the similarity of the circumstances with my husband who had died eight years before, I had special concern for this family.

Very early one morning the thought came to me, "If you will go at six o'clock in the morning and pray with his wife and mother he will be healed." I called and they said they would meet me. So on a cold winter morning I drove the twenty-two miles (it took on the roads at that time) from my home in Celo to Bald Creek. I remember feeling spiritually exalted as I drove along. We interceded for Fleet in the cold church basement and came out feeling certain that God had heard, and would answer, our prayer.

His mother said he was much improved when she cooked his breakfast that morning. She said, "All my life I have read about the miracles Jesus performed; but this is the first one I have seen with my own eyes." Later that week his doctors at Duke hospital agreed he was much improved.

But a few weeks later he was back in the local hospital. I visited him there and after one particular visit, on my way home, I reached the edge of town and felt irresistibly impelled to return to the hospital. Echoing over and over in my heart were Fleet's recent words to his young son, "If I had my life to live over I would answer God's call to the ministry."

As I drove back, I promised myself, "If he's alone in his room, that will be a sign to tell him, 'Fleet, it's not too late to answer God's call. You *can* be well.'"

He was alone, and I did say what I'd come to say. But Fleet just turned his back to me and looked out the window. "It would be a good day to go hunting," he said. And then he was silent.

He died the next week, and I wonder if it was all too much to face at his age.

This weekend I have attended two fiftieth wedding anniversary celebrations. Arle and I were married less than nine years, and our girls were four, six, and eight when he died. This year, my daughter Dena called to wish me "Happy Father's Day".

Yes, God does heal today, using the many means at His disposal; but sometimes death is the ultimate healing. Elisabeth Kubler-Ross said, "There is no need to be afraid of death. I think this is the key to the door of life. When you fully understand that each day you awaken could be your last, you take time *that day* to grow, to become more of who you really are, and to reach out to other human beings."[6]

I have witnessed the inexpressible joy on the face of two of my saintly friends, Sarah Hipkins and Joe Letterman, as they stepped from this life into the next, so I am not afraid to die; but I do need — like we all do — to be more aware of how to live.

NOTES

1. Derek Humphrey, *Final Exit*, (New York: Bell Pub. Co. (Bantam/Doubleday), 1992).
2. Matt. 22:37–39 (NRSV).
3. Richard Blanchard *Fill My Cup, Lord* (Romans 15:13), (Alexandria, Indiana: Gaither Music Co., 1987).
4. Richard Blanchard *Bread of Heaven, feed me 'til I want no more*, Lord (Romans 15:13), (Alexandria, Indiana: Gaither Music Co., 1987).
5. Agnes Sanford, *The Healing Light*, (New York: Ballantine Books (Random House), 1983.
6. Elisabeth Kubler-Ross, *Death, the Final Stage of Growth*, (Englewood Cliffs, NJ: Prentice-Hall, Inc., 1975).

Methodist Women I

W.S.C.S Exec.c. Asheville Dist. - L to R - Juanita Proffitt, Tillie Brooks, Fannie Crowell and Elsie Bancroft P. ~~298~~   about 1967

waiting for ferry to cross Ohio R. - top L to R - Winnie Lou Ray, Ona Davis - bottom L to R - Eleanor Hickok, Fannie Crowell, and Tillie about 1954

WNC CC Workers - L to R - Vera Falls, Tillie, Anita Benoy, Laura Wells and Virginia Miller P. ~~272~~   about 1967

Virginia and Jack Stone P. 305 Scarritt - Bennett Center

Methodist Women II

U.M.W. at Givens Estates

top L to R - Mary Gillespie, Betty Cathcart, Mildred Ray, Beverly Bard, Madge Fouts, Nell Rudolph, Phyllis Bailey, Doriscey Young and Kathy Ward. - bottom L to R - Virginia Shaw, Maxine Westbrook, Julia Ray, Mildred Turner, and Gladys Young.

U.M.W. at Crescent View Apts.

- top L to R -
Melanie Stallings, Frederika Sargent, Julia Ray, and Maxine Westbrook.
- Bottom L to R -
Mildred Ray, Madge Fouts and Phyllis Bailey.

Higgins Memorial - UMC I

- top L to R -
Ruby, Mildred, Beverly, Nozomi, Nora, Tillie, Minoru.
Bottom - L to R - Pat, Frederika, Renee,
Winston   5-9-90

June and Billy Hunter
5-23-93 - Retirement

Tillie
(Pulpit)
4-10-94

Betty Staley
5-19-93

The Wamplers
12-84

Lady Slippers

Higgins Memorial UMC II

Prayer group - home of Althea Proffitt.
Mildred Ray, Mae Young, Lizzie Young, Nell Bennett, Lena Laughrun, → Althea Proffitt, Winnie L. Ray, Dorothy Fall, Madge Fouts, Luella Honeycutt, Hattie Clevenger.

12-1991

↗ Becky and Charles Gillespie, hosts for special dinner for Higgins elderly. 11-25-90

Ralph and Miriam ↓ Jacks

at special dinner - Mary Gillespie, Phyllis Bailey, Dale Hagler, Betty and David Cathcart
11-25-90

MY TRIBUTE TO THE WOMEN OF THE METHODIST CHURCH

(Higgins Memorial Officers Installation, December 1, 1992)

Friends, I think you may be aware of the seriousness of your commitment to this unit of the United Methodist Women, because you know what it means to this church and the community; but *are* you aware of the scope and magnitude of the world organization? I once read that it is the largest women's organization in the world. Its main concern has been to see to the spiritual and physical welfare of its members and those whom it served, especially women and children. It is the most effective, efficient, compassionate, loving body I know anything about. It provides more than half of the financial support for the church's mission workers at home and abroad. It has been the thread of life for many small membership churches. And my hat's off to this unit. I have never known more dedicated members, or any who accomplished as much. I would like to pay tribute to this unique body of women who have contributed so much to my life and work through these fifty-four years.

It started with my sociology teacher at Morris Harvey College in Charleston, West Virginia. She had been personal secretary to Belle Harris Bennett, founder of the training school for missionary women that in 1924 became Scarritt College in Nashville, Tennessee. Miss Olmstead encouraged me to go to Scarritt to train for a life of service through the church. The women of the West Virginia conference provided full scholarship for the two years — 1938–1940. They also sent small personal gifts during the years, and gave me a Bulova watch for graduation. The women of the Bluefield District were generous in their support during the three years I worked in coal mining towns in Southern West Virginia, 1940–43.

Miss Mabel K. Howell, my missions teacher at Scarritt, requested that I be appointed to the Scarritt Rural Training Center at Crossville, Tennessee. I served one year. I married in October 1944 and spent the next eight years rearing my family. In June of 1953 I again started to work here in Yancey County. My husband died the sixth of July. I was left with the three girls — ages 4, 6 and 8 — no insurance, nothing but this job. Thank God it was for the Methodist Women of this Conference, and I had a Conference advisor, Fannie B. Crowell, who gave me encouragement and substantial help. She said the Wesleyan Service Guild (WSG) wanted to buy me a washing machine and sink. I said no because many of the women I worked with did not have such conveniences; and besides I did not have the money to put in running water. She said to pray about it. I did! Before the week was out the estimated amount I needed for pump, water line and septic tank came from an unexpected source — friends of Arle — so I told Mrs. Crowell okay.

To say thank you to the WSG annual meeting, I kept a diary of what I had done the previous month so they could appreciate the help running water and washing machine gave me. I was surprised to see many of them crying. I thought they would be happy. When asked, they said "and it only cost me an extra dime to provide that help for you."

During the mid-sixties I served on the District Executive Committee. Another member was Elsie Bancroft, a minister's widow. She retired in Michigan, and for many years sent me a Christmas card with a little check in it. Last week I had a letter from her sister-in-law. It said, "About ten years ago Elsie handed me a list of names and addresses (and stamps) and asked me to write to those people upon her death. She died November third, at age 102."

This Higgins society was most helpful after my husband died. After school started, Mary Gillespie kept Dena a couple of days a week. When I was transferred to Kentucky in 1968, you gave me this pin with WSCS on the back. That was the year of union with Evangelical United Brethren (EUB) churches and many of the Women's Division responsibilities were transferred to the National Division, including Church and Community Ministry and Scarritt College. I felt I was left dangling — the women had spoiled us. Finally the Louisville conference appointed H.H. Green — a black former District superintendent they didn't know what to do with — as someone to relate to in the Conference. He was a dear man, but the most memorable Methodist woman was "Billie" Hummel from Louisville. She found out about me through a promotional financial film strip I was not supposed to be on. She now lives in Florida in Chucky Morrow's city. She will be a hundred on May 19, 1994.

I moved to the Memphis conference in 1972, and received the same kind of support. I was ex-officio on the Conference Executive

Committee, and when I retired in 1980 they dedicated that year's Annual Report to me.

Now I have been approved for residence at Brooks-Howell Home in Asheville, and have said I would move when an apartment or suite is available. I don't know when that will happen. My income will pay my way until I have to go to the nursing unit, but the Women's Division will see that I am cared for. I think you can understand my gratitude for what all these women have meant to me. You are a part of this ongoing line of splendor.

SCARRITT COLLEGE AND SCARRITT-BENNETT CENTER

A talk given on September 19, 1993 on an article by Esther Madriz
from the magazine, *Response*,
Program for: Mildred Ray & Sue Brown Circles

Belle Bennett's visionary idea of a training school for young missionary women took form in 1892 when Scarritt (Nathan Scarritt) Bible and Training School was created in Kansas City, Missouri, by the women's organization of the Methodist Episcopal Church South. In 1924 the school was moved to Nashville, Tennessee, with the name Scarritt College for Christian Workers . . . They cooperated with the Board of Missions in the training of all missionary personnel.

From 1940–1964 the Women's Division provided appropriations and scholarship funds annually, but in 1964 the Board of Missions was reorganized. It became the Board of Global Ministries, and Scarritt became related to the National Division. . . . During the next two decades it struggled financially. . . . In 1981 it became a graduate school focusing on training Christian educators and church musicians. In 1984 the board of trustees voted to close the college.

A few months later the Women's Division voted to enter into a partnership with the Scarritt Foundation to use the campus mainly as a place for the education and training of lay persons. On June 1, 1988, the Women's Division assumed ownership of the property.[1]

I think the reason Margaret Tyner asked me to do this program was because she hoped I could add a personal dimension. As I thought about it I was *amazed* at the important points in Scarritt's history where I had some personal involvement.

MY PERSONAL INVOLVEMENT IN SCARRITT'S HISTORY

During the last years of the founder's life, Belle Bennett's personal secretary was Emily Olmstead, who was my sociology teacher at Morris Harvey College in Charleston, West Virginia, 1935–1937. It was she who encouraged me to go to Scarritt. My application was sent to Mrs. J.W. Downs, Executive of Rural Work in Nashville, Tennessee. She said a year's experience was required. By the time Miss Olmstead had convinced her that working for my room and board four years should equal a year's experience, I had decided to work a year at the State Agricultural Laboratory where I had previously worked part-time.

I went to Scarritt 1938–40 on a scholarship from the women of the West Virginia conference. During the last quarter of my second year, Mrs. Downs came to Sunday evening tea, when I was serving. She wanted to know *why* I had never been to see her, (I'd heard a visit with her was not always pleasant) and she requested that I come the next week. She wanted to know where I'd like to be appointed. Because of the scholarship, I said West Virginia. Our appointments were like appointments of ministers used to be — you didn't know until they were read where you were going. When mine said "Bluefield District, West Virginia" Mrs. Downs winked at me.

The article I just read mentions that Scarritt moved to Nashville in 1924. Jesse Lee Cuninggin had been president of the school in Kansas City since 1921. He decided to move the school because he felt professional Christian workers' education should come up to the level of other institutions. Nashville was chosen because of Vanderbilt and Peabody — and also because the main offices of the Methodist Episcopal Church South were there. Dr. Cuninggin was president of Scarritt when I was there. He retired in 1942. He was also my teacher in a two-hour course, *The Family of God*. Near the end of the course he asked for a written evaluation. When I compared it to A.E. Barnett's New Testament course that shook many people's faith, I found it repetitive, and said so. He called me in to thank me. He was a dear, gentle man with great vision.

A history of the college, *Yes, Lord, I'll Do It*, by Dr. Alice Cobb was published in 1987.[2] She also wrote most of the Church Community Ministry history, *A Tapestry of Service: 100 years Along the Way*.[3] Alice is a longtime friend of mine who now lives in a retirement community at Pleasant Hill, Tennessee. I have visited her there and planned to go there in September, but she fell and had to go to the nursing home.

Another place I feel I was involved in Scarritt's history was in the matter of integration. The first two black students — one from South Carolina and one from Texas — were admitted in 1952. In 1939 I did my field work at Bethlehem Center and worked with two young women from Fisk, who worked part-time and lived at the center. In my last year I did my master's thesis on an interracial theme, "The Relationship of Dolls to Race Consciousness and Attitudes." I visited many black homes of children I'd had at the center, and did much work at the Fisk library. The black Baptist publishing house typed my thesis. In the late seventies, in a roundabout way, the hostess of *Jump Street*, a black variety program on NBC in Nashville, heard about my dolls thesis and asked me to be on her program.

I got the nickname "Tillie" at Scarritt. In the dining room someone said "Who *is* that tall girl?" "Arthelia Hilleary," another answered. Did you say "artillery?" Then they pulled out the "Tillie" — like "Tillie the Toiler" and I've been Tillie to most everyone except my *two first friends* at Scarritt and my family ever since.

I also met my husband at Scarritt. At 5:30 one evening in March, 1940, I had a call from the switchboard that there was a young man to see me. (Most unusual — taxi drivers never wanted to bring pretty young girls to Scarritt, they thought it was a convent.) I went with nails on one hand polished (fortunately with clear polish). We had only fifteen minutes before call to dinner and I told him I could *not* do a Friend's work camp that summer, since I had not seen my family for two years. I was called because I was president of the student body, but he never asked to set up a meeting with the student body. I later learned that his report on his visit to me said "She could not be recruited, but I'd like to recruit her for myself." And I told my roommate, Mattie Lula Cooper, "I've met the man I'm going to marry," but when he came back a month later and proposed I said no, because I had promised to work four years or repay my scholarship.

One further connection with Scarritt's history. On that day in the Laskey Library, when representatives from the Women's Division and Scarritt Foundation were meeting to decide the fate of the college (would it be sold outright, become a part of Duke, or what?), our Church and Community Ministry History Task Force was meeting across the hall. Kathryn Mitchem, a member of both, left our meeting to attend theirs. In about an hour she returned with the glad news. The Women's Division had invested too much to let it go. They would claim ownership again! And Scarritt-Bennett Center came into being. We rejoiced because we were all firm believers in the women of the Methodist Church.

MEMORABLE SCARRITT CLASSMATES

Agenor Andrade. A small dark man from Brazil who planned to itinerate to youth camps in United States before returning to his country. He asked me to pray he would find a wife. I said, "A cute little blonde?" And he said, "No, one like you! If I had a wife as small as I am, we would sweep the children out with the dirt."

Akira Takage. Akira was from Japan. He and I worked in a youth camp in West Virginia after graduation; on our trip to Japan in 1966, he hosted Betty Motsinger and me in Kyoto. I learned when I went back there in 1985 that he had died. In my mind I'll always see him bidding us good-bye, holding his umbrella and in his hand the pink dish mop Betty had given him for his wife.

Mary McMillan. Mary was my Scarritt classmate and a missionary to Japan. When I visited her office in Hiroshima in 1966, I left her a note because she was in the States on furlough. She died while at Chautauqua, New York in the summer of 1993. In a phone conversation with Lois Marquart (the hostess at the deaconess home in Chautauqua) she said, "Mary was a blessing to the end. She had a great influence on the nurses at Jamestown hospital."

Esther Banks. My housemate the first year, Esther had dreamed of being a missionary in Africa from childhood on. Her father, a Tennessee farmer, was so prejudiced that he said he'd rather *see her dead* — he almost did. Coming back to Scarritt from Thanksgiving vacation, she was involved in a car wreck, and remained in a coma until after Christmas. She could not be accepted for the mission field. She went home and taught in high school and worked in her church. I visited her about eight years ago. She is one who never called me Tillie.

Sarah Bennett. A missionary to Brazil, who stayed at the Brooks-Howell home in Asheville, North Carolina, until she died. During her stay there, I visited her bi-weekly so I could read to her and write her letters for her. My youngest daughter is named for her co-worker, Dina Rizzi, who came to Scarritt and visited the youth camps. One weekend I took her on a visit to my parents' home in West Virginia.

Michiko Tonegawa Onuki. Scarritt sent her to be with me in North Carolina for ten days in 1962. Through her I met Nora Satsuma Yamada, and acquired my Japanese family. [see the articles, "The Far East–1966" and "My Japanese Families," earlier in this book.]

Virginia Dickson Stone. In the summer between my two years at Scarritt, I worked at Vashti School in South Georgia for girls from broken homes — fourth grade through high school. We tried to make the summer schedule different. One of my jobs was to tell stories for two hours, three times a week. It was a great blessing that children love to hear stories over and over. Their usual request was, "Tell us again about Virginia and Jack."

Virginia was a tiny blonde who had had a close call with death after a major operation and felt she was spared in order to be a missionary — and so was at Scarritt. Her father was a Methodist minister who served near Nashville. She had an attachment to me that made me uncomfortable at times, but I learned a lot about her. She wrote poetry. Some selections were published in a sailors' magazine. A sailor got her address from the publishers and they began to correspond. When he was home on leave he came to see her and proposed marriage. Her minister father said "no way," so he was sent away. There was a story about her love sustaining him through an ordeal in Alaska. She read me a poem that had been published in an anthology for beginning poets:

Rain Fell Last Night

Rain fell last night, soft gentle rain
That tapped upon my window pane
And called me back from troubled sleep
To soothe a heart too numb to weep.

My loneliness was deep and real
And like a wound that will not heal.
It throbbed within me, and I knew
My arms were empty without you.

But as I listened to the sound
Of soft rain falling to the ground

> You called my name, and oh, my dear,
> I threw the window open wide
> To let the sweet rain rush inside.
>
> It kissed my eyes, my lips, my hair
> And, love, I knew that you were there.
> Last night while gray clouds softly wept
> I held you in my arms and slept.

In early spring, when Virginia was sitting by me before New Testament class started, someone brought word from the switchboard that one Jack Stone was asking for her. I saw her reaction! Through the next couple of weeks I tried to help them sort out what they should do. I had no doubt they loved each other. Jack had gone to the Mission doctor and was told he would not recommend her for the mission field because of her previous health problems. So Jack begged me to use my influence to persuade her to marry him. So, one evening in the cloakroom, she told me she was making a decision that night, either to marry him, or send him away forever. "Tell me what *you think God wants me to do.*" "Marry him," I said, with real conviction. They were married secretly and she finished the term. I later had pictures of them and their beautiful children. I've lost touch with them since.

Alma Staggs. Alma was my first year roommate. She was short, a bit chubby with coal black hair, dark eyes and skin — a tiny little face I could cup in my two hands, *and* the worst inferiority complex I've ever encountered. Everyone in our house on 21st Avenue did all we could to boost her self-esteem, even to bragging like crazy on the little rhymes she liked to write. Our room was on the second floor with a big landing that led to the four bedrooms. Once I was coming up the stairs when she was ready to go into our room. She stood aside to let me go in first. I said, "Go on in, Alma. Don't ever wait for me!" And then I went to the dean of women to ask *what* I was doing to this person! She said if I knew her background I would understand, but just to do the best I could.

I thought she might be part Cajun, from a poor family that some women's society had seen leadership possibilities in, and had given her a scholarship, even as I had one. She was an undergraduate student.

In the spring, Scarritt was sponsoring a workshop, and since they were making definite efforts to include the black community, the two Fisk students who lived at Bethlehem Center were invited. I did my first year of field work there — helping with Saturday Bible school, and I knew the young ladies.

At the workshop, I was talking with Alma when one of the girls came by, so I said, "Alma, I'd like you to meet my co-worker at Bethlehem Center. Miss Staggs, this is Miss Cooper."

When I went to our room after lunch she jumped on me like a bantam rooster. "I'll have you know. Don't you *ever again* introduce a nigger to me as *Miss*!"

Well now, what was I to do? This was the first time she had shown any spunk, but I couldn't just let it go, so I said, "Alma, let's talk about this. I know you grew up in Mississippi where there are more blacks than whites, so I have no way of knowing what it was like for you. I grew up in West Virginia where I never saw a black person until I was in my teens, so I can't judge you. But there is one thing I do know. You are *now* in Scarritt College for Christian Workers, and will be leaving here to represent Christ, who is no respecter of persons. It is your responsibility to change your attitude."

I said nothing more, but noted that she took advantage of every opportunity to get to know the people in the black academic community.

The next year she lived across campus from me. One day she called me into a classroom and thanked me for what I had said to her the year before. She was a different person — outgoing and confident.

The lesson Alma taught me was "When you don't have to *look down* on anyone, you don't have to *look up* to anyone either!"

I've told this store many times — once on WTOE radio in Mitchell County where they used to brag, "The sun never goes down on a nigger in Mitchell County." I did have some repercussions, but I managed to live with them — *how* is another story [told in the article on the *Toe Valley View*, earlier in this book].

NOTES

1. An article by Esther Madriz, in *Response*. (Cincinnati: General Board of Global Ministries of the UMC, May 1992).
2. Dr. Alice Cobb, *Yes, Lord, I'll Do It*. (Nashville: Scarritt College Publisher, 1987).
3. Dr. Alice Cobb, *A Tapestry of Service: 100 Years Along the Way*. (unpublished manuscript).

FAVORITE SERMONS

During my twenty-seven years working with Methodist churches I was quite often asked to substitute for a minister who needed to be out of the pulpit. I'd like to include my favorite sermons: "Just One Chapter," "Womankind's Special Debt to Jesus," and "The Importance of a Name."

JUST ONE CHAPTER

If someone said to me, "To sustain your faith for the rest of your life you may have only one chapter of the Bible. You must choose. Which one will it be?"

I would, without hesitation, take the fourteenth chapter of John because: (1) It tells me whom to believe ("Believe in God, believe also in me,"[1] says Jesus).

And (2) these verses will provide the following: *solace* in any kind of trouble ("Let not your hearts be troubled, neither let them be afraid."[2]); *patience* with doubt and ignorance ("I am the way, and the truth, and the life . . . He who has seen me has seen the Father."[3]); and a promise of *eternal life* ("And when I go and prepare a place for you, I will come again and will take you to myself, that where I am you may be also."[4]).

(3) The verses give advice for living in this world today: *The power of prayer* — ("Whatever you ask in my name, I will do it, that the Father may be glorified in the Son . . . He who believes in me will also do the works that I do; and *greater* works than these will he do, because I go to the Father . . . you should rejoice."[5]) What are these "greater things?" *Communications* — The preached word of God reached just a *local* radio audience in 1979. Now it can be heard in most of the world simultaneously. *Medicine* — Organ transplants, the miracles that discovery of DNA have made possible, elimination of many diseases, and the realization that a *loving touch* from the *least of us* has power to heal and bless. I remember being told that

Mollie Robinson was out of the lunchroom (where she worked) at our school because of her swollen legs. I went to see her and was so moved with compassion at the sight of her swollen legs that I knelt, took her legs in my arms, and *implored* God to bring relief, because I loved her so much and was sure He loved her much more. Many months later Mollie told me how graciously our prayer was answered, because the swelling went down quickly soon after our prayer session. Then there was the day I shut my car door on the finger of one of the Grindstaff twins. Having experienced that agony myself, it made my touch of compassion and plea for mercy all the more urgent. As I remember, the finger of the Grindstaff girl did not give her any more trouble.

(4) "If you love me, you will keep my commandments . . . and I will pray the Father, and he will give you another Counselor, to be with you forever."[6] The Holy Spirit will not leave you desolate; will teach you, bring to mind all that Jesus taught; will convict you of sin; will give power for your service; and will give you peace. "He who loves me will be loved by my Father, and I will love him and *manifest myself* to him."[7]

When I looked up the verb *manifest* in the dictionary, it said "to make clear or evident to the eye or the understanding."[8] I did not take these words literally — as something that Jesus would really do — as an experience an ordinary human being might have — until I met Lura McMahan.* Shortly after coming to Yancey County, I had joined a Home Demonstration Club to get to know the local women, but since Lura did not belong to my club, I didn't meet her until we rode in the backseat to an area meeting of the Home Demonstration Club. I was drawn to her as someone very special. It was her *eyes*! What had she seen that I, and all the people I know, had not? It was not until, perhaps, five years later, in the summer of 1954 when we kept handicapped twin baby girls for a few days at my home, that she trusted me enough to tell me her personal story. We had become friends during those intervening years as I worked with the women of her church.

She told me that she had been a part of a very large, poor mountain family. She had not had much schooling and found reading quite difficult; but Jesus was such a friend. He was so real

---

*I called Lura on October 13, 1993 to check on some facts for this story, and later it occurred to me that it isn't only her *eyes* that are compelling, but her *voice* has a way of *caressing* you as she speaks.

to her! She said as a child she would lie on the hillside and "talk to Him up there."

She married and had children, but the great burden of her life was her alcoholic husband. She did not chide or nag — only prayed, believing that one day he would change; and her faith was finally justified; but not before the night their twin babies were born. Her husband was not at home, and she had no way of getting word to anyone or getting away herself. It was up to her. When the time came for her to be delivered, Jesus stood beside her to help. After the first baby came, He said, "Wait, there is another one." And then when that was accomplished, He was gone.

Lura said, "You are the first person I have ever told this story. I've been afraid anyone else would think I was crazy." I believed her! Now I know not *what* but *whom* she had seen, and the verse of scripture became real to me even though I had not had the experience, I knew it *could* happen to an ordinary person. Later, Genevieve Parkhurst told a small group I was attending that Jesus came to her in person and healed her of cancer.

(5) The rulers (or powers) of this world have no power over Jesus — nor over us if we are in Him. The last words of the chapter are, "Rise, let us go hence."[9]

We are to do His work in the world — equipped with the power of the Holy Spirit, bold in the knowledge that no earthly power can finally defeat us, and at peace with the assurance of his promise, "Yet a little while and the world will see me no more, but you will see me; because I live, you will live also."[10] Amen.

Note: In the *American Bible Society Record* for December, 1986, is the report of a survey of 100,000 readers as to *the chapter* in the Old or New Testament that they felt had made the greatest appeal to members of their congregation. The most popular was the fourteenth chapter of John, the only chapter to receive a higher number of votes than the 23rd Psalm. After it came Matt. 5, Romans 8, Ps. 91, Matt. 6, John 3, Ps. 46, Romans 12, and Hebrew 11.

WOMANKIND'S SPECIAL DEBT TO JESUS

(Given at the Good Friday evening service, South Pleasant Grove UMC, March 28, 1975.)

Scripture: Genesis 1:27, Luke 23: 44-56
Introduction, I am grateful for the invitation to be with you; even

though it has been a very full day. The three-hour service in the Lakeland Parish was energy-sapping. The four men on the staff and I shared the meditations on the seven last statements from the cross. I had the third one, "'Woman, behold your son!' Then he said to the disciple, 'Behold your mother.'"[11]

In thinking on this passage, I became intrigued with the part women played in Jesus' life and ministry — especially in the Holy Week drama.

Almost any church gathering I attend, the majority present are women, and it is so here tonight; so I am speaking mainly to you. First, to make you aware of your indebtedness to Jesus and second, to help you feel a sense of gladness at the faithfulness of the women who were His followers.

Background. The early Hebrew status of women. Edith Deen in *The Bible's Legacy for Womanhood* says, "One of the magnificent themes of the Bible is the orderly process of creation . . . moving ever onward and upward . . . man's and woman's creation is even more wonderful than the other creations, and only they actually resemble God and have the ability to communicate with Him."[12]

Genesis says: "God created man in his own image . . . male and female he created them."[13]

The Mosaic law gave just consideration to women. They had some property rights, and in case of seduction or rape certain provisions were made for them. In case of adultery both the man and woman were to be stoned to death.

Some women of status in the Old Testament were: *Miriam* — the sister of Moses and Aaron. Her song after deliverance at the Red Sea is in Exodus 15:20; *Deborah* — a judge in Israel; *Ruth* — the ancestor of Jesus; *Esther* — A queen at an important time in Israel's history.

Deen continues: "In the nation that ceases to build on coercion but patiently approximates the Kingdom of God, as did Israel in the beginning, woman gains her God-given rights and privileges, not as a woman but as a person. The status of women is a good test of a nation's civilization."[14]

As Israel became influenced by the cultures around them, they gradually changed the status given to their women — until in Jesus' day, it was low indeed.

Leonard Swidler said in his paper, *Status of Women in Palestine in Jesus' Day:* (1) "Women were not allowed to study the scriptures — 'Rather should the words of the Torah be burned than entrusted to a woman.'[15] (2) Women, children, and slaves were not obliged to recite the morning prayers, (3) In morning prayers, a male Jew recited a threefold thanksgiving — that God had not created him a Gentile, a woman, or an ignorant man, (4) In the Temple the women's court was five steps below the men's, (5) Women were separated in the synagogue and allowed no part in the service, (6) A Rabbi should not speak to a woman in public — in fact no man should speak to women in public. In some cases there was a division in the home. (7) A woman could not divorce her husband, but it was very easy for the man to divorce his wife, (8) There is a Rabbinic saying, 'When a boy comes into the world, peace comes into the world; when a girl comes, nothing comes . . . even the most virtuous of women is a witch.'"[16]

These were the prevailing attitudes when Jesus was growing up. In the beginning of his ministry, as recorded in Luke 4:16–21, when He commented on the scripture He had read from Isaiah. He said that scripture was fulfilled in Him — that God had consecrated Him "to preach the good news to the poor . . . to proclaim release to the captives and recovering of sight to the blind, to set at liberty those who are oppressed."[17] This included the women, and He was true to His promise. Let's look at some of His encounters with women.

His mother — He was more impatient with her than with any other woman. In Luke, chapter two, he says, "How is it that you sought me? Did you not know that I must be in my Father's house?"[18] In John his mother said, "They have no wine," and he answered, "O, woman, what have you to do with me? My hour has not yet come."[19] (But he provided the wine.) Recorded in three gospels, his mother and brothers came looking for him, and he said, "Who are my mother and my brothers? . . . Whoever does the will of God is my brother, and sister, and mother."[20] But at the cross (still calling her *woman*) he entrusted her to the care of the disciple, John.

Mary and Martha — He seemed to say that work in the home was not the only vocation for women. He commended Mary for her interest in intellectual and spiritual matters, and he later, in John 10:25, revealed to Martha the great spiritual truth that *he* was the *resurrection* and the *life*.

The Samaritan woman at the well who had many husbands — he revealed to her that he was the long-looked-for Messiah, the living water, and that God was a spirit and should be worshipped as such. The woman's life was changed, and she brought her village to Christ. See the fourth chapter of John.

Woman with issue of blood — He did not rebuke her for touching him (to any other male Jew, she was considered unclean), but rejoiced in her faith that healed her (Luke 8:43–48).

Woman taken in adultery — The Mosaic law said *both* should be stoned. They brought only the woman. It was a trap. Jesus did not fall into it, but put the responsibility back on her accusers. He did not condone her action, but forgave her with the admonition not to sin again (Luke 8: 8–10).

Crippled woman healed on the Sabbath — She "had had a spirit of infirmity for eighteen years; she was bent over and could not straighten herself."[21] Jesus healed her, saying, "Woman, you are freed from your infirmity."[22] The ruler of the synagogue criticized him for doing it on the Sabbath. He said, "You hypocrites! Does not each of you on the Sabbath untie his ox or his ass from the manger, and lead it away to water it? And ought not this woman, a daughter of Abraham whom Satan bound for eighteen years, be loosed from this bond on the Sabbath day?"[23]

Mary of Magdala — She is mentioned in Mark as one of the women who "when he was in Galilee, followed him, and ministered to him."[24] And in Luke we see: "And the twelve were with him, and also some women who had been healed of evil spirits and infirmities: Mary, called Magdalene, from whom seven demons had gone out . . . who provided for [Jesus and his disciples] out of their means."[25] Luke does not say what the seven demons were; but as in the case of the crippled woman, evil spirits and being bound by Satan was associated more with disease rather than with sinfulness. There is no scriptural basis for casting Mary Magdalene as a prostitute (*Jesus Christ Superstar* not withstanding)! Whatever Jesus rid her of must have lifted a terrible burden from her life. Her gratitude and devotion are phenomenal!! Many find it difficult to believe that it was *agape* and not *eros* love that she felt toward Jesus. Tradition has it that she was a cultured woman of some means — possibly a Greek.

From the moment she met Jesus until his final resurrection from the dead, she was his devoted and intimate follower; and together with Mary His mother (two other women), and John, the beloved disciple, she wept for him on Calvary. All the gospels say the women were there — three say they were at some distance. John names four at the foot of the cross. John is the only disciple mentioned as being at the cross. All the gospels say — or imply — that Mary Magdalene was at the cross. One says the women watched where they laid Him and that Mary Magdalene went there the next morning. All the gospels say Mary Magdalene was first at the tomb on resurrection morning. Three of the gospels say an angel (or, man in white) appeared to Mary and the women, and in John it is the Lord Himself who rewards her faithfulness.

All the gospels *entrust to these women* (who, outside the fellowship of Jesus, could not even read sacred scripture) the most glorious message the world has ever heard — He is risen!! Go tell the disciples. Death has been cheated of his prey. He lives and reigns forever!

We must remember that *all* these accounts were written by men who had grown up in the Palestine I described before; so we are indebted to them for the faithful recording of all these events. They had experienced the outpouring of the Holy Spirit on all flesh. Sometimes Paul lapsed back into the law, but in his highest moments, he could say, "There is neither Jew nor Greek, there is neither slave nor free, there is neither male nor female; for you are all one in Christ Jesus."[26]

All of us are indebted to God for what He has done for us through Christ, but I pray you can see how much more we, as women, owe Him. We can be proud of the way those who walked with Him were faithful all the way. May we be found following their example.

We *are* all one in Christ. I rejoice in that realization.

THE IMPORTANCE OF A NAME

(Given at Higgins Memorial UMC, Burnsville, North Carolina, April 10, 1994)

Hymn of Dedication: "Take the Name of Jesus with You".

How important is your name to you? Would you hear it if called amid the jabber of many voices in a crowded mall? Do you become irritated if your name is wrongly pronounced or misspelled? I do. Every month when I receive my tax shelter check with my maiden name misspelled it "bugs" me.

The author of the Holy Week meditations in my *Upper Room Disciplines* relates this story about her name, K. Chérie Jones, "My given name, Chérie, is uncommon. Thus it is frequently mispronounced and/or misspelled, which I have come to expect. However my name is part and parcel of who I am, and I expect those who know me well to both pronounce and spell it correctly.

I assume my family and friends will get it right . . . [that] helps me identify whether I am dealing with a friend or stranger."[27] I suppose she *should* be thankful her last name is *Jones*.

My three daughters were each named for a very special person. Marla was named for a famous concert pianist, Maryla Jonas. We read about her giving a concert at Carnegie Hall while we were waiting for the two-weeks overdue birth. Later I read about her tragic life. She saw her family killed in Nazi Germany. I'm sure her name was pronounced "Ma-re'-la," and that is what we intended for our child, but her classmates were inclined to say "Mary'-la." She had the *y* dropped from her birth record while she was in high school.

I was named Arthelia Marguerite Hilleary. I could identify with Chérie Jones, because my first name is also uncommon. It was my paternal grandmother's name, and most of my life I heard, "Will you please spell your first name for me?" And the first letter I had from my future husband, said "Dear A???". My family tends to say Arthe'-ya — omitting the *l*.

I got the nickname, Tillie, at Scarritt College. One day someone in the dining room said, "Who *is* that tall girl?" Another answered, "Arthelia Hilleary." "Did you say 'Artillery?'" Somehow "Tillie" evolved — like Tillie the Toiler in the funnies. The first two friends I met at Scarritt still call me Arthelia; but everyone else in all my working years since 1940, has called me "Tillie." I have enjoyed answering to that shortened name; but I do have a couple of quirks related to it — on anything official I want my proper name used (I even checked with Helene about this Sunday's church bulletin); and don't ask me why, but to see it spelled "T-i-l-l-y" makes me cringe.

How many of you were nicknamed? Has it stuck? Buzz and I are examples in this church. Our names *are* so important.

We have recognized this and tried to devise ways to help us know each other's names in this church. If I said I knew one fourth of all of you, I might be stretching it. I don't remember as well as I once did, and I don't try hard enough. Is there anyone here today who believes they know everyone else? Perhaps Buzz does. (My next best guess would be Beverly Bard.)

The writer for this year's April fourth meditation in *The Upper Room* expressed our dilemma. Her name is Gioia Catabriga. She wrote, "There are pictures of several church members, including me, on our church bulletin board . . . I was standing [there] when I heard a man next to me . . . reading the label identifying my picture. He turned to his wife and said, 'Do we know this person?' 'Oh, yes, if I see her I'll point her out to you.' The couple passed me as they spoke and wished me a cheerful good morning without recognizing me."[28] With a name like hers, they should have remembered. (With a name like Smucker's, it has to be good.) Our names are so important to us that at least three people in our congregation have held on to their maiden names, at least professionally: Diana Donovan, Pam Budd, and Ann Swift.

Why all this concern about a name? Do we have a biblical precedent? We certainly do! In my concordance, I found some form of the word "name" 386 times: name, by the name, His name, My name (God), Thy name, name as a verb, nameth and namely. "In the beginning God . . ."[29] In Genesis 2:19, "the Lord God formed every beast of the field and every bird of the air, and brought them to the *man* to see what he would call them; and whatever the *man* called every living creature, that was its name."[30] It was not until Genesis, chapter three, that the people are given their names. "The man called his wife Eve, because she was the mother of all living"[31] and the man is called Adam (the progenitor of the human race).[32] They were just *the man* and *the woman* before then, so the animals were given names before the people.

In my Bible dictionary I found these comments about names: "Names were important in the Old Testament society [remember all the begats?] . . . Originally the source of names was limited. Parents drew them from animals [Rachel means ewe]" or flowers . . . Sometimes the name described a trait [Esau - hairy] . . . or reflected foreign groups with whom they lived . . . Frequently they were further identified by appending 'son of' [Joshua - son of Nun] or the town from which they came [later, Mary of Magdala] or their occupation [Simon the tanner]."[33] Sometimes events changed their name — Abram to Abraham, Sarai to Sarah.

There were many names for God. When Moses asked in Exodus 3:13, "If I come to the people of Israel and say to them, 'The God of your fathers sent me to you,' and they ask me, 'What is His name?' what shall I say to them? God said to Moses, 'I am who I am'."[34]

The Hebrews were fearful of naming God, so they used different words to designate the deity: Elohim, El Shaddai, Adonai, Lord, Jehovah, and Yahweh.

Very early in the New Testament we are introduced to more of the naming process. There is a long list of the ancestors of Jesus in Matthew and Luke. Joseph is told "his name shall be called Emmanuel (which means, God with us)"[35] Elizabeth said on the eighth day, that her son should be named John. Her neighbors said,

"None of your kindred is called by that name,"[36] but his father, Zechariah, the priest, verified it by writing before he could speak. He had been struck dumb because of his unbelief — "How shall I know this? For I am an old man and my wife is advanced in years."[37] A reprise of the Abraham-Sarah story. Mary was told by the angel Gabriel, "you will . . . bear a son, and you shall call his name Jesus."[38] According to Paul, Jesus had bridged the gap between God and his people; so Christians need not be afraid to speak the name of God — we may even call him Abba (father, daddy).

In the New Testament we also have some name changing. Simon, the disciple who became Peter, or Cephas (rock). Saul, the persecutor who became Paul, the missionary. My favorite explanation of a name is that of Barnabas, "which means son of encouragement".[39]

The Easter story is also about a name. Each gospel tells the story differently; so for my purpose I shall use excerpts from John. "Mary stood weeping outside the tomb . . . two angels in white . . . said to her, 'Woman, why are you weeping?' . . . 'Because they have taken away my Lord, and I do not know where they have laid him.' Saying this, she turned around and saw Jesus standing, but she did not know it was Jesus. Jesus said to her, 'Woman, why are you weeping? Whom do you seek?' Supposing him to be the gardener, she said to him, 'Sir, if you have carried him away, tell me where you have laid him, and I will take him away.' Jesus said to her, 'Mary.' She turned and said to him in Hebrew, 'Rabboni!'"[40]

In Mark's version, the young man in white tells Mary: "'He has risen, he is not here . . . go, tell his disciples and Peter.'"[41] She went and told them "I have seen the [risen] Lord!"[42]

Why did Mary not recognize Jesus? She and the other women had followed him in Galilee and cared for the day-to-day needs of him and the disciples. She saw Jesus crucified, taken down from the cross, and she marked where they put him in the tomb. Did Jesus deliberately close her eyes to his identity? I think not. Then what distorted her vision?

Was it grief, weariness, fear, frustration at not being able to find the body and do what she had come to do, or was it the utter impossibility of believing that a person she had seen crucified, could now be standing alive before her?

Hearing Jesus call her name opened her spiritual eyes, and she called Him who He is — Lord.

What keeps *us* from recognizing Him? Do we look for him in

the wrong places? Jesus answered in Matthew, chapter twenty-five, to those who said, "When did we see thee?"[43] His answer, essentially, was, "in the hungry and thirsty, the stranger, the naked, the sick and those in prison. To whom you ministered in my name."[44]

Has He called *you* by name and given *you* instructions? Have you obeyed?

In 1934 I knew He called my name — "Go and tell the Peters of this world that even though you may have denied, persecuted or ignored me, I still love you and gave my life on the cross to bring you back to God."[45] I have tried to be faithful these sixty years. Only God knows where I have failed or succeeded.

We are Easter people! We know Jesus is alive, and through His promise of the Holy Spirit, is ready to help us meet our every need — both now and in the life to come. Will you say with me, Thanks be to God?

Amen.

NOTES

1. John 14:1 (RSV)
2. John 14:27 (RSV)
3. John 14:6,7 (RSV)
4. John 14:3 (RSV)
5. John 14:13, 12, 28 (RSV)
6. John 14:15, 16 (RSV)
7. John 14:21 (RSV)
8. Random House Dictionary of the English Language, Second Unabridged Edition.
9. John 14:31 (RSV)
10. John 14:19 (RSV)
11. John 19:26, 27 (RSV)
12. Edith Deen, *The Bible's Legacy for Womanhood* (New York: Doubleday, 1969), p.3.
13. Genesis 1:27 (RSV)
14. Edith Deen, *op. cit.*, page 223.
15. (Publication information on this reference not available.)
16. Leonard Swidler, "Status of Women in Palestine in Jesus' Day," (publication information not available.)
17. Luke 4:18 (RSV)
18. Luke 2:49 (RSV)
19. John 2:3–4 (RSV)
20. Mark 3:33, 35 (RSV)

21. Luke 13:11 (RSV)
22. Luke 13:12 (RSV)
23. Luke 13:15–16 (RSV)
24. Mark 15:41 (RSV)
25. Luke 8:1–3 (RSV)
26. Galatians 3:28 (RSV)
27. K. Chérie Jones, "Holy Week Meditations," *The Upper Room Disciplines* (Nashville, TN: The Upper Room, March 28–April 3, 1994)
28. Gioia Catabriga, April 4, 1994 meditation, *The Upper Room* (Nashville, TN: The Upper Room)
29. Gen. 1:1 (RSV)
30. Gen. 2:19 (RSV)
31. Gen. 3:20 (RSV)
32. Gen. 3:21 (RSV)
33. Madeline S.J. Lane Miller, *Harper's Bible Dictionary* (New York: Harper & Bros., 1952)
34. Ex. 3:13–14 (RSV)
35. Matt. 1:23
36. Luke 1:61
37. Luke 1:18
38. Luke 1:31
39. Acts 4:36
40. John 20:11–16
41. Mark: 16:6
42. Mark: 16:7
43. Matt. 25:37
44. paraphrase of Mt. 25:36–40
45. paraphrase of the Gospel by author.

A EULOGY FOR THE DEAR DEPARTED

Several times during my working years I have been asked to do the eulogy at the funeral of a dear friend. Mildred Ray, of Burnsville, North Carolina, tells me that I had that part of the service for her father, Gus Hensley, and for her husband, Hobart Ray, and I do not remember having done those eulogies. I do remember doing the eulogies for the funerals of Yates Bailey, Troy Howell and Stanley Boris.

Then, while I was living in Kentucky, there was Greta Maddox, whom I visited on June 4, 1981, and helped plan her funeral service. She said, "I can't seem to get it written down — how I want my service. I always get distracted when the thought intrudes, 'Now let's see what part will I have in this service?'" (She had been so used to being a part of programs.) We both laughed. "You'll be the star performer in *that* drama," I assured her.

On a subsequent visit on November 11, 1982, she asked me to do the eulogy for her service, and to be *sure* the last lines of W.C. Bryant's poem, *Thanatopsis*, were used, and she quoted them.

I did not get to see Greta again until after she was taken to the hospital, a couple of years later. She was in a coma for several weeks, but she did know me on the December day that I visited her in 1984. My daughter Marla was scheduled to have surgery on February 8, 1985, so I had to go back to North Carolina on the fifth to care for Marla's boys. Greta died on the sixth, back in Kentucky. I'm sorry I didn't get to do that last service for a very precious friend, but I include here, the poem she requested.

                (from the end of) Thanatopsis
So live, that when thy summons comes to join
The innumerable caravan, which moves
To that mysterious realm, where each shall take
His slumber in the silent halls of death,
Thou go not, like the quarry slave at night,
Scourged to his dungeon, but, sustained and soothed

> By an unfaltering trust, approach thy grave,
> Like one who wraps the drapery of his couch
> About him, and lies down to pleasant dreams.
>
> William Cullen Bryant

Juanita Brandon's Service: April 15, 1983, at Colliers' Funeral Home in Benton, Kentucky.

On Tuesday night I went to the hospital to tell Juanita good-bye — feeling certain it was the last time I would see her alive. She knew I was there. She acknowledged my questions and squeezed my hand. She was supported by the love of her family; and I was thankful that Lourdes Hospital allowed them to be with her in the ICU until the end.

I wept there, and when I passed her road on the way home, I thought I would have to stop the car because the tears came so fast. But I knew I was not weeping for Juanita. I was weeping for me and for all of us because I knew there would be a void that no one could fill.

In her family — She's been fortunate to have so many of her family around her. I know that "her children rise up and call her blessed."[1] They have been faithful in attending to her needs — not only in these last days — but through the years.

In her church — From where she lived she could see Mt. Carmel UM church. She was in a very real sense its custodian. She took its concerns to her heart whether they had to do with the physical or spiritual aspects. She supported the leadership in all good efforts.

In her community — She had a spirit of adventure — a willingness to take a risk. The Lakeland parish was a case in point. I was involved there for eight years, and I know she was an ardent supporter. I think this work repaid her. It helped to foster her creative abilities. She began to paint after she was seventy. In my estimation her work excelled that of Grandma Moses by far. Many of us here treasure her paintings. I have one, a picture of the oldest house in the county (which later burned).

Among her friends — What a marvelously faithful friend she was! It humbles me to think that after all the friends in her long life, I, who came so late, can dare to believe I was a little bit special to her. My birthday was the day before hers, which was February 12, and for at least eight years we have celebrated together. This year she prepared a lovely supper and invited the Ellenbergers and me.

It was a memorable evening with her daughter Ramona coming in to share later.

It is no use to say we won't miss her, but my weeping is over. It is now time to remember and rejoice. It is spring! It is resurrection time, and with the apostle Paul, "If the Spirit of him who raised Jesus from the dead dwells in you, he . . . will give life to your mortal bodies also through his spirit which dwells in you^2 . . . I consider that the sufferings of this present time are not worth comparing with the glory that is to be revealed to us^3 . . . We know that in everything God works for good with those who love him, who are called according to his purpose^4 . . . Who shall separate us from the love of Christ?^{5} . . . No, in all these things we are more than conquerors through him who loved us."^{6}

Note: When her family *numbered* her things to divide them among the many children and grandchildren there was one item left over — the painting she had done of the pyrocantha at the end of her porch. "Let's give it to Tillie," they said. Of those paintings that she had done, it was one of my favorites. It is now on the wall of my living room — facing me as I write these lines. I bless your memory, Juanita.

NOTES

1. Proverbs 31:28 (RSV)
2. Romans 8:11 (RSV)
3. Romans 8:18 (RSV)
4. Romans 8:28 (RSV)
5. Romans 8:35 (RSV)
6. Romans 8:37 (RSV)

Eulogy for the Dear Departed

Troy Howell and Elsie
P. 321
10-66

Tillie with
← Juanita Brandon
(her home)
P. 322
2-11-75

Greta Maddox
(her home Paducah, Ky.)
P. 321 →
8-77

A GOOD FRIDAY PRAYER

Higgins Memorial UM Church, April 1, 1988

Our Father, on this day, when only from our perspective can we call it *good*, we come again to live through these events and ponder anew their meaning for our lives today.

We try to imagine the horror of it all — the sting of the lashes; the pain of spikes being driven into wrists and feet; the agony of trying to breathe and the unquenchable thirst; and the trust of the spear. But could it be that greater than the physical pain was the feeling of utter *loneliness* — deserted by closest friends, betrayed and denied, and feeling deserted even by you his heavenly Father? It may well be that his speedy death came from a broken spirit!

Dear God, we are consumed with remorse that it was necessary for your Son to experience such suffering and humiliation in order for You to say once, and for all time, how limitless is your caring and love for a stubborn and wayward humanity.

No wonder the sun refused to shine on such an event; and the earth trembled at the fearsomeness of it. What a dark day indeed for those who experienced it.

But, Oh Father, we can call it *good* because we live on the after-side of Easter! We can thank You that every man-made barrier between us and You was torn in two and broken down, and through your Son, Jesus Christ, we are all set free! Father, please receive the thankfulness and praise of your grateful people. Amen.

Section VI
TODAY

Styles Hill I

My apartment 1985-1995 (?)

Irma Parsley and Theresa V Styles 11-28-86

Pat and Cristal Styles 3-14-92

Raymond Honeycutt and Pat Styles on Roan Mtn. 12-25-91

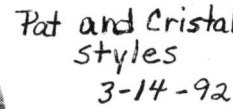

On Styles Hill - II - Styles family
Virgil, Theresa, Keith, Connie and Morris

50th Anniv.
← 3-14-92

Chris Hagler
+ Cassandra
Styles
3-14-92
↓

←"Storm of the Century"
3-14-93   P. 332

3-17-93
Marla
P. 334

WEATHERING THE "STORM OF THE CENTURY" ON STYLES' HILL

March 12 through 19, 1993

Fri. 12th — The weatherman on CBS, Mark McEwen, had given us plenty of warning on the morning weather report — a very serious winter storm was due to hit the Eastern states from Florida to Maine — including snow, cold and wind. The first flakes came in flurries at 1:30 P.M. on my hill. I hurried to get a package ready to send back, and wrote two birthday cards. I left at two o'clock in a brisk snow. I stopped at the grocery store to get a few items. The store was crowded. I said to Danny Hensley, who checked me out, "The threat of snowstorm is awfully good for the grocery business." It snowed all afternoon and night.

Sat. 13th — I had fifteen inches of snow, and it continued to snow. Then the wind started to blow! It was a blizzard. The poor birds ate all the food in both feeders, and I couldn't get out to fill them. I tried to devise two ways to get food to the birds, but was foiled by wind. Friday and Saturday I went through the letters that I had written to family from the 1940s to the eighties. (Elva had sent her copies back to me.) I made notes of the facts I might need to write about these years for this book.

I figured my friend, Muriel, in Oregon would have seen the national weather report and would be wondering about me, so I called her. She had been trying to get a call through, but all circuits were busy. I also called Dena and Paula on the west coast. Here in town, I called Mildred Ray, Miriam Jacks, and Lena Letterman (her birthday), Dorothy Robinson, and my daughter, Marla. My electricity went off at 6:15 P.M. Even though I heard the power had failed in many places, I did not have sense enough to have some water drawn.

I was thankful for the excellent flashlight that I kept plugged in to recharge. Gladys Young gave it to me several years ago. I had candles, matches, and batteries for my radio, but no heat or lights. I was fasting on Saturdays for Lent, so didn't have to worry about cooking. I lit five candles — one was a big white one that Kermit Ellenberger had made in a square milk carton that had been on my sewing machine since I moved here, just waiting for such an emergency. I read a couple of articles by candlelight, but it was too hard on my eyes.

When the room began to be cold, I put on more clothes. I got out the "snuggle bunny" I've had since living at Aurora, Kentucky. I remember trying to take a self-portrait in it — which was no easy thing to do — to get in it and zip it up before the timer went off. But I did it. I can't remember whether I bought the snuggle bunny, or if Paula gave it to me (it wouldn't help to ask her). I put on the "furry inside," roomy pink bedroom shoes Pat, my upstairs neighbor, had given me several years ago, my soft, warm outdoor jacket and crawled into the snuggle bunny. Since I didn't want to go to bed too early, I played six games of Yahtzee and one of solitaire. It was ten o'clock by then, and the wind had died down, but it was still snowing a little, so I prepared for bed. From the waist down I wore panties, panty hose, warm p.j.'s and socks; above the waist, a camisole, p.j.'s, and a sweater. Then I put the snuggle bunny under the covers, which included sheet, blanket, spread and the down comforter that the Yamadas had brought me three years ago. I slept warm. Dottie (upstairs) had called to offer help if needed. Marla reminded me of the hall door which, if I moved my chest of drawers, I could use to get to the woodfire upstairs.

Sun. 14th — I awakened at 3:00 A.M., went to the bathroom, and checked the temperature. It was fifteen degrees and still snowing a little, but not much more had accumulated since I had gone to bed. I stayed awake from then until six, took a little nap, and got up at seven. I ate an orange and cereal and went over in my mind how I would make it through the day. I was reading my devotional books when the lights came on at 8:20. I was *so* thankful!! I felt the tears come to my eyes as I realized workers had to have been out in the storm to restore the power to me. (I did write a thank-you.)

I had studied my Sunday school lesson, but knew I could not get out to teach it. I had heard on the radio that most of the churches were closed and finally heard that Higgins was also. (Buzz doesn't give up easily.)

Miriam Jacks, Dorothy Robinson, and Marla all called to find out how I made it through the night, and later my neighbors, Connie and Pat, also called. I was glad to report that I was fine.

My big concern had been for the birds, and my satellite was so full of snow that I had no TV. So before dinnertime I put plastic bags over my bedroom shoes with elastic bands around my ankles and knees and a big garbage bag to catch the snow that fell in when I opened my sliding door, and waded over to fill the bird feeders. Then I took the shovel and one of the staves I use to balance myself when I take step exercises on the cement blocks, and waded through drifts well over my knees to remove satellite snow.

From more than one source I began hearing this called "the storm of the century" — Marla's weather-buff friend, Henry Ray, for one. This was the most pervasive storm to hit the whole Eastern states since 1888. It went from Florida to Maine and probably did more damage in Florida than anywhere. There was snow and cold, very high wind — even tornadoes, high tides, and flooding. There were real blizzard conditions in many areas.

Mon. 15th — The temperature was fourteen degrees. They announced this morning on TV that the count of the dead was 112, many of the fatalities caused by heart attacks suffered while shoveling snow.

Muriel called at 10:10 from Oregon to check on me. At eleven o'clock I put on my high-top boots and waded out to measure the peak of the drift in my driveway — thirty-eight inches; then I waded on out where I could see Style's driveway, most places the snow came up over my knees. Keith was outside. He said some drifts were twenty-three inches, and even if we could get out our driveway we couldn't go any place because Green Mountain Drive had not been plowed. One reason for this is that there was a seven-foot drift where Green Mountain Drive enters Highway 197. The snow there was level with the banks beside the highway. At three that afternoon, someone came with a tractor and scraped some of the snow off our driveway.

Tues. 16th — It was twenty-four degrees and cloudy this morning. At 9:30 I put on my boots and shoveled the snow from my patio in front of my door. While I was getting it off my car, I saw the scraper go by (9:45). Connie called to say there had been some damage to Roses department store and to the BiLo grocery — heavy snow on the roofs. I spent most of the day working on the chronology of the log house at Celo from 1947 on — who was there, how long, etc. I also made some preparation for Marla's birthday tomorrow — in case she can come for supper. I decided not to try to bake a cake. Instead I cut a small cottage cheese tub down to one-half inch and covered it with foil; then I put five "buckeyes" (peanut butter, margarine and powdered sugar balls dipped in chocolate) in it. In the middle one I put a candle and on the four others the numbers, 1, 9, 4, 7 (the year of her birth). That was her cake! I wrapped the gift Paula and I had for her. So I was ready if she could come.

Wed. 17th — Marla said to call her at work (in Asheville). She hoped to know by noon if she had to go to Morganton to pick up some Amway products she had ordered for some of her customers. I called, but she didn't know. I called again at 4:15 P.M. She said no one was home at the distributor's in Morganton (Randy's mother had died), so she said that she would come. I asked her to stop at the Fresh Market in Asheville to get some salad stuff. She was able to get here, and parked in the side yard where Keith had had his truck. We had pork chops, potatoes with cheese cream sauce, sliced tomatoes, our favorite half-runner green beans and my special slaw, which I had frozen. We had herb tea and "buckeyes" (I had only one), but not from her "cake." She took that home to share with her son Jamie. She was wearing the pretty sweater Jamie had given her. Robbie (her son) called while she was here, and Derek (her son) called later. I gave her a box of "aplets and cotlets" fruit candy, a package of thank-you note paper, and a half share in the lovely clothes that Paula had sent — which she loved!! And why shouldn't she? A skirt with matching top and a long, divided skirt with coordinating blouse. When it was time to leave, she was afraid she would have trouble driving back up the bank by the barn. I watched. She had to back up three times but made it. I took her picture walking in from the car through the drift with her "plastic leggings", and later, one of her with her "cake."

Thurs. 18th — At 3:45 I shovelled the width of my car tracks behind my car. It took me a half-hour to shovel forty feet through drifts eight to twelve inches deep (I measured them — didn't guess). I used a five-inch-wide shovel, but each block of snow I moved was twice or more as wide as the shovel. The temperature was forty degrees. Then I started typing this article.

Fri. 19th. — Connie, who lives next door, called to ask about the dogs. I had not seen them. She said they would come over to see if Keith had shut them up. I asked if Morris would run his truck in behind my car. He did. I went out at 1:40 and dug down to the gravel in the tracks where it was slick. I intend to go out this afternoon to get my mail — I have a package at the post office — and I will also get a few groceries. One week I have been snowbound! The latest death toll from the storm, I have heard, is 219. I fared better than most. Emergency vehicles, helicopters and snowmobiles had to come to the aid of many.

The last vestiges of snow from the drift in my driveway vanished under the sun's power at 1:45 P.M. on March 24, 1993. The streak near the top of the mountain finally disappeared Friday, March 26, I presume, (fog covered the top on Friday and Saturday).

I wanted snow. Well, I guess I got it.

Styles Hill II

3 sq. ft. of my shrub bed next to my patio ← P. 337

The Stones
#1 - Rutilated quartz 10-1-91
#2 - Rutilated quartz 10-22-91
#3 - Rutilated quartz 10-23-91 ↓

Actinolite #4 in Foliated Talc 10-23-91
Biotite Mica #5 10-23-91 →
Amethyst #6 (tumbled tear shape) 10-23-91

Two pages from Luke Miller's book "The Mysterious Stones"

"Another theory was that a meteorite fell from the sky." ↓

"I think that the 'Little people' brot the stones. And I think ← Tillie is a good person."

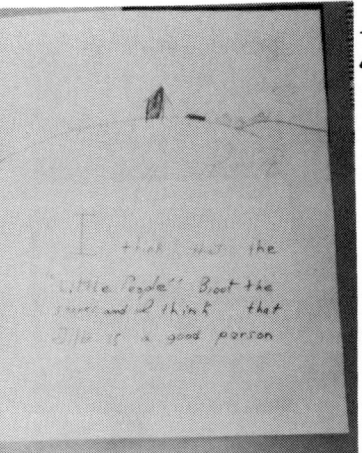

THE UNSOLVED (STONES) MYSTERY

I moved into the ground floor apartment of Keith Styles' home on April 29, 1985. There were shrub beds (rhododendron and azalea) on either side of my concrete patio. Keith had hauled soil from the woods to plant them in, and then covered the soil with heavy, black plastic topped with wood chips. When I came about five years after the shrubs were planted, the chips were all decayed, along with the leaves and roots to form a very solid mat. It took two years to get the poison ivy out, and the last two years I've pulled up the prolific jewel weed. I have watched the holly seedlings grow (from seeds dropped by the birds from the holly branches I brought from Mildred Ray's tree to hang by my front door), and have fed the dogs scraps on the large flat rock in the bed.

This is all to explain that when an unusual stone appeared on October 1, 1991, in the three square feet of matted surface next to my patio — all clean and lying on top of the ground, it did *not* come *up* (from beneath) and had not been there for any length of time.

The next day I called Rings and Things, a shop nearby that specializes in gems. When I described the stone to Mr. Young, he said it sounded like rutilated quartz. On the fourth of October, I took the stone for Fritz Young to see. He verified that it was rutilated quartz and made this comment, "I've never seen any from this area. If you want jewelry made from it, I suggest that you take it to Dick Johnson at the head of Crabtree Creek." On the eighth, I took the stone to Dick hoping he could get from the stone a sizeable ring for me and three "pinkies" for my girls.

On the morning of Oct. 22 (my wedding anniversary) I went out to throw a banana peeling under a shrub, and there, nearer to the patio than the first rutilated quartz I had found, was a smaller stone of the same kind, rutilated quartz. The next afternoon about four o'clock, I was sitting on the patio eating an apple. I suddenly decided I would take a *good, bi-focal look*. Down next to the wood posts around the bed, I found an even larger rutilated quartz *and* a nicely shaped, clean piece of biotite mica and actinolite in foliated talc (I later glued pins on them myself). On the same occasion I found at the base of one of the shrubs a tumbled, tear-drop shaped amethyst. I bought a gold cap and chain from the Johnsons and I made the amethyst into a necklace for myself.

Dick Johnson and his daughter, Theresa, cut and set the jewelry made from the quartz. So then I had five rings, three different sizes (mine was the largest): six stick pins, five mounted on silver backs and one on gold: one cluster pin set with seven stones; and a necklace for which Dick cut the stone and Fritz Young did the stone setting using the gold and diamond from the engagement ring of my daughter, Marla.

When the making of the jewelry was finished, I asked Dick Johnson to tell me what price he would put on the finished products. He said, "Three thousand, six hundred ninety dollars." (The diamond raised the value of the lot.) I estimated that I paid $1,159.96 to have the settings done.

I have had many people offer ideas about how the stones got in that three-square-foot-sized corner: (1) they came up out of the ground; (2) they were washed down from the bank above; (3) some child (*what* child?) threw them there; (4) the jewelers put them there to get the business of making jewelry from me. To me all these theories seem ridiculous. So are there any theories that are not? Not really! But in November my next-door neighbor, Connie Styles, said she saw a man on Asheville TV who said he was going to give his address and phone number — if anyone had found rutilated quartz and would like to sell it, he would like to buy it. He showed a piece the size of a gallon milk jug and said he had paid two million (?) dollars for it — that it fell from the *moon*, and pieces had fallen over a large area of northeastern United States. Connie ran for a pen, but when she got back to the TV, the man who had spoken about the rutilated quartz was gone. She didn't think to make a note about the time of day or the program. I was away in Texas at the time. When I returned home, and she told me about it, I wrote to the TV station, but they were unable to help without more specific information.

My "bus friend," Muriel Clark in Oregon, told me a nice story about "First Crow" bringing the stones to me as a reward for my past goodness to him. (Crows have been known to steal and hoard bright objects.) Then my friend, Herbert Robinson, surely one of God's beloved servants, and one who has Cherokee Indian ancestors and is inclined to believe their legends said, "It is no mystery to me. *The Little People* brought them. They reward people they care about."

Peg Neal had another theory: "The people from outer space

wanted to make contact with an earth person. I think you would be a good choice."

In early December, 1991, Libby Miller had a Christmas party for the volunteers at Reconciliation House, which she runs. Her son, Luke, attended and heard me tell the story and show the stones. This past school term (late winter, 1993) Luke's fifth grade class was asked to write a book. Luke's was "The Mysterious Stones, a True Story, Written by Luke Miller, Illustrated by Luke Miller." The teacher had their books nicely bound. Luke's schoolmates derided the *true story* part. He brought the book and gave it to me. By one illustration (of my house on a hill) he wrote, "Another theory is that a meteorite fell from the sky," but on the next page, he wrote, "I think that the *Little People* brought the stones, and I think that Tillie is a good person."

I used the extra blank pages in the book to add pictures and facts; then I had him handle all my jewelry and gave him two leftover pieces of stone and gave the book back to him. I said to him, "Tell your classmates it really *is* a true story."

For a long time Marla and Connie had been saying they would like the holly seedlings in my shrub bed to transplant onto their properties. Connie also wanted some of the wild Monkshood plants, but they never came to get them. On April 23, 1993, I decided to dig them up and take the plants to Marla and Connie. I worked an hour or so on the other end of the bed from where the six stones were found. The next afternoon I was doing step exercises on the two cement blocks in the corner. I looked into the bed and said to myself, "*That* stone was *not* there yesterday!" I picked it up and found it very strange and lovely — also smooth and clean. It measured 6½ inches by 3¾ inches. The next day I took it to Fritz.

"I never saw anything like it; but it is a fossil formed in the sea — there's a shell," he said.

On April twenty-eighth I took it to Dick Johnson. He had never seen anything like it either. I had decided I would have a pendant, ring, and earrings for myself, and earrings for the girls, made from the stone. Dick said he would cut the pieces but suggested I have Anita Lawson, in the shop below his, silver-wire them for me. She did a lovely job, and the pendant *may* be my favorite of all the jewelry. It is a real attention-getter.

The shrubbery on the *other* side of my patio has been dead about three years, and I had planted tomatoes and flowers in the bed with pine chips around them.

The tomatoes had been so disappointing the past two years that

I had decided that this year it would be flowers only. My friend, Jean Quinn, and I decided we would go together to Troy's, a local greenhouse, to pick up flower plants on Friday.

On Wednesday (May 23) I moved my bird feeder back to the rock wall and raked the remaining chips next to the patio and made marks where the rows would be. When I looked at the bed on Thursday *there* in the middle of it was *another strange stone*! I sent it for Herbert Robinson to identify. He said, "I believe this is bauxite mineral. It comes in white, gray, yellow, red, and brown (mine was gray) . . . it's found in Alabama, Mississippi, Tennessee, Virginia and Arkansas. (His stone book didn't mention North Carolina, and neither did two other stone books I consulted.) It is the principle ore of aluminum."

I call it my "Pirate's Skull," and I had Herbert's and Dorothy's daughter Diana silver-wire it for me. I am very fond of this gruesome piece.

These days I speak of my "latest stone" — not the last. David Salstrom once asked, "Why in *your* garden?" I flippantly answered, "Why, because I'm such a good girl, of course!" But really, there is no sensible answer. I feel my pastor probably came the nearest to an answer that I will ever know, in his "A Message from Buzz":

> I remember a very large white pine that had a prominent limb just a few feet above the ground. This limb made a perfect arch out from the tree, then turned upward to the sky. The arch formed a seat, perfect for a little boy's body . . . he was fascinated by this unique limb . . . and had a sense that he had discovered it — therefore it was put there for him. . . . Like the stones that Tillie Brooks found by her door . . . we have an experience of discovery . . . The power of this discovery may be that we are graced and thus loved in particular. That is, God has in a moment distinguished us from all of the clutter of His creation and sent us the message that we are unique and are uniquely loved.[1]

Who knows how or why they appeared in *my* garden? I'm just thankful and have tried to enhance their beauty to show my appreciation by making them into jewelry for myself, family and friends.

NOTES

1. Higgins Memorial Church, *The Bell Ringer* (February 1, 1994).

AFTERWORD

The following books have had an enduring impact upon my philosophy of life and on the maturing process of my faith. I offer them to my readers as a gift.

The Bible.

Toyohiko Kagawa. *Songs from the Slums.* (Nashville, Tennessee: Cokesbury Press, 1925). [God's presence amid squalor.]

Thomas R. Kelly. *A Testament of Devotion.* (New York: Harper Brothers, 1941). [The effects of inward prayer.]

Gerald Heard. *A Dialogue in the Desert.* (New York: Harper Brothers, 1942). [The temptations of Jesus dramatized.]

Agnes Sanford. *The Healing Light.* (New York: Ballantine Books (Random House), 1983). [Healing through prayer.]

J. Allen Boone. *Kinship with All Life.* (New York: Harper Brothers, 1954). [Love and understanding connects all life.]

Carrie Ten Boom, with John and Elizabeth Sherrill. *The Hiding Place.* (Old Tappan, New Jersey: Chosen Books, Fleming H. Revell Co., 1971). [Perfect obedience — resurrection.]

David Wilkerson, with John and Elizabeth Sherrill. *The Cross and the Switchblade.* (New York: Pillar Books, 1976). [New York City gangs and the Holy Spirit.]

Ernest Gordon. *Through the Valley of the Kwai.* (New York: Harper & Row, 1962). [Sacrifice is redemptive.]

Leroy Augenstein. *Come, Let us Play God.* (New York: Harper and Row, 1969.) [Who shall live? Who shall die?]

Elisabeth Kubler-Ross. *Death and Dying.* (New York: Collier Macmillan Publishing Co., 1969). [Dignifying death as a part of life.]

Elias Chacour. *We Belong to the Land.* (San Francisco: Harper Collins, 1992). [Reconciliation of Palestinians and Israelis.]

SCHOENBAUM LIBRARY
UNIVERSITY OF CHARLESTON